One of the GUYS

THE WISING UP OF AN AMERICAN MAN

BY

HARRY STEIN

Simon and Schuster

NEW YORK

LONDON

TORONTO

SYDNEY

TOKYO

DESIGNED BY IRVING PERKINS ASSOCIATES
MANUFACTURED IN THE UNITED STATES OF AMERICA

10 9 8 7 6 5 4 3 2 1

LIBRARY OF CONGRESS CATALOGING IN PUBLICATION DATA

STEIN, HARRY.

   ONE OF THE GUYS: THE WISING UP OF AN AMERICAN MAN / BY HARRY STEIN.
   P.   CM.
   ISBN 0-671-55704-1
   1. STEIN, HARRY—BIOGRAPHY. 2. AUTHORS, AMERICAN—20TH CENTURY—
BIOGRAPHY. 3. MEN—PSYCHOLOGY. I. TITLE.
PS3569.T366Z47 1988
818'.5409—DC19
[B]   87-32629
                                                CIP

The author gratefully acknowledges permission to quote from the following works:

The Groucho Letters, by Groucho Marx. Copyright © 1967 by Groucho Marx, Simon and Schuster, New York. "He's Still Not Home Free," by William Nack. *Sports Illustrated*, October 13, 1986, pages 104–108. *Home Before Dark*, by Susan Cheever. Copyright © 1984 by Susan Cheever, Houghton Mifflin, Boston. "There Used to Be a Ballpark," words and music by Joe Raposo, © 1973 by Jonico Music, Inc., and Sergeant Music Co. Used by permission.

ACKNOWLEDGMENTS

A great many people contributed to the making of this book, but I will hold the list down to those without whom it would not, in tone or substance, be what it is: Priscilla, Sadie and Charlie, natch; Alice Mayhew, for her quite extraordinary guidance; Kenny Rotner, for his smarts and vast generosity; Jay Acton; Lisa Bain; David Black; Dan Brooks; Lee Eisenberg; Henry Ferris; Lisa Kaplan; Philip Moffitt; Michael Noble; David Shipley; Amanda Urban; and my father, for his encouragement, forbearance, guts and love.

For Charlie

"I CAN'T HELP IT IF I'M SHORT. BUT
YOU CAN HELP IT IF YOU'RE MEAN."

*Sadie Stein, overheard admonishing a boy
in her kindergarten class*

One of the GUYS

THIS book was going to be a snap. Why not? I knew exactly what I wanted to say: that, dammit, enough lip service, it's time that we men take seriously the proposition that our lives are profoundly out of balance; time, at long last, we begin to rethink our very definitions of success.

Oh, yeah, by all means, I was prepared to acknowledge how difficult such a recognition can be. The proposal for the book spoke of the great contemporary male dilemma, "the need to be more and somehow, often, in our own eyes, less than we have ever had to be before." But, I concluded with a flourish, what it had to come down to was the simple understanding, accepted not only in innumerable individual lives but as a cultural truism, that change is a matter of self-interest: that such a choice can, in fact, do nothing less than bring us to life—often, for the first time.

All right, I knew there were a lot of abstractions in there, and even more generalities. But what the hell, I figured then, the book wasn't due for a long time. I'd get to the details later.

And yet—and this was a first for me—the words just wouldn't come. Over the course of a year, I made innumerable false starts, each of which felt, almost immediately, labored or insincere or self-aggrandizing.

How, I finally began to wonder—*how had I gotten myself into this?* Reflexively, I'd blame my wife. If we hadn't needed the money, I'd inform her, there's no way I'd have involved myself in so thankless a task. Sometimes I'd start to blame my kids, too; but they were so winning, and so awfully nice to me, that instead, I'd blame my wife again. I used to write *humor*, I'd tell her. Before I met her, things *amused* me. Back then, I had a life of my own. Almost no one is writing decent humor stuff these days—and everyone who is is making a fortune! That should have been me. I hate this goddamn project!

My wife is not the sort who simply takes this kind of thing. If she happened to be in a benign mood, or exhausted, as both of us had frequently been since the birth of our second child, she might merely offer me a severe look and a dismissive remark. ("Fox's mom," I was wont to taunt at such moments, quoting the line that turned up in every one of my daughter's "Fox" books, "gave him one of her looks.") But more often, there would be between us an angry exchange of some duration.

I was, she would snap during the worst of these, constitutionally incapable of taking responsibility for anything; and more than that, a hypocrite. There I was, writing about the emotional liberation that had come with commitment and fatherhood, and I didn't mean a word of it.

Screw you, I'd point out, I *did* mean it. What I didn't like, what had no business being part of the bargain, was that I— who so loved being around the kids, who had grown so in this new role and had contributed so much to their growth— was saddled with having to write this stupid book, while she brought in not a dime. And by the way, maybe she ought to start thinking about where we're going to live after we have to sell the house.

"Hypocrite!" she would change the subject. How many times had I argued in print that it was best for children to have a full-time parent? How many times had we remarked, wonderingly, at how astonishingly curious, humorful, generous-spirited our children had turned out to be? Did I actually believe that was all on account of me? Hah! I had the easy part, the fun part. If I had her job—that's what she always called it—I'd go stir-crazy in a day.

It was true, I had written those things. That, I'd reflect

miserably at the worst moments, was part of the problem: that while my professional contemporaries, my erstwhile friends, were shooting ahead professionally, I'd gotten myself typecast as this thoughtful guy who writes serious things. Who the hell needed that as an identity? Where, in a culture that lionizes Madonna and Lee Iacocca, was the future in *that?* Or the dough?

There was the day I heard from a guy I know that he had just signed to ghost the autobiography of a well-known industrialist—for so much money that "I'll never have to write anything I don't want to ever again.

"But, then," he added a moment later, self-protectively, condescendingly, admiringly, "it's a project *you'd* never do in a million years."

"Yes, I would."

"No, you wouldn't."

Nah, in retrospect I guessed I wouldn't—not only because the idea is kind of sickening but because, at this point, it would represent so pointed a betrayal of my public self. Dammitall.

It was Lee Eisenberg, the editor of *Esquire,* who had gotten me into this god-awful fix. Eight years before, when the magazine had changed hands and the new proprietor had gotten it into his head to create a column called "Ethics," it was Eisenberg, shuddering at the potential of such an enterprise to be pompous or pedantic, who had lobbied to have me write the thing.

"But I don't know a thing about ethics," I'd initially argued, gently. "I never even took an ethics course in college."

"That's all right. Write it funny—then, every now and then, throw in an ethical point. We'll call you Shecky Spinoza."

Before terribly long, however, the column became, in large measure, something else—a chronicle of my own effort to behave with a semblance of honor in an amoral world. Which was not only why, all this time later, I continued to receive admiring letters from strangers who, it seemed to me, were generally more decent than I was, but why experienced publishing people were willing to give me the opportunity, and a fair amount of money, to purport to represent so many of my contemporaries in print.

I had taken the money; that was not hard. But from the outset, I had a problem with the purporting. When it came right down to it, who the hell was I to presume to speak for others? Weren't the specifics of their lives as unique as my own? I confided my doubts to my brother-in-law, a smart-aleck Midwesterner of German descent, who responded with a suggested title for the alleged work-in-progress: "Growing Up Male in America—as Harry Stein."

In fact, he had it wrong. At the juncture, the book wasn't going to be about me at all; not so that it would be apparent, anyway.

Indeed, in desperation masquerading as professionalism, I was already deep into research of the traditional kind: scanning periodicals in the library for useful bits of information and data; reading books by psychologists, sociologists, feminists; conducting interviews with other men about their lives, and with women about the men in theirs. For a few weeks there, I even had a researcher to help me out.

To be sure, some of it proved helpful—the interviews in particular. On the one hand, they added credence, as if any were needed, to notions about men that, in this angry, confused age, have in many quarters achieved the status of assumptions: that we are often selfish, childish, so utterly unconscious that were such behaviors not also hurtful, they would be comic.

"What in the world is the matter with you men?" a woman lawyer put it to me one evening early on, over what had started out as a lighthearted dinner at the Carnegie Deli. She shook her head. "I mean, I know it's a cliché—for years I refused to accept it myself—but I'm starting to think it's true. Maybe, as a sex, you're *all* screwed up. Maybe it's innate."

Gnawing at my immense corned-beef-on-roll, avoiding her eye, I moved to shift the conversation from the general (everyone with gonads, including me) to the particular individual with gonads who'd occasioned this outburst (and whom I didn't even know). "What happened?"

"What happened?" She fairly snorted. "What's the difference? He was a creep who didn't know how to make commitments, someone who was unable to deal with his own inability to deal with things. That sums it up." She offered a mirthless laugh. "That sums up most guys."

But, too, face to face with the perpetrators—individuals speaking with greater or lesser insight about who they are, how they got that way, the extraordinary obstacles involved in trying to be anything else—the clichés took on a different character, the extenuating circumstances vast new meaning. More to the point, over and over I saw myself in these people, men who had passed into their twenties, thirties, forties abiding by a value system that was suddenly discredited.

Still, I remained stuck—not only over the issue of content but, increasingly, that of style. Over and over, in start after false start, my prose was hopelessly constricted; the kind of spiritless, self-serious writing that constitutes the new male confessional tone. I had always despised it and yet, almost of its own will, it was clattering out of my typewriter.

It was easier to figure out what was up here than to get back on track stylistically. Quite simply, that endlessly earnest prose, already the object of so much scorn among women, generally so heavy on *mea culpa,* reflects the continuing uncertainty men feel as to exactly where we stand with the opposite sex. Anxious to meet women on their own terms, desperate to reveal ourselves as good guys and assume our place in the new social order, we are ready to plead guilty, in retrospect, to all manner of transgressions, emotional, moral, intellectual. All we want is to be told we're okay.

Yet I recognized, too, that the scorn was merited—for such prose, finally, tends to be characterized not only by self-contempt but by self-delusion. That is why even in its more benign manifestations—I'm thinking of the guy who wrote an "About Men" column in *The New York Times Magazine* telling of unexpectedly finding himself in the midst of a bunch of attractive single women, with everyone discussing community business, and no one deferring to anyone else, and there not being even the merest hint of sexual tension, and, well, how wonderful it was that at last everyone could be *equal* in every sense—it rings so utterly false. That just isn't the way men behave or feel, certainly not the way we talk.

The truth is, virtually every man I know regards the changes of the last twenty years with at least a touch of ambivalence. Sure, it has always been easy to endorse the broad social objectives of the women's movement. As the father of a six-year-old daughter who unhesitatingly lists banking as one of her potential careers, along with ballet, bareback riding and pottery making (and never mind that she figures she'd get to *keep* most of the money in the bank), I feel a personal, daily debt of gratitude to those who have, in so short a span, dramatically expanded the scope of female possibility in this culture. But, too, particularly at the beginning, there was an inflexibility to feminist dogma, and an air of moral rectitude, that occasionally even now puts a crimp in a good day.

Moreover, though the thought rarely occurs consciously, there is a subtle but pervasive understanding that the movement never delivered on its most grandiose promise, its most audacious challenge to the social order. Women, we used to hear, were not merely going to move in numbers into male preserves, but would *feminize* them, pushing men to be as emotionally connected as women, in their role as nurturers, had traditionally been. Instead, so very nearly the opposite has occurred that the anthropologist Desmond Morris began referring to the phenomenon at hand as the "masculinist movement." By the literal millions, women are doing very well in the marketplace by having proved themselves as aggressive, as tough, as unrelentingly focused as their male counterparts. There is much to be said for this—for a while there, it was said all the time—but it is not for nothing that we have heard so much lately about the dramatic rise in stress-related illnesses among women. "It has now been clearly doc-

umented," as Dr. Paul J. Rosch, president of the American
Institute of Stress, put it, noting the appalling increase in
breast-cancer deaths among young and middle-aged white
women during the past decade, "that emotional stress is associated in a decline in immune-system parameters responsible for defenses against cancer. Inability to express anger,
frustration, loss of important emotional relationships and social isolation have been particularly incriminated, especially
for breast malignancies."

As yet, there seem to be no statistics to reliably measure
heightened alienation.

Still, the trend Morris characterized so archly seems, if not
precisely on the wane, in the process of dramatic alteration.
For there are vast numbers of women who, having pretty
much gotten what they thought they were after, are now facing
up to it; wondering, at long last, what it was that once, from
the outside looking in, had seemed so terrific in the first place.

We men, meanwhile, though we have been living out those
very lives from the start, almost always, even now, including
those of us who have lately made a point of appearing not to,
find ways to get around asking the really hard questions out
loud.

There are, of course, excellent reasons for that, most of
them having to do with what we in this culture take to be
self-respect. Who wants to be caught speculating around the
office on the possibility of investing more of himself in family
at the expense of career? Who wants to own up to the turmoil
within when quick-fix reassurance can be found in confirmation from without? Who needs to be thought of, even passingly, as a loser or a wimp? Where—for how often does the
contemporary mind work otherwise?—is the percentage in
it?

And yet the truth is that a lot of us have been quietly
struggling in recent years with precisely those dilemmas: re-
evaluating old attitudes and modes of behavior that rarely
brought anything more than glancing satisfaction; surprising
ourselves with our capacity for emotional intimacy; *changing*.

And if we would certainly never describe ourselves as "new men"—indeed, regard the very term with amusement and disdain—neither are we any longer at the stage of emotional adolescence where, it now seems a harrowing thought, we might under other circumstances have lingered forever.

It was almost a year after I'd signed to write it that it became evident what the book had to be about: not just that struggle in general but—for how else to get it down right, with all the shadings and nuances?—my own in particular.

Still, for literally months more, I hesitated. It is true that I had exposed bits and pieces of myself in print before, but always there had been lines of defense. Now my life—the emotional trek from where I used to be, to where I am, to where the best in me wants to continue heading—would be at the very center of the book, and there could be no evasions. Did I really want to come clean, expose the daily duplicities, large and small, that had always eased my way through life; and the flaws, the intense self-doubts, that people like me construct entire personalities in order to obscure? My children would one day read this stuff! And close friends. And colleagues. And women who had known me at my most devil-may-care. And what would they think of me then?

Eventually, inevitably, all of that made its way into the text—the continual hesitation, the ambivalence, the sense so many of us have of our best instincts' being at war with other, safer perceptions of self. And I was surprised at the degree to which the business of setting it down honestly proved cathartic. Indeed, the book quickly, for me, became something alive, not merely a record of an emotional landscape in flux, but a catalyst to further movement.

Then again, I should have known—for in fact, that is part of the point. Once undertaken in earnest, such a process almost always assumes a momentum of its own.

Along the way, too, another quite obvious something at last began to sink in: I was an idiot to worry about what others thought. Most of them already knew, anyway, and so, eventually, would my kids. In the realm of self-presentation, no one is ever so readily fooled as oneself.

Indeed, not long ago a friend of mine, just returned from a wedding in the Midwest, mentioned that he'd encountered a woman I'd known slightly way back in college, a friend of my then-girlfriend. "And, boy, does she hate your guts!"

I was shocked, mortified. "What are you talking about? I hardly knew her. I haven't seen her in sixteen years!"

"Apparently, you didn't treat her friend very well." He smirked. "That part rang true."

It rang true to me, too. It had, after all, been the Sixties, I had been at my *most* devil-may-care, temptation had occasionally come my way, and, all right, I'd been a jerk! "Hey," I offered, "it was the Sixties. Did she happen to tell you about *her* boyfriend? The guy was constantly stoned out of his mind. One day, on acid, he actually stuck up a 7-Eleven with a water pistol and tried to make his getaway on a bicycle. The cops nabbed him struggling up a hill."

My friend laughed, and the moment passed. But what he'd said continued to bug me. What the hell was wrong with her? Didn't she realize that what she'd seen all those years ago was adolescent strut; that even then, there was so much more than met the eye? But, my God, if she'd been on to me, had I fooled anyone?

That night, in bed, in the dark, I was going on about it to my wife. She seemed to understand, and, comforted, I moved on to the story of the bicycle thief; and then to reminiscing about the college girlfriend; and finally, to blow-by-blow accounts of a couple of long-years-ago infidelities, one-nighters with (a) a girl at a party during a light show and (b) a girl encountered at a silent vigil for peace. I tried to keep my narration of these stories breezy, even played for laughs at my own expense, but the braggadocio occasionally peeked through. "I am not sure," I noted at one point, "I even knew their last names."

"Sounds great," observed my wife, into the darkness. "Every boy's dream—good, clean, anonymous sex."

"Oh, forget it," I snapped, falling silent.

But a moment later, lying there, reaching for her hand, no longer caring to deny the point, I was grateful beyond measure to be known and loved anyway.

THOUGH it occurred in the first year of the Eisenhower Administration, the moment remains among the most vivid I've ever lived. I recall the feel of my father's arms around me, the harshness of the light off the white tile of the bathroom walls, the sight of the two of us reflected in the mirror above the sink. I was five years old to the day and, though it was past my 7:30 bedtime, still wore the clothes—navy blue shorts; white shirt; a clip-on bow tie, bright blue with red stripes—in which I had celebrated the occasion. From downstairs came the rush of the vacuum cleaner, my mother straightening up.

"Harry," said my father, "there's something I have to talk to you about."

"What?"

"You're a big boy now. A very big boy. Do you know that?"

"Yes."

In retrospect, it is not only the words that so impressed themselves upon me, but the tone. I am quite certain it was the first time my father had addressed me even remotely as an equal.

"Mommy and I would like it if you stopped crying so much. You're a big boy now, and big boys don't cry."

I nodded: a trooper taking note of a superior; a football player crisply acknowledging a coach's order before sprinting back to the huddle. I knew he was right. I did cry all the time—when someone spoke crossly to me without clear provocation; when my older brother picked on me; whenever I found myself losing any kind of game. The reaction had always been visceral, almost beyond my control.

"All right."

"Will you do that? Will you try?"

"Yes."

That was pretty much all there was to it: man-to-man stuff would never be my father's long suit. Years later, when I was twelve and had just returned home from summer camp up-state, I begged him to tell me about the birds and the bees; and then listened as, awkward as Robert Young at a crossroads with young Bud, he attempted to do his fatherly best by his middle son, tossing around so many euphemisms that the message was all but indecipherable. What I failed to mention to him at the time—indeed, still haven't—is that every bed-time for two months my camp counselor had regaled us with stories out of his own carnal history, sparing not even the minutest detail.

This last is hardly something of which I am proud. It is, let's face it, the sort of stunt associated with the smart-ass teenagers who today overpopulate the nation's movie screens, a company with whom I would otherwise never willingly iden-tify myself.

But then, these things do not occur by happenstance. In the years between those two conversations, something had been going on between my father and me, the same something that so routinely characterizes father-son relationships in this culture—an imperceptible lengthening of the gap between us, born of nothing more dramatic than who each of us was. My father insists I have it wrong—perhaps I do—but it is not insignificant that I recall his holding me close so infrequently that when he did, I'd always be momentarily startled by the feel of stubble against my cheek.

Why, women friends occasionally wondered years later, why aren't you two closer? You're both nice guys. You have an incredible amount in common.

It was something no man has ever asked.

"I recently read," noted one of the men I spoke to, in

discussing the dynamic in his childhood home, "that there's a tribe in New Guinea whose word for 'father' translates as 'stranger.' That about sums it up, doesn't it?"

Journalist Perry Garfinkel, whose book *In a Man's World* was the one the guy had been reading, takes note of a recent study in which three hundred seventh- and eighth-grade boys were asked to record over a two-week stretch the time they spent alone with their fathers. The average was seven and a half minutes per week.

All right, all right, this may not qualify as big news. The Greeks knew every bit as much about fathers and sons as we do, with all our studies, and Shakespeare got more mileage out of the subject than O'Neill and Miller combined.

But for those caught up, on both ends, in private dramas of their own creation, that hardly makes it any easier.

"Father hunger," they have come to call it in psychoanalytic circles. Dr. James Herzog of Harvard, who coined the term, initially meant it to apply to those men without fathers at all, postulating that the absence of such a figure in a young male's life can come to bear dramatically upon "matters as diverse as caretaking, sexual orientation, moral development and achievement." But it rapidly came to be used to characterize the longing of the far greater number of men who had fathers who were absent psychologically or emotionally. "We can define father hunger," writes Andrew Merton, who has interviewed extensively on the subject, "as a subconscious yearning for an ideal father that results in behavior ranging from self-pity to hypermasculinity and frustrates attempts to achieve intimacy."

For a lot of us, that hits painfully close to home.

Indeed, in conversations with men in their twenties, thirties, forties, even those who say they normally focus on such matters hardly at all, the subject, once it arises, often comes to dominate the discussion; and though the stories vary considerably in specifics and tone, they move, with astonishing regularity, toward the same conclusions.

"My father owned a grocery store just around the corner

from our house," recalls one guy, "so it wasn't like he was
Willy Loman, off on the road all the time. The thing is, I
don't recall ever having a conversation with him about anything important—*ever*—or even thinking that such a thing
was possible. When I'd watch TV and the father would sit
down with the son and say, 'Well, Beav' "—he offers a small
smile—"well, that was as far removed from my daily reality
as *Gunsmoke*."

"I remember," notes another fellow, a research scientist,
"that once, when I was four, I made a deal with my father:
I'd take a nap if, while I was asleep, he'd build a castle out
of my favorite blocks. I'll never forget it: when I woke up
there was nothing there but two rows stacked haphazardly on
top of one another. It must have taken him all of fifteen seconds." He stops. "It took me a long time to realize that my
relationship with my father is something I have to overcome."

"What are you talking about?" inquires his wife, sitting
nearby. "You don't *have* a relationship with your father."

It is hardly coincidence that, even around one another, we
are so much less guarded about our fathers than about perceived shortcomings in our children, for instance, or persistent doubts about ourselves. For it is a brand of vulnerability
that, being so readily identified with, is rarely turned against
anyone. Every day, throughout the country, in bars and offices, over pinball machines and white linen tablecloths, the
subject turns relative strangers into temporary soulmates. "At
least," laughs a lawyer I know, on particularly sour terms with
his father, "they're good for *that*. I've found it's kind of like
hemorrhoids. When you've got a sonofabitch for a father, you
only meet people with sonofabitches for fathers."

Recounted from the sons' point of view, the stories are
almost always persuasive. Beyond question—for once in a
while one hears these stories, too—emotionally absent *mothers* tend to leave in their wake an even greater sense of dis-
location, an even vaster array of doubts. "If your own mother
doesn't seem to give a damn about you," as one guy thus
tormented put it to me, "then you figure, 'Who will?' " But

then, such a thing is not remotely the norm. "Obviously," as a woman who has done a lot of commiserating with men sums it up, "mothers can be a real pain—especially for daughters. But in most families, the children at least feel they're her highest priority; she will love them for themselves, not simply for what they achieve. So the girls grow up identifying with the nurturer. But look who the boys get to identify with. Can you blame them for being bitter?"

And yet, for so many of us, the bitterness eventually comes to obscure an elementary truth: that, their frailties notwithstanding, and even their clear failings, our fathers, almost all of them, in the ways they knew how, *loved* us.

Until we grasp that fact, not merely as an intellectual proposition but as a matter of the heart, so that somehow, at long last, we can begin to set aside the hurt and the disappointment—recognizing that it too is born of the most primal kind of love—we will remain emotionally incomplete; still, in the most fundamental sense, children.

For a long time, the incident struck me as innocuous enough, one of those family legends good for a quick laugh.

There my parents were, sitting in an expensive restaurant late on that Thanksgiving afternoon—November 25, 1948—when my mother felt the first, faint contraction. "It's probably nothing," she decided, returning to her fruit cup. She was not due for another couple of weeks. But within half an hour, the waves were coming in earnest, three minutes apart, and leaving behind full plates, my parents hurried from the place, grabbed a cab and checked into the hospital uptown.

"Joey," called my mother, as she was led toward the labor room, "could you run out and get me a couple of magazines?"

So my father reemerged into the cool fall evening and, four or five blocks away, found an open newsstand. As he headed back, bearing *Life, Look, The New Yorker,* he passed an appliance store, its window ablaze with eight-inch television sets. And there he stood, the magazines under his arm, watching.

The show was *Holiday Star Varieties*, a two-hour special on WJZ-TV hosted by George Jessel and featuring, among others, Morey Amsterdam, Jerry Colonna and Marge and Gower Champion. My father, you see, had written a sketch for it.

The thing is, while he was gone, watching his show, I was born.

Not that, early on, this seemed anything to hold against anyone. I mean, it had been his *first* television exposure. Here was a guy who a mere half-dozen years before had been laboring full time as a social worker, someone who had forged a writing career for himself virtually by force of will, turning out free-lance radio comedy material between the cracks— during lunch breaks, late at night; and now, suddenly, on this night, he had the opportunity to actually *see* his stuff. Who could pass up *that?*

In any case, hadn't he already been through the hospital routine? I was his third kid. And what difference would his presence have made, anyway? Back then, even the most involved fathers were obliged to play stock characters in a *New Yorker* cartoon, their options reduced to sitting in the waiting room or pacing.

All of which remained as valid as I moved into my teens and twenties as it had ever been. Still, somewhere along the way, for reasons no less obvious, the story stopped striking me as cute; indeed, came to seem a metaphor for so much that had happened since.

This is something else I never confided to my father. Though, as these things go, we even then had what passed for an okay relationship, the ground rules had been in place a long, long time. Almost always, even when we were talking with seeming ease, what passed between us tended to be by the numbers. "How's your work going?" "And yours?" "Did you catch Seaver the other night?"—and we'd rarely linger longer than momentarily on matters close to anyone's heart.

It's just the way it was, immutable. For my father, in particular, good conversation has always consisted of good stories or, if there aren't any to be had, what Hollywood likes to call action/adventure—reports and analysis of what's going on in one's life, especially the professional side, or the world at large. He has never been introspective; tends to discuss even his own past, when it comes up at all, in anecdotal terms, wringing a laugh, or at least a smile, from an episode that otherwise presented, might be taken as harrowing.

"For him, the possibility of discounting childhood experiences was a matter of great consequence," wrote Susan Cheever of her novelist father, John. "He had spent his life escaping the past; he wasn't about to return voluntarily." That struck me as awfully familiar. So, in an altogether different sense (and though my father, who takes the progressive side on almost all subjects, on the face of it subscribes to a virtually opposite view), did a letter from Groucho Marx—by all accounts, even more difficult as a father than he was in other respects—to a writer friend:

> . . . it's about time someone spoke up about Freud and his disciples. I'm so sick of that nonsense. To wit: (a) Parents are responsible for all children who turn out badly. They hated either their mother, their father or both. (b) All people in show business had unhappy childhoods and compensated for it by going on the stage. . . . If analysis did nothing else, it left a lot of people with a hell of a lot less money than they started with.

It is not for nothing that in his writing, even when dealing with highly charged emotional issues, my father has usually kept the interplay between characters light; it is the way he has lived his own life.

And I, let's face it, was of essentially the same stuff—even after I'd begun ostentatiously professing an interest in getting to the bottom of things. More than once, as a child, I'd be sitting at the dinette table with my brothers early on a Saturday morning when all at once, from upstairs, we'd hear my mother's voice, insistent at first, then angry, then furious.

Only my mother's voice, seemingly arguing with herself. My brothers and I—listening, learning—would smirk. Then, at last, we'd hear our father: "Ah, you're crazy"—spoken with finality, his voice at once agitated and controlled. A door would slam, and a moment later he'd join us downstairs. "Good morning, boys."

"Hi, Dad."

Then too, hardly incidentally, my father happens to be (and it is a word I have often heard used to describe him) a nice man, someone who never consciously wrongs others; and the issues at hand—neglect, unresponsiveness, emotional absence, mutual betrayal—are hard to be glib about. When it came right down to it, face to face, neither of us wanted to make the other feel rotten.

Moreover, objectively, in many senses, my father's approach to the world has served him well. "I've never met anyone who seems to worry as little as he does," an old girlfriend of mine once observed. "No wonder he looks so good."

In fact, with an unlined face and a head of luxuriant salt-and-pepper, he remains astonishingly vital. Married to an attractive woman considerably younger, very much engaged by the world around him, he has always been one of those people, rarer than one might think, capable of spontaneous and unbridled delight.

One evening a couple of years back, marooned in the city after a business dinner that had gone on too long, feeling beat, I showed up unexpectedly at his apartment. He answered the door in a bathrobe and slippers, his hair even more unkempt than usual; he and my stepmother had been reading in bed. But the moment I had thrown myself into a chair in the living room, he was perched on the edge of the one opposite, a magazine in hand, eyes alive. "You want to hear something marvelous?" The question was, of course, rhetorical; already he had the magazine folded back to the page he wanted: the results of a "meaningless proverbs" competition. " 'The slowest way to kill an anteater,' " he intoned, " 'is to starve the ants.' "

He looked up, caught my eye, offered a broad grin, returned to the page. " 'The dying man makes a poor traveling companion.' 'I wept because I had no shoes, till I met a man who had no Porsche.' " He laughed. "I mean, they're so *stupidly* wise." A beat. " 'It is not mannerly to be cheerful in the presence of the doomed.' "

If I had run across it on my own, I'd have been laughing hard; but as usual, I held back, offering only a small smile.

Oddly, it was moments not unlike this one that I even then recalled as among the happiest of my childhood; times when I'd lie sprawled on my parents' double bed, my father propped up against the headboard behind me, watching something funny on TV that I would know was marvelous from the size of his reaction. And if, from time to time, even then, he would occasionally glance my way to make sure I was laughing also, seeking not only companionship but a bit of corroboration—well, back then it only made me feel better.

I was not, in any case, as a child, inclined to think very much about it; or, for that matter, about much else that happened around our home. Like just about every other kid, I just sort of assumed that the way we did things was *normal*.

Nor, in a general sense, was I wrong. My father worked hard. My mother ran the house. My brothers and I went to school, played, watched TV, fought a lot. How was I to know—it dawned on me only much, much later, on picking up details from others about their childhoods—that each of our homes is uniquely *abnormal?*

Back then, in any case, the ways in which we differed from those around us seemed to be mostly fortuitous. My father had always done at least reasonably well financially—even as a social worker in the early Forties, he had pulled in $80 a week—and by the time I was in nursery school, the numbers on the checks arriving in our mailbox were beginning to strike my mother, like her husband a first-generation kid out of the Bronx with a social conscience, as "obscene." By then the checks were coming from NBC, where my father was among the writers making what turned out to be television lore, pounding out weekly scripts for Sid Caesar's *Your Show of Shows*. It was, not so incidentally, a circumstance that conferred upon his sons, uncertain of ourselves as we may have been, a kind of status by association—if not among our friends, certainly among some of their parents; and it became even more pronounced when my father, eager to strike out in new directions and in spite of Caesar's legendary wrath, left the show to write Broadway musicals. If, from this distance, it seems to me quite extraordinary that every time I visited my seven-year-old pal Jimmy Lucas, his mother asked me about a forthcoming cast change in *Plain and Fancy*, or my father's progress on *Mr. Wonderful*, or what he might be planning to do next, at the time it seemed altogether natural.

The fact is, I was able to answer most of her questions; and was even prepared, on request, to get up and belt out a song from one of my father's shows. Once, I was actually called upon by my father himself to replicate, in a kind of hum-sing, the entire overture of *West Side Story* in our living room for the edification of composer Jerry Bock and his wife.

In retrospect, I suppose I should be glad that it wasn't Leonard Bernstein himself. But the truth is, I found the experience, and others like it, quite the opposite of humiliating. At the time, it was my intention to become a professional singer—that or a veterinarian—and I was certain that my parents' evident pleasure when I performed was fully justified by the facts. In fact, I did have a pretty good little voice, as well as considerable sincerity, and I was pleased to flaunt both even when my parents were nowhere in evidence. On one memorable occasion, in my eighth year, I won first prize in a camp talent contest, and the monster watermelon that went with it, with my rendition of "Young and Foolish," the love ballad from *Plain and Fancy*.

But of course, what I wanted most to win was my father's sustained interest. My mother's I had—we all did—but somehow, as these things go, that made it less important. In retrospect, she was a quite extraordinary woman; sharp, thoughtful, full of humor; among those who knew her, every bit my father's equal. But her domain was tiny, his the whole world. Ferociously devoted as she was to her brood—and she was a maniac in the matter—her efforts were, even in her own home, incessantly, subtly devalued.

Surprisingly early, and, it now seems, to a greater extent than my brothers, I had begun to become my father's son, having inherited not only his enthusiasm for the theater and the Brooklyn Dodgers but his pointed lack of interest in science, ice hockey, anything mechanical. He read the newspapers avidly—had once, in fact, hoped to become a journalist himself—and by nine or ten, so did I, becoming the founder of my school's Current Events Club. Above all, I learned, as we all did, that a functioning sense of humor is among the most valuable of human traits; not simply because it feels good to laugh but because, in a world that is frequently the opposite of welcoming, it makes for such excellent protection.

My father himself seems always to have known this. One evening when I was fifteen, burrowing through some cartons in the attic in lieu of doing my homework, I came across an antique school notebook, "BRONX SPECIAL" printed on its soft brown cover—the diary that my father had begun at about the same age. In it, there appears an entry dated July 15, 1927, in which, following a lengthy description of a prolonged, fruitless effort to land a summer job in one of the city's innumerable newsrooms—one he desperately hoped would launch his career—he tells of looking into an extraordinarily unappealing job, at $12 a week, at a used-awning shop near his Bronx home.

> *The boss explained that he was the only one there, and that his helper would have a good chance for advancement. He expected to teach the helper the business so that he could stay in the business—practically forever.*
>
> *Could I answer the telephone?*
> *I assured him I could.*
> *Would I go back to school?*

To night high school, if I got a good job.

I'd apparently passed the oral quiz, so he started to test me on my ability to hear and talk over the telephone. He had a dilapidated old house telephone which he must have built himself and through which you could hear sounds, but could make out only about one word in ten.

He went upstairs and started to talk to me through the house telephone. At first, I just repeated the sounds. If he said "Orchard 4367," it would sound like "Awahd aw ee ix ehen." And I would repeat it as I heard it.

But after a minute of this, I noticed that if instead of putting my ear to the telephone, I would listen through the stairway, I could hear quite clearly.

When he came down, he said, "Well, you didn't do it so good at first, but you got it all right later."

He seemed quite pleased with me, and told me to come back the next morning at seven.

"At seven?"

"Why, yes. You will have to stay from seven to six, six days a week, and part time Sundays during the busy season."

I am writing this in the middle of my new job—answering the telephone at a doctor's office.

Still, after reading through the diary in a single sitting and then locating my father in his workroom, I did not even think to mention that delightful episode.

"Dad," I asked instead, "what did you think of Sacco and Vanzetti?"

"Sacco and Vanzetti?" He looked at me, bewildered.

"I mean, when you were young."

"Why, I thought it was awful what happened to them, of course. I was a very liberal kid. Why?"

"Because"—I held up the BRONX SPECIAL notebook—"I want to read you something."

I began with August 10, 1927: " 'A subway station has been bombed in London. Two have been killed!! The efforts to save

them have resulted in damage more costly than the lives of
these two men, it seems' " . . .

. . . then moved on to August 23: " 'Sacco and Vanzetti are
executed at last. It is about time. All these reprieves only
excited radical sentiment all the more. Now there will be a
hubbub which will gradually simmer and die down. Then,
the case will be forgotten' " . . .

. . . and, finally, to September 19, his last word on the
subject: " 'A month, and the Sacco case is no longer mentioned
in the press. The execution did it!' "

My father, in reaction, was gratifyingly abashed; and I continued to get reasonable mileage out of it for a couple of weeks.

Indeed, it is only recently that it's dawned on me that that
particular bit of adolescent upmanship had been an extraordinary opportunity lost; one of the few chances I had back
then, when knowing might have meant so much, to find out
from my father something of how he had evolved into who
he was. For the thing that is actually most striking about the
diary is that the boy on those pages is at once a stranger and
eerily familiar; not only a fledgling conservative and confirmed
goody-goody, *Family Ties'* Alex Keaton sixty years before his
time—"*A policeman was arrested for murder!*" he exclaims
at one point, aghast; *"Next a fireman will be arrested for
starting a fire! What is the world coming to?"*—but someone
marked by a sense of wonder that seems, by today's standards,
nothing short of astonishing. Though, for example, this child
of non-English speakers is exceptionally well read, going on
at length about Shakespeare, Dickens and Shaw, marveling
at the bits of wisdom to be gleaned from the classics, he is
equally delighted by passing items in the daily papers or by
a hot streak by one of John McGraw's New York Giants.
Though his judgments are sometimes harsh, his indignation
is always that of the absolute innocent. *"I sent* The World *six
teams for 'Babe Ruth's All American Selection Contest,' "* he
grimly notes at one point. *"For my reason for including
Hornsby, I wrote 'His timely hitting has put the Giants in the*

race.' Today, I read those exact words *in* The World *in an article about the contest. They stoop so low!"*

What passed me by entirely in my initial reading of the diary, however, what back then probably would not have hit me if I'd studied the thing for weeks, was how seldom my father made reference to his parents or siblings, or, for that matter, any internal life of his own. If, in retrospect, such an omission is certainly not rare in journals of this kind, at least not in those composed by boys, it is nevertheless not without considerable significance.

I did not know my father's parents well—both died before I was thirteen, and seemed to me, in any case, so foreign as to be unknowable—but the reports on each are consistent. My grandfather, by trade a maker of handbags, was, according to everyone who knew him, a man of great sweetness, humility, quiet humor. My grandmother, according to everyone who did not happen to also be her child, was sharp-tongued and emotionally forbidding. Neither, in any event, was much aware of, or remotely interested in, the vast, very American world outside their neighborhood about which my father obviously cared so desperately. In a very real sense, and to an even greater extent than most first-generation kids, my father, without distinct role models or particular support at home, was obliged to invent himself.

But if I squandered my shot at getting into all of that with him, however superficially, I made a conscious choice not to mention the other material I discovered in the attic on the same foray: that which dealt with my dead brother, Genie.

Genie was a shadowy presence in our house, someone who influenced all our lives, and the life of the family itself, but whose name was rarely spoken. Which certainly has more than a little to do with why, for me, he was of virtually mythic stature. Though he'd been only nine when he died, hit by a truck on Amsterdam Avenue on a spring afternoon in 1950, when I was a year and a half old, I continued, even as a teenager, to think of him as older than I; truth be told, I still do. Once, when my younger brother and I discovered a miniature pool table buried away in the basement, a seemingly ancient thing, with real netting in the corners and the green felt mildewed and ratty, and our older brother Danny told us it had been Genie's, it became an instant icon. Neither of us would even touch it. Sometimes, when no one was around, I would study the one photograph of Genie displayed in our home, hanging in my parents' bedroom in the midst of a half-dozen other family portraits. He was professionally posed, alongside three-year-old Danny, and I never stopped being struck by how much more he looked like me than the brothers I saw every day.

That remarkable cache in the attic contained countless other shots of him, from baby photos to several that I guessed had been taken shortly before the accident, and they confirmed that impression. Then too, there were other artifacts—birthday cards, health reports, school attendance sheets and the like—in sum documenting the seemingly extraordinary proposition that my brother had in fact been a regular little boy. "Eugene enjoys dancing and music tremendously," read a report written by his kindergarten teacher. "He is singing better and usually tries hard, though he sometimes gets very excited and forgets to listen to the pitch and rhythm. He can concentrate well but only for a short time. He has excellent ideas and is most dramatic."

But even more than that, I was struck by all that had to do with the relationship between my father and this vanished child. For there they were, in shot after shot, playing together: my father, so very young then, arms extended, face radiant with love, holding Genie up in the air; or crawling with him on the floor of someone's apartment; or smiling broadly as they sat side by side in a rowboat. *That's about all that's new on this end,* my father started to conclude a very ordinary letter to a casual friend that, however, suddenly came back to life. *"Except, of course, for our Genie. He is a delightful and delighted little boy. ('Am I big yet? When can I be big?*

*I want some coffee.') Genie has his third birthday coming up,
and he figures when he blows out the candles, he can light
up a cigarette."*

To us, when we were away at camp, my father wrote chatty
letters; they got somewhat personal only when composed in
the voice of Buttons, our soulful almost-beagle, whose sen-
timents they ostensibly contained. But here he was in 1947,
in a postcard from California:

> *My darling, darling little boy,*
>
> *I haven't seen Roy Rogers or Gene Autry or any of
> those people or even their horses, because I guess they
> stay home mostly. Or else in their stables. But I bought
> you some post cards, and one of them has a picture
> of Gene Autry and his house, but not his horse.*
>
> *I have to do some work now, Gene boy, but I will
> write you again tomorrow. And please write me again,
> because I love you and love to hear from you. Tell
> Mommy, please, to kiss you for me . . .*

In late 1973, a year after my parents separated, shortly after
my mother became bedridden with the cancer that would kill
her, she and I at last got around to discussing Genie and his
death. We had been kicking around the notion of writing a
book together about herself and women like her of her generation—"The Girl with Potential" was the working title—
and so there happened to be a tape recorder going when we
found ourselves in the midst of that awful day: Genie, it seems,
had stayed home from school with a sore throat, and my
mother had given him strict instructions not to leave the apartment; but when she stepped out, with me in tow, to run a
couple of errands, he decided to surprise her by picking up
Danny from his nearby nursery school. Apparently—all these
years later, she was unclear about it—he must have spotted
her on the other side of the broad avenue. Evidently, he called
to her, and when she didn't hear, he dashed into the street
toward her. . . .

Had she and my father ever talked about the extent of their loss? I asked.

"No."

Not even to console each other?

Just the previous year, she offered, sighing, just as her thirty-five-year marriage was coming apart, she had raised the subject of Genie with my father. "He kept saying, 'I don't want to talk about it, *I don't want to.*' The tears came to his eyes and he got very upset. 'I don't want to talk about it, and that's all there is to it.' " My mother began to cry herself. "A day or two after Genie's funeral, we were sitting in the living room, just sitting there, paralyzed in our grief. Joe hadn't shaved in nearly a week, had practically grown a beard. And little Danny came over to him and asked, in a tiny voice, 'Are you my Grampa?'

"Joe looked up. 'Of course not, I'm your Daddy.'

'You look like Grampa.' And he climbed up on Joe's lap and started to comfort him, stroking his cheeks and hair. It was the most beautiful thing." My mother paused a long time, wiped away the tears. "And I remember thinking we'd pull through, after all. Joe and I were strong, we were adults, we loved each other. Somehow or other we would make it."

It was not long ago, as I was listening to that tape more than a decade later while just beginning research on this book, that it suddenly hit me: there were good reasons I cried all the time as a small child, the best reasons in the world. They had to do with the altered atmosphere in our house and the subtle and unsubtle ways, in the aftermath of my brother's death, that the grown-ups around me changed in self-protection.

My father and I rarely discussed my mother anymore. He was caught up in his new life and is, in any case, constitutionally unable to dwell on the past.

But, too, there were the specifics of what happened between my parents toward the end: their decision—more his than hers—to separate after all those years of marriage; her illness; his subsequent return to the household and the long, uneasy truce, marked by outbursts of anger and recrimination (never, from his end, returned in kind) that preceded her death. He remained uneasy about all of that, felt that I judged him harshly. And, of course, he was right.

Yet, curiously, as I listened to my mother speak, I found myself identifying with my father as I never quite had before. He had been thirty-seven when Genie died—my age at that moment exactly—and as madly in love with his kids as I was with mine; and who could say whether, if the unspeakable were to befall me and mine, I'd deal with it any better?

Indeed, a few days later, as I heard yet another guy berate his father, maintaining that not only does the old man refuse to take responsibility for how his children turned out, "he doesn't know why I'm so upset," I caught us both up rather short with my reply. "Don't knock it," I heard myself saying, through a smile; "it's a tactic that might come in handy for us someday."

That kind of glibness has always come to me easily, by inheritance and habit, and for years I was proud of it. But of course, in the end, it is part of the problem. All at once, I found myself wishing that I could express the same sentiment to the person who most needs to hear it—but honestly, without muddying the moment by looking for a laugh; that I could let my father know, simply, at long last, that I understand; and that, eventually, from such a beginning, the phrase that had never come easily to either of us—"I love you"—might become both meaningful and routine.

"**MY** very first love," the guy was saying, "was Olive Oyl. This was when I was three or four. I had this Popeye record, and whenever Olive Oyl's voice came on—this incredibly girlish voice, the essence of femininity—I'd get this weird, thrilling sensation."

"I won't ever forget it," notes another guy, a friend of mine, and since it's already been thirty years, it's easy to believe him. "Her name was Wendy. She had flaming red hair and green eyes, and I think I fell in love with her the first day I saw her in kindergarten." He pauses. "In fact, I've had a thing for redheads ever since."

"I guess," says someone else, an accountant in his late twenties, "I was fairly indiscriminate as a little kid. I seemed to have a crush on a different girl every week. But, then again, why not? They *were* gorgeous."

Not, of course, generally speaking, that these are things we confide nearly so readily as children. Social expectation weighs heavily even on the very young, and aware as we may be that this perception that boys have no interest in girls is utter nonsense, right up there among the great myths about childhood with the notion that the early years are the best time of life, we learn early to pay it its due. "My friends and I used to act like the guys in *The Little Rascals*," recalls the fellow with the thing for Olive Oyl. "Remember how Spanky and Alfalfa had all the others banded together in the He-Man Woman Haters Club? But every time Darla showed up in one of those cute little dresses, flashing that come-hither smile, they were instantly gone? That was us."

But then, why should it be otherwise? As children, we hear the same stories at bedtime that girls do; and it is every bit as easy to identify with assorted princes as with Cinderella or Snow White or Rapunzel. We are just as keenly aware of the loving couples who populate the breath-mint ads, and the elegantly attired ones who make eyes at each other in those for luxury cars and perfumes. We have a pretty good idea what takes place between the sexes on the afternoon soaps, and even before we can read, we can tell a lot about romance novels and all those publications on the supermarket checkout lines by their covers.

All of which certainly serves to confirm that a certain kind of girl—feminine and decidedly on the demure side—is highly desirable. Still, it is an open question how much reinforcement from without we actually require in reaching that determination. For from the outset, there is also the evidence of our eyes and ears and hearts—and as a species, girls strike many of us not merely as different from ourselves but, in important ways, as *better*. Instinctively subtle where we are obvious, reflective in contrast to our loutish impulsiveness, fine where we tend to be so terribly crude, they seem, in many cases, to have been touched by something approaching the divine. "Everything girls did always seemed so graceful," a next-door neighbor of mine recalls. "Why is it that their letters were always so neat and mine were always crooked or smudged?" He pauses. "I mean, could *that* be innate?"

In fact, it may well be. Not to get too arcane here, but the geneticists make a powerful case that the distribution of X and Y chromosomes—two X's for a girl, an X and a Y for a boy— has everything in the world to do with fine and gross motor coordination; and now they are even daring to speculate that it may also figure prominently in how we think and feel. In the past couple of decades, biology, chemistry and medicine have edged into the act as well, looking into the ways subtle differences between the male and female brains seem to impact upon behavior. It has been noted, for instance, that while the average male brain is ten to fifteen percent greater in both weight and volume than that of the average female, the bundle of fibers that connects its left hemisphere (which governs verbal ability) to its right (the emotional center) is markedly smaller; a circumstance that some scientists believe is responsible for women's seemingly greater capacity to express emotion.

Then too, there is the matter of hormones. Recent research has established that androgen, the male hormone, is related to aggressive behavior. In one characteristic study, performed at the University of Wisconsin's Regional Primate Research Center, female rhesus monkeys receiving a stiff dose of androgen not only took up fierce roughhousing, but actually began mounting their companions. According to another study, conducted by the New York State Psychiatric Institute, girls who, through a genetic disorder, received abnormal levels of the male hormone while in the womb tended to be more inclined to rough-and-tumble play and less to nurturing behavior.

Obviously, such research is in its infancy. Some of it remains controversial. But beyond question, science is at last getting around to confirming what most of us have sensed since grade school: that quite simply, males and females often approach the world—and each other—with different things bouncing around within their heads.

Not, all in all, that this should be big news. We have long been aware of the striking differences in the durability of the sexes. Possessed of bodies measurably more fragile than those of females—less prone to survive premature birth, less resistant to a wide variety of diseases, less apt, finally, to keep going as long—there is little reason for surprise that we males might also be stuck with less resilient psyches. It is, for example, among the more revealing of contemporary harrowing statistics that while twice as many adolescent girls as adolescent boys attempt suicide, the boys succeed three times as often.

Quite simply, it appears—hell, the fact has been confirmed by the specifics of many of our own lives—that though it is females who are alleged to be unduly preoccupied with romance, it is males who more often give ourselves over fully to grand passions; who are more chronic brooders; who suffer in greater silence; who tend to take more time to recover from disappointment.

What makes this last a bit strange, sometimes even comic, is how frequently those passions are based not on what's in the love object's head and heart but on how she looks and moves, and how readily we are able to rationalize away real shortcomings, even gargantuan ones, on that basis.

Most females, on the other hand, even when they are very young, have at least some small sense of priorities. A few months past three, my daughter requested a play date with a boy with whom, she insinuated, she was smitten. "He looks like a prince in my books." And so he did—angelic features framed by a halo of blond curls. But after a single afternoon at his side, her infatuation was no more. "He's not very interesting," she explained. "He only likes to play with Go-bots."

"I've come to think of it as a Darwinian thing," observed a friend of mine, whom I'd been badgering to come clean about some of the sorrier episodes out of his youth. "Since females are responsible for the preservation of the species, it's their job to be somewhat judicious in their choices. Our job, on the other hand, is to improve the stock in more obvious ways"— his smile approached a leer—"which is why we go crazy for anybody that looks good. Let's face it, if there were no social niceties, we'd all be like Harpo Marx, tearing down the street after every sexy blonde we saw."

Indeed, one reason I was so struck by my daughter's enlightened sense of priorities—"Last time she'll be a sucker for a pretty face," as my wife put it—was that it stood in such stark contrast to my own performance as a child. My first crush, and it was a doozy, was on a certain Nancy Bell, who had doelike brown eyes and waist-length black hair, and who made me sweat every time she glanced my way. I can still summon up the way she cocked her head when listening, and the soft, tentative voice in which she answered teachers' ques-

tions, and the gray skirt she wore at least once a week in the
first grade, the one bearing a single strand of pink yarn shaped
like a poodle. At night, tucked in bed after my quota of stories,
I would lie awake thinking of her. I would think about the
other pretty girls in school also, but in my most persistent
fantasy they were mere supporting goddesses, their smiling
faces, each in a kind of bubble, rotating in the air above me
like so many Busby Berkeley girls until, finally, they made
way for the exquisite Nancy herself, who assumed the place
of honor in the middle.

The thing is, throughout it all, I am quite certain I never
spoke with her. Not a word. In fact, I rarely even got within
talking range. And when I did—say, if I'd been ordered to
work on an adjacent finger painting—I made sure to be otherwise engaged, thrusting myself into conversation with someone less intimidating. Like, for instance, a boy.

Undoubtedly, this went beyond conventional shyness. For
me, growing up in an all-boy house, a place where I was
surprised to find a toilet seat anything but up, having passed
my earliest years devoid of sustained contact with any girl
who wasn't also my cousin, this was perhaps inevitable. Certainly, my brothers felt the same way about girls that I did.
Together, we would sit before the vintage black-and-white
TV, ogling the youngish blond housewife types who appeared
in commercials for kitchen appliances and cake mixes. These
we referred to as "wreet-wrio girls," the sound being our
verbal imitation of the appreciative wolf whistle none of us
knew how to fashion with our lips.

Nancy, of course, was considerably more than a mere "wreet-
wrio girl," but, in retrospect, I had no idea what I wished to
have transpire between us. I didn't particularly want to touch
her. Or play with her. Or find out where she lived. I never
even told my brothers about her. It was enough to know, in
the privacy of my soul, that she existed, and that there was
indeed such a thing as true love.

I felt this way, without equivocation, for almost two years;
until, to be precise, a fall afternoon in 1955. Our class had

been assigned that day to work on our food scrapbooks, and I was just pasting a picture of a pear on my fruit page when I chanced to glance up and saw my beloved, two rows to the left and one in front, raise her hand and wave it frantically toward Miss Miller. Unacknowledged, she rose from her seat and walked with uncharacteristic speed to the front of the room; then, after a frantic, whispered conversation with the suddenly attentive Miss M., she began moving briskly toward the door. I was watching closely, of course, filled with both curiosity and that familiar sense of wistful wonder, when she suddenly stopped, doubled over and threw up. Right on the floor. Right in front of the whole class.

And for the next ten minutes, long after Nancy had been hustled off to the nurse's office and we were supposed to have returned to our food books, there remained the puddle, a silent, stinky rebuke to romantic love.

After that, of course, it could never be remotely the same between Nancy and me. Soon, however, chastened, I moved on to lesser crushes: Michele, who seemed more interested in horses than in people of either sex; Barbara, whose mother, to my stupefaction, turned out to be as red of hair and freckled of face as she was, and even prettier; Karen, the best reader in the whole class.

Eventually, too, I became aware that there existed girls who actually had crushes on me. This remarkable circumstance was, in large measure, the inadvertent handiwork of Mrs. Levin, my fourth-grade teacher. She was fond of my singing voice and, like Miss Crabtree with Alfalfa, occasionally had me come to the front of the room to sing for the class. It was in the midst of one of these sessions, while I was crooning my specialty, "Young and Foolish," that I became aware that Amy G. was gazing at me with what can only be called dreamy eyes.

My most disquieting, titillating suspicions were confirmed a month later when Amy made me the sole male invited to join her and two friends for her tenth-birthday extravaganza, an afternoon at a local amusement park, followed by dinner at her father's club and a stage show featuring the ventriloquist Paul Winchell. All day long, there I was, shuffling from venue to venue in my white shirt and bow tie, a child version of the guy on the wedding cake. Except when prompted by a grown-up, I spoke not a word to anyone, the nearest thing to a comrade being Amy G.'s father. A small, round-faced man who toted a large camera, he several times clapped me on the back and said embarrassing things about my having all the women to myself.

But I'll be damned if he wasn't right! True, I had no idea of what to do with them all, or even with one, but I could not help noting that they were continually vying for my attention. And even through my mortification, I recognized that this was not a bad thing. Though I respected their judgment not at all, Amy G. and her pals had much to commend them. One of them, Amy A., had once actually played the role of a supporting goddess in my Nancy Bell fantasies. If only she—they—had not been so full of high jinks, so forward, I might have gotten a couple of serious crushes of my own going that day.

But the fact, as undeniable as it is awkward, happens to be that many of us, including some who grew up in ostensibly enlightened homes, were drawn to girls who came off as pliable, even passive. Flesh-and-blood wreet-wrio girls.

It was this recognition that was the genius of *Playboy*, the reason that way back when, as a newcomer on the publishing scene, it generated so visceral a reaction. In it could be found precisely the sort of women we'd always adored from afar— but now they were available, willing, *naked*. And the *Playboy* men—*well*—not a trace of awkwardness there, not even in the presence of staggering beauty.

It is, in sum, hardly a matter of happenstance that within four years of Amy's birthday bash, I, like so many of my contemporaries, was passing a fair number of hours every month in some very private place, communing with that illicit publication; relying on it not only as a source of titillation but for counsel. Given the circumstances of my youth, I had,

before running across it for the first time, not even been
certain what a female minus clothing looked like. Though it
was common knowledge that the magazine went heavy on
anatomical touch-up, though the prevailing expression on the
faces of the women who adorned its pages—vulnerable, yet
unmistakably come-hither—bore little relation to anything I
had ever noted on the face of a girl at school, it was nonetheless
a treasure trove of info.

But more than that, far more, *Playboy* spoke, though the
word had probably not yet been coined, of *lifestyle*. It seemed
to represent the world at its most unutterably sublime. The
Playboy Mansion. The Bunny barracks. The underground
grotto, in which Bunnies allegedly took midnight swims. In
recent years, in response to the women's movement, it has
been maintained that there was little connection between
what went on in our pants during sessions with that magical
publication and what was happening within; that, as someone
recently wrote in the pages of *Playboy* itself, a healthy male
merely "searches for beauty wherever he can find it." Yeah,
right. . . .

Not that there weren't still big surprises. There was, as a
case in point, the morning, midway through my twelfth year,
that I awoke from a truly remarkable dream to discover immense quantities of sticky gunk all over my pajama bottoms,
sheets, belly. Wow. If a girl at the onset of her first period
begins to regard herself, in some unspoken way, as having
come of age, a boy in the wake of his first wet dream leaps
from childhood to the animal kingdom. All at once I knew
exactly what a healthy man did with the kind of beauty to be
found in *Playboy*. And I began doing it incessantly. Com-
pulsively. Alone in my room—after school, at night; all right,
just about anytime the coast was reasonably clear—I was wont
to imagine myself in carnal association with any number of
female schoolmates, including some I'd merely glimpsed in
passing in the halls.

The annual appearance of the Playmate Calendar occasioned particular excitement in bedrooms and bathrooms throughout the land. "If I heard it was in the store," says one guy, "I'd start to feel horny hours before I got there. Yet when I finally got it home, I'd play this masochistic game. I'd tell myself I could pick one Playmate to do anything with I pleased. But I had to make my decision on the basis of limited information. Once I had flipped past someone, she was eliminated as an option; and if I chose someone early in the year—say, Miss March—I wasn't allowed to choose anyone who followed. There was *so much* riding on intuition and instinct." He grins. "Isn't that crazy?"

"Not really," I offered. "I did the same thing."

"You're kidding."

"Nope. A couple of times I passed by some unbelievable ones, holding out for perfection—and got all the way to December, and she'd be horrible."

We laughed.

"I know. That's when you had to bend the rules. . . ."

I had more than an inkling, of course, that there existed males my age who probably did more than just fantasize. I was aware, for example, of a wisecracking jerk in my homeroom named Johnny Phewick. Once, in the hall, between classes, I personally observed him grab someone's breast and give it an affectionate squeeze. I was stunned: this guy was human in name only. But *she* merely laughed and offered a protest that seemed more an invitation. *"Johnnnny*, stop that."

Was this, then, what it took? I pondered darkly. My God, I'd be celibate forever.

During this period, my outward appearance, as if mirroring the turmoil within, was undergoing drastic, seemingly daily alteration. The same thing was happening to most of my friends. Almost to a man-child, we found ourselves suddenly gawky and possessed of voices that cracked at odd times, and massively preoccupied with pimples and B.O. But in one important respect, at least, we felt reasonably secure. The makers of teenage boys' undergarments had done their job admirably, and even the most ferocious boner—prompted, say, by a quarter-second glimpse of bra through an armhole during a biology lab—was invariably held in check.

Summers, however, presented a problem, at least in retrospect. *In retrospect* because, incredibly, at the time (and I am thinking most particularly of the summer of 1963, much of which my family spent at a beach resort), I managed to persuade myself that the bulge straining my drip-dry nylon bathing suit to the breaking point was invisible. Goodness knows, no one ever commented on it. In fact, it was only twenty years later, when I happened to run into a woman on the crosstown bus who had been a neighbor of ours that summer, that I learned the truth: among my female contemporaries, I had been the object of ribald comment from late June to Labor Day.

But then, I hadn't really had all that much say in the matter. Penises, especially adolescent ones, are not only vital parts of what we are, but also totally distinct entities, with habits, customs, points of view of their own; it is not for nothing that so many of us bestow on them pet names. And they can be almost as much a source of consternation as of pleasure.

As small children, confronted with our fathers', we tend to be taken aback, even a little horrified. "It seemed grotesque to me," one guy straightforwardly put it, "this huge hairy thing, one part protruding, the other part hanging there. It looked like it ought to have been attached to an alien, not a human being."

But in fact, even then we have a real bond with our own. "Bye-bye, penis," a woman I know tells me her two-year-old calls out, a plaintive farewell to a pal, every time his diaper goes back on; yet, enlightened mother that she is, she wonders why he so infrequently slips his hand into the diaper to *hold* it, as she's heard boys are wont to do.

Still, it is usually not until well into grade school that one comes to the understanding that the world at large places vastly more significance on this particular appendage than it does on one's fingers or toes. All at once we are sneaking peeks at others' equipment in the locker room before gym, exchanging stories about those of the famous—John Dillinger's alleged 24-incher, supposedly preserved in a bottle of formaldehyde at the Smithsonian; Napoleon's shriveled 2-incher, purportedly in a private collection in London and responsible for the way its former owner, desperate to prove his manhood, turned the world upside down—and remarking on those of others immediately at hand. "I'll never forget," says one fellow, thinking back on his junior high school days in suburban Milwaukee, "there was this guy in gym who had the original soft eleven inches. The rest of us were fucking mesmerized. It was one of *the* landmark events."

All of which, of course, often masked a very real concern: how did we measure up ourselves?

"I used to measure it with a ruler," confesses someone else. "The goal was to get up to six inches erect; that's what was supposed to be necessary to do it right."

In fact, I used to do the same thing myself—feeling just as isolated in my concern as he did.

Still, the odd new physical yearnings, even the confusion itself, could also be curiously pleasurable, simply because they were so dramatic a break with all that had come before. We were, most of us, suddenly leading secret lives. Good kids on the surface, accommodating to our elders, we were also sex maniacs, as inexorably drawn to the lurid illustrations on the covers of paperback potboilers as, just a couple of years before, we had been to D.C. Comics.

And no one suspected a thing—no one, that is, except, in my case, perhaps my mother, who had to deal with my sheets.

Indeed, it never even occurred to me that publicly at least, it was suitable to be anything other than a gentleman; that especially in the presence of a female, I or anyone I knew might display anything but exemplary manners.

And then Jeff Ireland, as polite a boy as any, explained to me how it had come to pass that he felt up Lois Diamond.

We were at camp. It was the summer of 1964, mid August, a time of serious escalation in Vietnam and unusually ominous headlines. And one evening after dinner, he just came out with it. "She thinks there's gonna be a war"—he snickered—"so I comforted her." He went on to note that he had used this technique before; had, in fact, copped his first feel on the bleakest day of our young lives, the twenty-second day of the previous November. About this last he seemed somewhat apologetic, but also defiant; it was his belief, he said, that at least President Kennedy's death had been "good for something."

If I needed any further reminder, in contrast, of my own ineptitude on the amorous front, I was presented with one in depressingly short order. There was another girl at camp named Laura, like the fearful Lois a denizen of Bunk C, who had let it be known that she "liked" me. She was hardly subtle about it. Indeed, several times over the previous couple of weeks she had, in my actual presence, made remarks whose meaning had been clear even to me; once, after we'd watched a friend of mine and a friend of hers disappear into the woods to do God-knew-what, turning to me and pointedly asking, "What about you?"

In fact, she was so up front about it all that I was finally approached by a counselor who, throwing a muscular arm around me, confided, man to man, that in his estimation Laura was a dish, and asked what I was waiting for.

Thus it was that a couple of evenings later, I took Laura up on her suggestion that we share a blanket during a folk concert on the sprawling lawn before the main house and, in short order, allowed her to wrap the blanket tightly around us into a kind of cocoon. And there we lay for fully two hours, motionless, arms around each other, my heart going like a tomtom, but managing to soar nonetheless. At long last, I too had a girlfriend! Afterward, walking her back toward her bunk, I was aware that dozens of our fellow campers spotted us holding hands.

It was only the next morning, when I turned up outside her cabin to walk my new girlfriend to breakfast, that it dawned on me that perhaps my performance the evening before had been less than exemplary. She brushed by me without a word. *"Dear Harry,"* she would write in my camp yearbook, *"I'm really sorry things didn't work out, and sorrier if I seemed to be taking you for a ride. That wasn't the case at all. I think you're great, and really nice."*

Nice. It was the bane of my existence. All around me, it was harder and harder not to note, big things were happening: things that, totaled up by the news media, would shortly come to be known as the sexual revolution. By my junior year in high school, even kids I knew were beginning to get laid. Not just guys like Johnny Phewick, either, but regular kids, kids who walked the halls in neatly pressed corduroys and madras shirts; who watched *The Dick Van Dyke Show* Wednesdays at 9:30 and *The Fugitive* Tuesdays at 10. Kids who had adored President Kennedy and would, within another couple of years, come to loathe Lyndon Johnson.

The first guy I knew about for sure was someone named Theodore Beck, known, with no particular affection—indeed, behind his back—as Beaver. Occasionally, Theodore and I would sit at the same lunch table in the cafeteria and talk, usually about sports—often, for this was the spring of 1965, about Bill Bradley, the extraordinary forward on Princeton's nationally ranked basketball team. Bradley was Beaver's favorite player. For reasons of his own, he had always loved Princeton, and dreamed of going there. But this was our junior year, and the dream was fading; he was smart enough to know he wasn't smart enough to get in.

Which, to get to the point, is what took him to Washington, D.C., one weekend—to spec out George Washington University.

"So, how'd you like it?" I idly inquired the following Monday.

He leaned forward and dropped his voice. "Never mind that. I've got something to tell you." And instead of student-to-teacher ratio and course offerings, I heard about Theodore's female cousin—the one who was a freshman at G.W.U.— and the fact that the cousin had a roommate, and that Beaver himself, sitting there before his spaghetti and chocolate pudding, grinning stupidly, was no longer a virgin.

Once again, and hardly for the last time, I found myself caught short. How could it be? Beaver Beck? I mean, look at him. If he could do it, you know, maybe it was possible that . . . *Nah,* c'mon, get real.

THE first time I laid eyes on the guy who was to become my best friend, he had a pillow slung over his shoulder and a look of mortification on his face, and I decided instantly he was jerk. I mean, it was bad enough that on this, the evening of the very first day of camp, before any of us had even finished unpacking, here were these idiots from the next bunk, these mindless yahoos, attacking us with goose down and foam rubber. Talk about juvenile. But this one guy—the skinny one, in the neatly pressed pajamas— was the worst of all, because he was so obviously *insincere*.

In fact, as the fighting got under way in earnest, as his companions, grinning crazily, filling the air with war whoops, flailed away, he held back, off on his own in the corner, his weapon trailing limply behind.

All of this I observed from the sanctuary of an upper bunk. Independent thinker that I prided myself on being, *I* was certainly not going to get dragged into the fracas by peer pressure.

Still, as the days passed and we settled into the camp routine, I found myself regarding this kid—Paul turned out to be his name—with reluctant interest. It was not that my initial impression had been wholly incorrect. In fact, in the thirteen and a half years I had passed upon the planet, I am not sure I had encountered anyone so essentially awkward around a group of contemporaries who was nonetheless so dogged in his determination to fit in.

But this is what most struck me about the guy: around *grown-ups*, he was wholly transformed. Articulate, poised, with even the body language under control, he seemed, incredibly, very nearly their equal. And to someone like me—someone who approached sixteen-year-olds with deference—it was hard to know whether this trait was more repulsive or impressive.

The grown-ups in question had no such difficulty: clearly, it impressed them. Invariably, almost immediately, he was accorded the respect he seemed to demand. Which, of course, could make the whole business even more repulsive as far as the rest of us were concerned.

There was, to dredge up a particularly memorable example, the morning those junior campers going out for drama first assembled on the lawn beyond the ball field. Not so incidentally, the camp was one that emphasized the arts—our softball team would eventually come to be known as the Culture Vultures—but as a rule, the kids who concentrated on drama, as opposed to music or dance or the fine arts, were the ones without any real skills; were, indeed, like me, kids who had been packed off to the place by parents intent on giving them a dose of culture before it was too late.

So when the drama counselor began outlining his plans for the summer, noting that we would probably begin by working on a couple of short plays by Shaw, and offhandedly wondered whether any of us might be familiar with the Irishman's work, he was as startled as we by the erudition of the squeaky little guy sitting, cross-legged, in the front row; and even more so when Paul evidenced a familiarity with Shaw's countryman J. M. Synge, whose *Riders to the Sea* was to be our second production.

I, for one, decided he was probably bluffing.

For the fact happens to be—and this is an admission that does not come easily even now, and certainly one I have never made to Paul himself—from the start I was a little bit envious of the guy.

Objectively, that might seem odd. His polish notwithstanding, any tally of the pluses and minuses would have indicated that I had at least as much going for me; probably more. For

starters, I was a good athlete, no small matter in early adolescence, while he was what was known, colloquially, as a
spaz. I was, moreover, favored not only with reasonable looks
and a fair degree of personal appeal, but with a father who
made his living writing for television and the Broadway stage,
which conferred upon me a minor celebrity by association.
Paul's father, who made his living in insurance, was, more
directly to the point, married to someone other than Paul's
mother. And in an era when divorce was not yet routine—
was, in fact, for the children involved, almost as much a public
embarrassment as a personal tragedy—this must have been
for him a burden of incalculable weight.

Still, to me, uncertain to the very core, his ready assertion
of confidence seemed absolutely the real thing; and the guy
seemed slicker, better able to get things to break his way,
than anyone I'd ever known.

We did not actually exchange a word until the fourth or fifth
day of camp. That afternoon, we junior drama types were
assigned to help clear debris from a camp construction project,
a half-completed outdoor stage, and I suddenly found myself
toting the front end of a plank of wood with this intriguing,
infuriating Paul guy on the other end. For a good three minutes, we walked in silence. Then—the moment seemed op-
portune—I began casually whistling a tune entitled "A Secretary
Is Not a Toy."

"Hey," he exclaimed, "that's from *How to Succeed . . .*"

"I know" . . . and went right on whistling.

"It's a terrific show. Have you seen it?"

"Sure."

This, of course, is precisely the point I'd been laboring to
make—that, goddammit, I knew theater, too, only had the
good grace not to flaunt it. But my hauteur seemed to escape
him entirely.

"I saw it just before I came here," he said. "Wasn't it great?"

"Yeah. I liked it a lot."

"I live in Springfield, Massachusetts. But I was down in

New York with my mother, and we hit four shows in three days."

What could I do? The guy was so open, so eager, his enthusiasm at having run across me was so intense, that suddenly all I had been feeling seemed petty beyond measure. And by the time, five minutes later, we deposited our load on the lumber pile beyond the dance studio, we were friends.

Which, of course, is certainly something else I had had somewhere in mind all along.

After that, we were always together; during drama and at mealtimes, swimming at the lake and on Sunday-morning jaunts into the town nearby. Indeed, within a week and a half we had contrived to get him moved into my bunk. He took possession of the lower bunk bed beneath my upper.

THERE is a certain Dr. Michael McGill, a researcher in the field of human behavior, who has concluded, on the basis of an extensive survey of male attitudes published under the title *The McGill Report*, that, in essence, the majority of men don't even know the true meaning of friendship. "To say that men have no intimate friends," he writes, "seems on the surface too harsh, and it raises quick objections from most men. But the data indicate it is not far from the truth."

What men tend to have, he observes, is utilitarian friends, buddies with whom we share particular, limited aspects of our lives, but no part of our innermost selves.

Often, as he puts it, "even 'best buddies' reveal so little of themselves that they are little more than acquaintances. There is no intimacy in most male friendships and none of what intimacy offers: solace and support."

Of course, his data merely lend weight to assumptions that have been bandied about, especially among women, for quite a while. A quarter-century ago, Margaret Mead was already observing that the sort of intense male interactions we're so routinely treated to on the screen or the printed page are, if not precisely counterfeit, mere "accidents of association"; that guys in foxholes or on the lam or in the midst of pulling off some kind of financial coup generally have little of substance in common, but are bound only by temporary self-interest; that, to carry it just a bit further, were the film to run another reel and the guys in uniform to make it safely home, they'd end up having nothing to do with one another.

Aware as we are that these kinds of things are being said about us, we tend to pay them little mind. We see ourselves getting along just fine with other guys, can little fathom why anyone would maintain otherwise. If we appear to be more comfortable with banter than with heart-to-hearts; if we keep to familiar subject areas and avoid more demanding terrain; if, in brief, even those of us who regard ourselves as reasonably sophisticated often come off like characters in beer ads, well, that's just the way we do things. *Just because we're not demonstrative, or gushy, that doesn't mean there's no communication. We know what we feel.*

All right, sometimes—lots of times—guys we hang out with turn out to be less than wholly dependable; but what's the big deal? One man I spoke with tells a story about the time, back in law school, when he went to a party at the home of a fellow student and presumed pal, where he was offered an artificial substance "which turned out to be elephant tranquilizer. Lying there, unable to move, I heard this guy ranting about how I had to be moved somewhere else, otherwise he'd never be admitted to the bar." The guy begins laughing. "I knew right then that he was going to make one terrific lawyer."

"I don't want to talk about it," a man I've worked with for years likewise managed to make a joke of it, when I pressed him to talk about the marital difficulties that were so evidently affecting his disposition. "I'm a guy, I want to talk about baseball."

And sure enough, baseball—or more precisely, life's vagaries as they are reflected in baseball—is what we did talk about that recent evening. For although we like each other, we do not fully trust each other. Over the years there have been too many thrusts and parries, too many hurtful remarks passing as innocuous fun. And so, finally, we tread delicately.

Had I heard, he asked, half an hour into the Braves broadcast going on on the TV set in the corner, about the Reds' pitcher who'd gotten arrested last night in Atlanta?

"You're kidding."

"Apparently there was a brawl in a restaurant after the game. According to Skip Caray"—a Braves announcer—" 'a waiter's hand collided with his fist.' "

We laughed.

"Has he been suspended?"

"Nah. They said he'll go on trial the next time the Reds come to Atlanta. Don't you love the way the law treats ballplayers?"

I smiled. "What, you think they'd treat *you* any differently?"

He hesitated, and for just a flicker of an instant, something more showed. "Me? Hell, no, I always get the breaks."

It begins early, this reflex to tough it out. Even as very small children—though by subsequent standards, wildly indiscriminate in our choice of companions; finding ourselves tight for weeks or even months with kids with whom, it is later apparent, we have zero in common—we are aware of the subtle competition to be the strongest, the fastest, the cleverest; and know, before we know how to ride a two-wheeler, that to be anything other than a winner is to feel somehow like a loser; and understand, too, that in the end, most people don't *care* how you feel. And so we soon learn, as a matter of emotional survival, to be ever quietly on guard, especially among others of our sex.

Which is why, for many of us, preemptive attack is so obvious a tactic. At the age of six, I was the leader of a neighborhood band known informally, almost formally, as "Harry's Gang." Our principal activities—climbing a large tree in our front yard; running fast as the wind; throwing dirt bombs for distance, for accuracy and at one another—served also as our initiation rites and, more vitally, as a means of maintaining a pecking order. Robbie Aarons, who did those things second best, was my lieutenant; a couple of kids were sergeants; my

three-year-old brother was the private. We regarded ourselves as comrades of the highest order and talked a lot about
nobility and honor—but, too, all along we had a secret agenda.
On the next block, we had it on good authority, on Wykagyl
Terrace, there existed another gang, one led by a kid named
Roger Slater, and we were forever planning for the clash we
took to be inevitable; until, that is, the day that Roger Slater
showed up, *his* three-year-old brother at his side, to ask if
they could join our gang.

Quite simply, it was never enough to be just good; the point
was to be *better* than someone. As any number of my contemporaries will recall, there was a pseudo joke that made
the rounds of schoolyards and ball fields in the late Fifties. It
was not intended to get a laugh, merely to stick it to the
unfortunate soul hearing it for the first time. "Hey, Andy,"
one guy in a group might pipe up, "did you hear the one
about the two elephants in the bathtub? See, they're taking
a bath, a mother and a father elephant. And the mother elephant says, 'Please pass the soap.' But the father elephant
looks at her and says, 'No soap radio.' "

At which point everyone in the group would absolutely
crack up—invariably joined, after an awkward moment, by
the pigeon. Then, abruptly, the laughter would cease. "Why
are you laughing?"

"At the joke"—though of course there would already be a
glint of panic in his eye.

"It's not funny, stupid. We just wanted to see if you would
laugh because everyone else did."

And half an hour later, the joke would be tried on someone
else, the recent victim invariably joining the perpetrators.

And so it went. Countless Americans still shudder at the
memory of the ritual choosing-up prior to long-ago games,
and never mind that the scene is among the great coming-of-
age clichés, that they now understand that it really *didn't*
matter when one was selected. At the time the procedure
seemed to make one's place in the social order as evident,
as irrefutable as was a telltale red splotch during the Great

Plague. And if one doesn't have what it takes, there is solace only in the approval of those who do.

In September 1957, two new boys entered my fourth-grade class: one quiet and well mannered; the other a skinny little guy named Richie Zucca who within a week distinguished himself as the best softball player in our class. For the life of me—and I have tried—I cannot remember the first kid's name. But a few weeks ago, when I ran into a guy at a party who turned out to have gone to my elementary school, we spent fifteen minutes talking about Richie Zucca.

"He was so incredibly fast!" recalled the guy, now a fourth-grade teacher himself. "I was a little kid—too little to play myself—but I used to hang around the field after school watching him play. His brother was good too."

I smiled. "Nicky Zucca."

"Yeah, Nicky. But Richie was even better. What a short-stop! I remember he was the first one I ever saw to use one of those six-fingered gloves."

"It was a Harvey Kuenn model. I used it a few times my-self."

"You did?"

"Sure. Richie was a friend of mine."

But of course—for this comes on the heels of the other—friendships can prove useful in another, more cynical sense. Decades before "networking" came into vogue and comedians began getting laughs with lines like "I've got friends I haven't even used yet," kids of my generation were forging relation-ships with the notion, occasionally conscious but more often so deep in the mind that the idea only partially revealed itself, of personal advantage. I know a guy, twice unhappily married, who now confesses, laughingly, that as an eight-year-old he was less interested in one of his constant playmates than in her father, who was in chocolate-covered cherries. "But," he says, "I was ready to marry her."

When, as a sixth-grader, I myself was nominated to run for president of the student council, I selected as my campaign manager not one of the kids from my own circle—each, somehow, as offbeat as I was; kids with whom, in the spring, I played softball on the patch of Elizabeth Road before my house dubbed Stein Stadium; with whom, in the fall, I competed at Leaf Catching—but the immensely popular, athletically gifted Bobby Merchant, who not only possessed a tiny printing press (needed, as I told both my slighted friends and my conscience, to produce "DON'T BE HESITANT, VOTE HARRY FOR PRESIDENT" flyers), but headed another, tonier circle, one that suddenly seemed more appropriate to a kid of my stature.

From the outset, and this is hardly a pleasant admission, or an easy one, there was much of this in my relationship with Paul. I recognized, even if he seemed unaware of the fact himself, that he had what has since come to be known as star quality, that his good opinion was something of value. To be singled out as his special friend was more than simply flattering; it suggested that maybe I was better than I thought I was. Oddly, I am quite certain I fulfilled very nearly the same function for him—for though I never knew exactly why, though the discovery continually surprised me, in group situations I had always been much liked and was often perceived as a leader.

Then too, there was the matter of my father. Among all the enduring memories of that summer, none remains more vivid than that of my friend, at my side, awaiting my parents' arrival on visiting day in a state of high excitement and anxiety that even then seemed comically out of character; and holding back when, once the familiar Peugeot had pulled into the camp parking lot, I was hugged and kissed by one and then the other; and then, at last, timidly stepping forward to be introduced and, to my astonishment and considerable pride, asking my father for his autograph.

But if, beyond question, each of us relied on the other to confirm his best hopes for himself, I like to think there was far more to it than that. We were, after all, living out early adolescence together, our joys and disappointments, expectations and sadnesses as intense, as vivid as the colors on a

palette. Even as we were self-consciously beginning to em-
ulate adults, surprised to occasionally find ourselves treated
that way—and surprised, too, having been much protected
and intensely idealistic, by the astonishing degree of insin-
cerity, duplicity, stupidity to be found in the world—we were
immensely grateful for the companionship of another in like
circumstances with whom to begin sorting things out. And
with each other, Paul and I could be honest; even, very occasionally, vulnerable.

Only once before, the previous summer—also at a summer
camp, where, for a couple of months, the normal rules of
boyhood can be somewhat suspended—had I shared a comparable intimacy with a peer. The kid's name was Chet, and
I vividly recall the afternoon when we walked back to our
cabin from Bass Lake, our trunks dripping chilly water, our
arms around each other, talking about how good we felt.

Not that with Paul the feelings came nearly so easily. Having both been wounded early—not so that it was apparent to
the naked eye, but in the usual ways—we were both prone,
at least as much as others of our sex, to covering up; and
almost always, our most meaningful exchanges caught us by
surprise. One early evening, for instance, right after dinner,
we were hacking around outside the main house, trying to
stump each other on show tunes, when on the road beyond
the camp perimeter, a car swerved to avoid a dog. Which
somehow led to my telling him about my dead brother. And
then, in emotional kinship, he began telling me, for the first
time, about his parents' divorce; and his mother's remarriage;
and his father's; and the things he loved and resented about
each of the four of them.

To be sure, neither of us spoke that evening with anything
resembling real self-knowledge; unaccustomed as we were to
thinking about these things, we weren't much good at talking
about them. But of course, that is precisely the point.

I don't mean to overdramatize here, or mislead as to our
day-to-day behavior. For if it is select extraordinary moments
that I recall best, it is probably the case that neither of us

came across to others as a notably sensitive soul. We were, for example, both of us, principals in the cabal that more than once reduced Lucille Redmond, the unfortunate charged with forging a junior chorus, to tears—not only by our inattention but, a couple of times, by singing off key on purpose. And in drama, intent as we were on making good, we were the ones constitutionally incapable of not snickering particularly dumb improvisations. And the ones who, on every camp trip, hunkered down in the back of the bus to loudly sing songs from obscure Broadway musicals, unable, for all our relentless good cheer, to obscure the impulse to show each other up. (I recall being particularly struck, even at the time, by my friend's disconcerting tendency to race ahead to the next line before it came along naturally, thereby ruining the song in the interest of establishing his credentials.) And the ones who, in concert with half a dozen others, were supposed by some to have taken good fun several steps too far in the matter of Donald Hough.

This last, by the way, I continue to regard as a bum rap. I actually tried to help Hough, did my damnedest to protect him from the others. But then, it's also true that, given the prevailing mood, I was considerably less adamant in the guy's behalf than I might have been.

It was at least a week into the summer before any of us had the slightest idea about Hough. Sure, he *seemed* a bit odd, with that brush cut of his, and his shirts buttoned up to the collar, and the most intense stare this side of Bela Lugosi, and his custom of going around mumbling to himself, waving a finger as he walked, conducting an imaginary orchestra; but, well, he assured us that he was a musical genius, and we just took it on faith that this was how geniuses behaved. Then one night, perhaps ten days after we'd arrived, shortly after the light had been turned out, there came a low, ominous chant from his lower bunk.

> Big fat hunk of dirt,
> Big fat hunk of dirt,

      Big fat hunk, of a big fat hunk
        of a big fat hunk of dirt.
      Big fat hunk of filth,
      Big fat hunk of filth,
      Big fat hunk of filthy, dirty . . . Steve Bergman.

There was a long, long silence. "Who's Steve Bergman?" someone asked finally, into the blackness.

"He's the kid back home who always beats me up."

After that Hough was fair game. He was the butt of a hundred jokes. His bed was short-sheeted, and a tube of toothpaste squeezed under the covers. The six of diamonds from his prized set of plastic playing cards mysteriously disappeared. Seemingly every time he entered a room, someone would start humming "There's a Place for Us."

I was, as reported, considerably less involved in all of this than most of the others. The guy was pathetic, destined, at best, to be the perpetual outsider, and it seemed to me that that was more than pain enough. While his tormentors became increasingly brazen in their meanness, and increasingly unembarrassed by it—while more and more routinely their names found their way into his sad-comic chant: "Big fat hunk of filthy, dirty . . . Michael" (or Joel or Paul),—I hung back; never, to be sure, saying what needed to be said, but persuading myself that I was something of a moderating influence.

That my friend participated so enthusiastically in the business at hand gave me only minor pause. That was altogether natural. Every group of boys to which I'd ever been attached, at school, in the neighborhood, at other camps, had operated by the same set of Darwinian rules, the normal and the quick finding a sense of community at the expense of the weird and the weak.

In any case, any small credibility I might have enjoyed as a finger pointer vanished for good the late-July morning that Paul and I discovered that we were both familiar with the score of *Oliver*, the London hit that had not yet opened on Broadway. It was, in fact, I, seizing upon a variation of a routine I had used over the years to show up my brothers, who suggested that we try a few numbers out on Hough, claiming to have composed them ourselves; and I who did most of the singing, while our patsy, sitting on a tree stump, listened attentively, nodding his head to the beat; and I who, once he had offered an only moderately enthusiastic critique of what he had heard, informed him that in short order it would be turning Broadway on its ear.

And, yes, there was also my involvement in the final episode of the Hough saga, the incident, on the eve of parents' visiting day, that abruptly terminated his stay at the camp.

That day began innocuously enough. We were in the midst of a thorough bunk cleanup when I suggested to Hough, who gave new dimension to the term "slob," that he replace the single sheet, ripped nearly in two and gray with grime, that had covered his mattress for a month with a pair of fresh ones.

"No," he replied coolly.

"Why not?"

"Because."

"Because why?"

"Because I like it this way."

"Goddammit, Hough, our parents are coming. We want this place to look neat for a change. Look, I'll lend you a pair of my sheets."

"No!"

"Well, I'm sorry, but I'm not going to let you screw up the whole bunk."

And with that, I began ripping off his bedding; was, in fact, in the process of shaking out a fresh sheet; when the blow, subsequently determined to have been struck with a two-by-four, caught me in the back of the head.

Had Hough's victim been anyone else, the punishment might not have been so swift, or so final. In spite of the fact that by his own perverse admission, he had once been forced to depart another camp for pushing someone down a flight of stairs, Hough enjoyed a certain sympathy among the staff, who appreciated his considerable musical gifts. But it had been I, as close to an ally as he seemed to have among his contemporaries, and that clinched it. Deemed a danger to his fellow campers, he departed that very afternoon with his parents, as sad-looking a pair of middle-class grown-ups as I had ever seen.

Neither Paul nor I ever saw Hough after that day, the same one my parents showed up in the Peugeot, and it may well be that my friend too thinks back on how he handled himself then with a degree of self-reproach. It is not insignificant, however, that in the twenty years that followed, through literally thousands of conversations, as our friendship grew even more intense before beginning to dissipate, neither of us has even once spoken of that doomed soul as anything but a comic figure.

FOR those who find themselves still preoccupied with their fathers—still given to brooding about what they did to them, handicapped by it in ways that most of us never know—the resentment, in its assorted guises, is likely to surface anytime, prompted by almost anything at all.

One morning several years back, for instance, I spotted a tiny item in the *New York Times* sports section. "You don't see strong arms like he has much anymore," Hall of Fame fireballer Bob Feller was quoted as saying of Dwight Gooden. "That's because dads don't play catch with their boys like they used to when I was a kid. Now the fathers sit in front of the television with a case of beer."

I snickered and read it aloud to my wife.

"Hmm," she replied, not looking up from the crossword puzzle.

" 'Hmm'! What's that supposed to mean?" It was, after all, good stuff—a bit of endearing crotchety locker-room wisdom that actually approached the profound.

I patiently explained this to the woman.

"I know," she said, "but is it true?"

"Is it true? Of course it's true!"

How could it not be true? Didn't she know what things were like? And all right, even if it was a bit of an exaggeration—the Waltons, after all, were never your average American family, even down on the farm—its spirit was accurate. "We're not raising grass," noted former slugger Harmon Killebrew at his induction into the Baseball Hall of Fame, recalling his father's admonition to his mother when she'd worry over cleat holes on the front lawn, "we're raising boys"; and by the hundreds, those of us in the audience were as moved by the innate wisdom of it, and the selflessness, as was the speaker himself.

Sure, observed my wife, but let's not forget that back then, far more routinely than today, fathers used to beat hell out of kids. And weren't parents once encouraged to apply child-raising techniques that strike us in the era of Dear Abby and Dr. Ruth as nothing short of medieval? Hadn't I, in the course of my own research, run across a certain Dr. Emmett Holt, the Benjamin Spock of sixty years ago, a man so alarmed by the prospect of thumb sucking that he advised parents of two-year-olds to strap them down in their beds? Why, her own father, as a child, used to have his right hand tied behind his back by her grandfather, the idea being that as a lefty, he'd have a better chance to make it as a pitcher. All true. "Now I can't write decently with either hand," my father-in-law once told me. "And I've hated baseball all my life."

But of course, for those of us walking around profoundly resentful of perceived past wrongs, there almost always remains the impulse to fix blame; and more than that, in one way or another, to get even.

The world is full of people who, unaware of it as they may be themselves, live their lives in daily rebuke of their parents; children of the excessively achievement-oriented who pointedly underachieve; the ones who, in anger masked as indifference, deny their parents full access to their own children; most commonly of all, the ones who, having failed to get what they needed as children, systematically make a shambles of their personal lives.

Nor is the mere recognition of the tendency always sufficient to overcome it. I happened to be watching a Mets game recently with an old friend, someone possessed of both a longtime passion for the home team and a recent degree in psychiatric social work. As we watched, this guy—like so many mental-health types, initially drawn to the field by the impulse to sort out personal issues; in his case, those involving an extremely overbearing father—began ruminating on Darryl Strawberry. His point was that the young outfielder's notorious moodiness had everything to do with the fact that he grew up fatherless. "It's something you see a lot in people with that kind of hole in their lives," he said. " 'Crippled inside,' as John Lennon called it, and he knew all about it. With Strawberry, there's such an obvious desperation to be respected—remember when he anointed himself 'team leader'?—but when things don't go his way, he just seems to have no emotional resources to fall back on."

Okay, I could see that. But I pushed on to the far more intriguing case of Keith Hernandez, the Mets' immensely talented first baseman, him of the movie-star good looks. Here we have a guy who seems to have everything going for him— but who chain-smokes his way through every season and seems to curse himself after every failed turn at bat; a man who, indeed, appears to the naked eye all but incapable of joy.

"Ah, Keith . . ." replied my friend; "now we're talking. In my professional judgment"—he smirked—"the man has a very serious problem. Talk about a guy whose father is too much with him . . ."

"What—you examined him, I suppose?"

"Nah. I read an article in Sports Illustrated. And there we had it, a classic case of accommodation—a son driven, at his own psychic expense, to live out the dreams of the father."

When I read the piece myself the following day, there seemed to be no denying it. Here was the mysterious Hernandez up close and personal, suddenly as familiar as the kid up the street suffering through another fatherly tirade in the wake of a Little League loss. And here was his father, John— once, until an errant fastball put a sudden end to his career, a big-league prospect himself, also a first baseman—riding the younger man ceaselessly, belittling, cajoling, bullying him toward ever-greater achievement. "I'd tell him," says Keith, " 'Dad, I'm a man. I don't want to be reliant on you for my career. Dad, I'm 28 . . . Dad, I'm 30 . . . Dad, I'm 31 . . . Dad, I'm 32; I'm a man.' "

Concludes the son, "He wants to take credit. He's told me, 'You wouldn't have made it without me pushing you.' You mean to tell me that of all the professional athletes in the world, all of them had a father that pushed and pushed and pushed on them? I find that hard to believe."

"But you know what?" noted my friend, when I called to discuss the piece with him: "When your father tells you stuff like that, you do believe it. Even if it's contradicted by objective reality"—he paused, and suddenly I understood that he was also talking about himself—"even if everyone else tells you otherwise. Your father just has this incredible power to swat you down."

It is not, of course, inadvertent that I set this business of the interplay between fathers and sons alongside the playing field. Even in an age when sports are less explicitly a male preserve than ever before, many women still wonder at the intensity of interest so many men bring to athletic competition; a fuller, more vivid passion, indeed, than some of us bring to anything else, or anyone, in our lives. " 'We're number one, we're number one,' " a woman friend parodied the faces screaming at us, wild-eyed, from the TV screen one fall afternoon, following a victory by football's Giants. "Why doesn't anyone ever tell them that *they* haven't done anything?"

But what such a view fails to grasp is the extent of the escape provided by sports from all in life that is mundane, from incessant low-level pain; that the games are someplace where one can lose oneself, even feel confirmed, with no demands made in return; that, above all, in a sports environment—a locker room or an asphalt stickball field, in the right-field bleachers at Shea or in a bar among strangers staring up at a 15-inch screen and commenting on the action—one is curiously free, unburdened by the constraints, often self-imposed, so evident elsewhere in our daily life.

Which is why, edging back to the matter at hand, it is so frequently through sports that fathers and sons come to reveal themselves most fully to each other. The psychological professionals talk, as they will, about the subliminal life messages fathers pass on to sons; and "dream dissonance" (in which the son fails to conform to the father's notion of what he *ought* to be); and "doubling," the capacity of a father to identify with his son's pain and joy. Average guys talk about exactly the same things—except they recall a father's reaction after they've scored a winning touchdown, or screwed up in the bottom of the ninth, or failed to make the team entirely.

Indeed, it is intriguing to note how often, when speaking of their fathers even in other contexts, men fall back on sports metaphors. "Conversation with him is like a fencing match," one guy told me, "except it always seems to start off with my sword on the ground." "For years, every Saturday afternoon," recalled another, whose parents divorced when he was a toddler, "he would take me to a cowboy movie. That was so that he wouldn't have to talk to me. It was like he was the club owner and I was some player with a long-term contract who couldn't be cut." "My father desperately wanted me to join the family business," noted a man who opted, instead, to become a college teacher. "He still thinks of me as having quit the team."

There is a footnote to this last. Once, long, long ago—for this is the way these things so often work—this guy *had* quit a team, a Pop Warner football squad run by an overbearing, win-at-all-costs coach. "That really teed my dad off. He didn't give a damn about my reasons—as far as he was concerned, I'd let *him* down. He's still that way. Last year, when I accepted a job seven hundred miles from where he and my mom live, he didn't for a moment see it as a good career move; he saw it as a personal slap in the face."

For of course, the depth of misunderstanding between fathers and sons is often beyond measurement; the mutual capacity to wound, even by inadvertence, limitless. Until a full and conscious effort is made to change patterns set early, they will play themselves out literally till the end.

I know a guy, a business associate, whose father was the last doctor in their Midwestern town to make house calls.

"Everyone regarded him as a saint, because he always made
time to listen to other people's problems. But he never made
time for me—never even came to watch me play the year my
high school basketball team won the regional championship."

Though I do not know this guy terribly well—an occasional
business meeting here, an even more occasional lunch there—
I have heard this story of the father and basketball team several times. "At the end of the season," it concludes, "I invited
my uncle, who used to go to some of the games, to the awards
dinner instead of my father. My dad was very hurt by that."

Pay-back time.

But of course, slight for slight, wound for wound is no
solution at all. "Very good," as my own father had *Fiddler*'s
Tevye admonish a fellow villager who, in the face of trouble,
reflexively cited the biblical dictum of "an eye for an eye":
"that way the whole world will be blind and toothless."

Ultimately, even the doctor's son came to realize that. Not
that it changed things. Relentlessly driven professionally, he
always made a point of lording his greater material success
over the father. And when the older man died not long ago,
he made sure the chapel was filled with ostentatious wreaths
sent by his business associates—showing up the old man one
last time, at his own funeral.

It was never that way between my father and me. The rift
was never so explicit. Had I played big-time ball, he'd certainly have made it to at least a couple of games; he'd certainly
have been beside me at that dinner. Indeed, I am not sure
at that age I was conscious of any resentment toward him at
all.

No, what distanced us from each other was something far
subtler; something I began only recently, well into my
fourth decade and with children of my own, to see for what
it was.

The incident is so humiliating, I have never confided it
even to my wife. That now, with this in print, my children
will someday learn about it bothers me even as I set it down,

the possibility that perhaps by then I'll have found a way to wring from it some kind of character-building moral striking me as the very essence of small consolation.

Not, looking back upon it with a semblance of objectivity, that it was really so gruesome, after all. So I flunked a Little League tryout. Big deal. That's life. It happens to everyone.

Only, see, the thing is, I was a good ballplayer. A very good one. Maybe not good enough to dream of the majors—I was smallish and Jewish and not crazy—but good enough that when the kids in the pickup game on the Roosevelt School playground, the one that daily came together between lunch and when we had to be back in class, would spot me coming, there'd invariably be an argument. "We got Stein!" "No, we got him!" Always, as I heard those words, glove in hand, loping toward the diamond from the playground entrance, chicken sandwich and chocolate milk sloshing around within, my heart would soar.

All right, it's true, I hadn't played much hardball. All right, again, I had long been secretly afraid of new situations, new people, anything that felt like a test of character. Still, I had dreamed of this afternoon for weeks, was ready for it. Little League! The big time.

The odd thing, in retrospect, is that I did fine during the initial phase of the tryout—the batting evaluation. Some grownup was doing the pitching, overhand, which took a bit of getting used to; speeding toward me, the ball looked unnaturally small, and at the start, I took a couple of healthy cuts and was surprised not to make contact. But soon enough I got the timing down and was ripping liners to left.

No, the roof caved in fifteen minutes later, during the fielding segment. Normally sure-handed—I was *known* for that—I was auditioning at shortstop. First I botched a pop-up, fungoed directly my way; off the bat, it seemed to go almost straight up, disappeared momentarily against a cloud and suddenly was hurtling downward, landing on the infield dirt behind me. And then, astonishingly, so did another. All around me, kids were smirking. Next came a ground ball. I booted it. I caught a glimpse of my father behind the batting cage; he looked stricken. I fielded the next grounder cleanly, my final opportunity to impress, and, picking up the first baseman with eyes already filling with tears, desperate to show off my arm, I winged it hard—five feet over his head.

A couple of minutes later, head down, tears streaming down my face, I was walking beside my father toward the parking lot.

I sensed he was disappointed, but not really surprised.

"Don't worry," he said, "you did fine."

"No, I didn't. I stunk."

He placed a tentative hand on my shoulder. "So you made a couple of errors. So what? Everybody does. Your hitting was great."

To this I made no reply. We had reached the car, the old Chrysler convertible. I flung open the door and slumped in the passenger seat.

"Harry."

No reply.

"Harry. Look at me."

"What?"

"I'm going to tell you something, and I want you to listen."

His face a blur. "What?"

"You did fine. Are you listening? Just fine."

"No, I didn't."

"You did." A beat. "And anyway, I'll tell you something else. It really isn't that important. Over the long run, it really doesn't matter whether you make the team or not."

Did he actually expect me to be consoled by this? Obviously. And in a vague, small way I was. There was, after all, something nice, something so effortful in the attempt. Still, it was a lie. *Wasn't important? Didn't matter?* What was he talking about? It mattered more than *anything*. If it didn't matter, *I* didn't matter.

But then again, maybe I didn't. Maybe I'd been an idiot to suppose I could play Little League ball to begin with, with kids who were bigger, faster, better than I.

An excessive reaction, perhaps. But I knew what I felt. I was a failure. And terribly, irredeemably alone.

It is only now, reflecting on that grim afternoon all these years later, perhaps working out a bit of future strategy of my own, that it occurs to me what might, under ideal circumstances, have taken place between us. There'd have been some talk about that awful sense of inadequacy and how it comes upon the best of us. But even more vitally, we'd have kicked around the legitimate difficulties involved in trying to adjust, without so much as a moment's preparation, from softball to baseball, with special emphasis on how timing and trajectory are screwed up in so precipitous a move from a larger, softer, lighter ball to a smaller, harder, heavier one. And then, maybe, we could have dug up one of each, headed for the backyard and, with an eye on the future, seen for ourselves.

Then again, we were who we were.

By the time we arrived home, my eyes were dry. The rest of the family was out. I went into the dining room and flicked on the TV; my father retreated to his upstairs office. Over the next half-hour, from above, came that familiar pattern of sound and silence: a staccato burst from his Olivetti, a long pause while he thought, fifteen or twenty seconds more of clatter. It may have been *Take Me Along* he was working on; or *Enter Laughing;* or, just possibly, a very early draft of *Fiddler.*

I stared at the screen. The detestable Yankees, in fuzzy black-and-white; the Dodgers had gone, the Mets were yet to come and we needed a new picture tube. That damn set always needs a new picture tube. As it happens, this game, against the woeful Senators, will turn out to be glancingly memorable. Along around the fifth or sixth inning, Mickey Mantle belts a titanic blast off the facade in deepest right field, reputedly among the longest shots of his career. An inveterate Mantle hater, in the immensity of my self-preoccupation I am even more than usually unmoved by the moment. *I have never, not once, gotten to hit a hardball for a home run— and now I never will.*

A while later, Dad appears in the doorway. "You okay?"
"Yeah."
"Good."
But a week afterward, when I get the postcard from the Little League informing me that I've made the minors—the minors! I hadn't even known there existed such a thing—I crumple it up forthwith, lest it be spotted by some enemy, and stick it at the very bottom of the outgoing trash.

IN the wake of that first summer at camp, my friendship with Paul remained somehow undiminished—this in spite of the fact that the couple of hundred miles between New Rochelle and Springfield might as well, for a couple of thirteen-year-olds, have been several thousand. Although it wasn't quite what it had been back at camp, this business of exchanging letters and an occasional phone call, we quite readily made do.

To my old friends, the intensity of my association with this mysterious guy from so far away must have seemed odd, and to his old friends also. What they could not know was that for each of us, the other represented a fundamental break with the past. Until then, we had always been *kids;* around our families and those we had always known, we still were. But together, we could be as worldly as we wished we were, and know we would be taken utterly seriously. True enough, at home I continued to spend a lot of time poring over guys' batting averages and, huddled under the covers, listening to West Coast games on my portable radio; and Paul, for all I knew, was doing likewise. With each other, though, we were as sophisticated as Rodgers and Hart.

Here, in its entirety, is a letter, scrawled on a sheet of looseleaf, that showed up in the mailbox one spring morning in 1963:

> *Dear Harry,*
>
> *It is now definite that I will arrive in New York on Friday night. (I'll take the train down after school.)*

79

What should we see? How about Never Too Late, *or*
Oliver *or* Pal Joey *or* Boys from Syracuse?

I just got the record of She Loves Me *and it's great!*
Barbara Cook is in finer voice than ever.

I saw Milk and Honey *in Boston, and it was dis-*
gusting compared to the original, which I saw two
years ago in New York. Robert Weede puts nothing
into it at all, and most of the rest of the cast is equally
bad. Also, for the road, sets have been simplified into
drops. Yecch!

Take Her, She's Mine, *with Tom Ewell, is there*
now, and I hope to see it next. Then (goody, goody)
The Sound of Music *for two whole months.*

I'm glad The Dick Van Dyke Show *won so many*
awards. It's my favorite show on TV by far.

When, periodically, I journeyed up to Massachusetts for a
visit—the first trips I had ever taken anywhere on my own—
we would spend whole afternoons listening to reel-to-reel
tapes or records, and a third of every night talking about camp
or school. And I would come to know, to the extent to which
a grown-up could be known, those people who had shaped
my friend, noting how Paul's odd, almost-Southern inflection
echoed that of his easygoing, Georgia-born mother, and in
his father, the same hint of formality that had always set the
son apart from his contemporaries.

His sorties to my place, characterized though they were by
a frantic round of theatergoing, long sojourns at the musicals
bin at Sam Goody's record store and leisurely strolls through
Shubert Alley, where we would decorate the enormous post-
ers for current shows with our own critiques ("*A helluva show*"—
H.S.; "*Barbara Cook is extraordinary*"—P.L.), were likewise
enlightening for me, although in a different sense. More readily than any other kid I had dealt with, Paul identified my
parents as ordinary human beings; as flawed, even comically
so, as we were ourselves, and only intermittently more sensible. This he did by silently observing the behavior in our

home, which, though it had always seemed to me altogether reasonable, often struck him as the antics of confirmed wackos. Indeed, much of what he witnessed, only slightly embellished for effect, soon found its way into our repertoire of shared anecdotes, right up there beside the best of Hough. There was, for instance, the morning of the heated argument in my parents' bedroom over whether my sixteen-year-old brother should be permitted to drive to an adjoining state, thereby slightly breaking the law. My mother, once again on the losing end, stalked angrily toward the door.

"Where are you going?" called my father after her.

"To do the dishes"—and she continued on her way.

A beat. "Wait a minute; there are no dishes."

She turned, offered a baleful stare and spoke the soon-classic line: *There are ALWAYS dishes, Joe.*

Then there was the family dinner that had been preceded by a brief dispute over which record should be placed on the stereo in the adjoining room as background music, my brother's brand-new *Meet the Beatles* LP or something out of my mother's small classical collection. Eventually a compromise was struck: first hers, followed by his. Thus it was that throughout the soup and into the chicken, my parents seized upon lulls in conversation to exclaim at the magnificence of certain harmonies and bits of virtuoso musicianship. "Listen, children, listen," implored my mother: "isn't it beautiful? Now, admit it, this is better than your rock 'n' roll." It was not until the first record ended and the Beatles slid onto the turntable that we abruptly learned that the machine had been going at the wrong speed all along. And there sat Paul, his eyes bright with amusement, literally gnawing his lip to keep from exploding in laughter.

Though neither of us would ever have thought to verbalize the feeling, such moments represented, in our common view, the very essence of friendship. All these years later, I continue to think back on them, when I think of them at all, with terrific fondness. And yet even then, in retrospect, had either of us known to look, or cared to, we would have discovered something missing.

"I grew up," another guy told me of a similarly pivotal relationship in his life, "just down the street from Larry. We met when we were five.

"It was a lower-middle-class neighborhood in a small Long Island town, and it had a kind of timeless quality. Kids were well brought up, mores were strict. I go back to that neighborhood now and it's exactly the same, with the tidy houses and the neat lawns; it's frozen in time.

"Maybe that's why as Larry and I grew older, the friendship seemed eternal in my mind. It was for life. We shared the same interests—not only the usual boy things, but literature and music. He was someone with great humor and great finesse—qualities his father also had. The father was a meter reader, very low-key and terrific with kids; the opposite of my father. I'd hang out at their place all the time. They had a pool table, so we'd do that; or go out and play some stickball; or play the piano; or just get a pizza and hang out. This kind of operation occurred until we were well into our teens.

"But there was always something I regarded as an anomaly. His mother was totally without class. Loud. Never read a book. And she was always after her husband to make more money. Once—I'll never forget it—she had him go to the blood bank to get thirty dollars for a pint."

He paused. "But this is what I'm leading up to: when Larry got married, at twenty-two or twenty-three, it was to someone exactly like his mother. I was best man at the wedding—but most of the people there only emphasized the gulf between us.

"We tried to keep the friendship alive. At the beginning, we exchanged Christmas cards. But after a while, she'd always write theirs—in a flourishing hand and without any content. And, I don't know, eventually we just lost contact."

He stopped, shook his head. "It still lives with me, this strange loss. And the most difficult part is, I find myself wondering how well we really knew each other all those years, after all."

In fact, a surprising number of us have Pauls and Larrys in our past: once-close friends who have somehow dropped from sight; or at any rate, from week-to-week, month-to-month consciousness. We take it to be just the way things are, accepting that even the closest of friendships simply peter out; we've changed, goes the thinking, and so have our life circumstances and, as a consequence, the way we look at the world. Sometimes, one hears it said outright, without the merest trace of embarrassment: someone maintaining that he has "outgrown" someone else.

It is hard to know whether such a view is more chilling for what it says—that no bond is so strong as to ultimately be immune to indifference—or for what is implicit: that in the current social environment, it is not merely the occasional friendship that tends to be so cavalierly set aside, but the very meaning of the term.

And yet, even in the midst of so dismal a trend, there are vital distinctions to be made. Beyond question, what has always been true continues to hold: women are generally less casual about the obligations of friendship, and more conscious of its rewards, than are men. Preoccupied as we invariably are with the business of getting some large or small something done, we men tend, quite simply, to possess less patience for the minutiae of daily life, the incidental give-and-take through which, finally, people come to slowly reveal themselves to one another.

"There's an interesting contrast between the diaries of Charles and Anne Morrow Lindbergh," notes Thomas Mallon, who recently wrote a book on private journals. "Hers were quiet and focused on things less celebrated women have written about too—childbirth, her house and so forth. His are very preoccupied with history and making sure people have his place right. By the way we usually judge the world, what he writes should be more interesting, but it isn't."

Which, oddly enough, is not surprising at all. The contrast in the Lindbergh diaries is between a show of ego and a display of quiet vulnerability; between the impulse to impress and the impulse to communicate; between a self-preoccupied demand for universal attention and something that, inadvertently, truly does speak to the entire human condition.

It is safe to assume that Anne remains richer in friends than was her husband even at his most celebrated.

In the end, as too many of us know, what pass among men for friendships are often simply extended relationships of convenience; pleasant enough, in their way, and perhaps even passingly fulfilling, but built, finally, on quicksand.

Paul returned to camp the following July, but I skipped a year, not heading back until the summer of 1964. From the perspective of the here-and-now, two years is less than an instant. But at the time, the gap between thirteen and fifteen seemed infinite. We were *big* kids now, among the very oldest on the premises; principals in the *senior* drama department, who got to live in the bunks adjacent to the ball field, pretty much without adult supervision; who even, on occasion, though God knows we didn't need to, shaved.

Then too, as it happened, these *had* been a couple of extraordinarily eventful years. That summer of 1964, we remained very much shaken by Dallas. John Kennedy had been our Pied Piper, so fully mobilizing the best within us that we had begun to feel, quite literally, blessed. So much so that even today, for many of us November 22, 1963, stands as a great divide: the moment that we understood, with chilling clarity, that nothing is as permanent as it seems; and that evil sometimes does triumph over good.

This was something else my best friend and I shared.

More than once, over lunch or relaxing after drama class, the question would be asked, as our parents had asked of one another in the years after the shocking news from Warm Springs: Where were you when you found out? The sense of moral community was immensely heartening and, more than that, an ongoing necessity. Already, as the summer progressed, new crises loomed, and together, secure in a shared vision of the way things ought to be, we scrupulously charted events. In Philadelphia, Mississippi, three young civil rights activists participating in a statewide voting-rights project, one of them from New Rochelle, were murdered. In San Francisco, Republican presidential nominee Barry Goldwater, addressing an angry, divided convention, idealized right-wing extremism as a virtue. In early August, there began appearing ominous headlines about a curious incident in the Tonkin Gulf; and Congress, with a mere two dissenters, obligingly handed Lyndon Johnson extraordinary war-making powers.

We followed all this through *The New York Times*, which arrived, scrunched up in my mailbox, six days a week, a couple of days late. Paul's copy of *Variety* turned up on Friday or Saturday. Between the two of us, we had the whole world covered.

Not that there were no big doings right there at camp. The two of us reigned supreme in the drama department, although he somewhat more than I: in the year I'd been gone I'd lost ground and, one counselor advised me, though not intending to be cruel, a bit of onstage panache. So while, for example, in the summer's principal opus, a production of *Li'l Abner* staged for visiting parents, my friend played the title role, I was assigned to impersonate the heavy; and when, during rehearsals, facing each other down in a climactic scene, spouting dialogue that seemed so ludicrous in our mouths that we'd crack up every time we caught each other's eye, it was I who almost got canned.

But on the other hand, it was I who was selected to be the editor of the camp literary magazine—no small distinction and, I suspect, a disappointment for my friend, who planned to be an important literary personage. With a flourish and a touch of the *grand seigneur*, I appointed him co–associate editor, along with a very pretty dancer he had his eye on, then allowed him to be represented in print not only by a longish short story, but by a series of meditations on fate, destiny and human possibility.

Then again, I myself, who had never so much as read any verse beyond Mother Goose, elected to cast myself that summer as a poet.

> What for, he did not know.
> He only knew he had to go.
> What was the fighting for?
> His mother thought, and cried.
> And so he went to war,
> And soon she heard he'd died.

I mean we were, both of us, guys with *things to say*. And not unnaturally, each of us hoped to say them better than anyone else, including the other; or, at any rate, get credit for doing so.

Still, just before the magazine was to go to press, when the owners of the camp moved to censor another of my contributions—a light essay expressing my skepticism toward those of my contemporaries who professed to adore classical music—on the altogether sensible ground that it might prove embarrassing to a camp that provided classical-music training, Paul joined me in provoking a staff revolt that very nearly sabotaged publication.

In fact, this odd mix of conspiracy and competition, which had characterized our friendship from the start, would, as time passed, be ever more discernible in its distinct parts. The very best times, the most fulfilling both back then and in retrospect, were when we were onto something together, the Hardy Boys loose in the real world; or, just as often, in our case, running around some theater.

There was, for example, the steamy August afternoon, just a few days after the end of camp that summer, when we sneaked into a rehearsal of *Fiddler*, then in the process of setting up for its pre-Broadway tryout at Washington's National Theater. There, on the distant stage, was Zero Mostel, an odd green bandanna around his head, a cigarette dangling from his lips, seeming to walk through his paces; and *mumbling*, so that the plot was all but impossible to follow. At the back of the house, in the shadows, I was disconsolate. "My father's got a disaster on his hands," I said softly. "Don't worry," tried my friend, without much conviction, "maybe they'll fix it"—all the while, neither of us realizing that what we were watching was a *technical* rehearsal. Or the time, a couple of weeks later, when, jointly smitten with the show's original Chava, we picked flowers from the park near the motel where we were staying with my family and had them sent backstage—only to watch the object of our infatuation swooped down upon by a duplicitous counselor from the camp we'd just left, to whom we'd made the mistake of pointing her out.

The opposite sex, one will note, was already a big thing with us, and as time passed, girls figured ever more prominently in our private universe. Paul knew the name of every female after whom I lusted, which is often just about all I knew about them myself. If he was shy also, he was considerably more adept than I at hiding it—which, in fact, is virtually the same as overcoming it—and by my standards, he did extraordinarily well.

Emphasis here on *my standards*.

"*Things have been going great with Jan,*" he wrote in the fall of his senior year in high school.

> *Thursday we watched* The Glass Menagerie *on TV— excellent, if not as fabulous as* Death of a Salesman— *and I got* au deuxième étage, *as they say in the trade! Details when you come up for the demonstration.*
>
> *Which reminds me, something really funny happened when William F. Buckley was on* Johnny Carson *last week. Carson: Did you see Henry Cabot Lodge's statement about "the war in Vietnam gradually fading out and dying"? Buckley: Yes, I saw that. Uh, I think Mr. Lodge is confusing the war with his own political career.*

This, of course, as time passed, was increasingly our other bond—an intense shared interest in current events, and most particularly the unsettling events in Southeast Asia.

There was, indeed, one remarkable day in the late fall of 1965, in the course of one of my visits to Massachusetts, when we managed to indulge all three of our obsessions in a single afternoon. We began with a couple of hours of picketing and vigorous chanting before a Boston University hall where Dean Rusk was speaking, which ended when Paul's stepfather picked us up at the curb and chauffeured us to a matinee performance of Anthony Newley's musical *The Roar of the Grease Paint, the Smell of the Crowd;* after which, while waiting for the stars to emerge through the stage door, we got to ogle, for a full fifteen minutes, Newley's wife, the young Joan Collins.

But all along, we never stopped knowing that we were also rivals. Not, to be sure, in the obvious ways. We were geographically too far apart to be interested in the same girls. Even at camp, we'd never competed in sports. Nor, frankly, would either of us have risked full-blooded, head-to-head competition. One of the men with whom I spoke described coming upon his date, in the back room at a party, "messing around with my best friend"; and though I certainly sympathized with his enduring hurt, it was hard to fully relate. No one purporting to be a best friend of mine would ever have thought of doing such a thing.

No, my ongoing rivalry with Paul was subtler than that, and in its expression infinitely more complex. Though, through adolescence, the only real argument we ever had was utterly trivial, prompted by a game of License-Plate Initials (when, with the contest on the line, we spotted an "EW" and my "Eudora Welty" edged out his "Ed Wynn," and he got so adamant about playing again that he refused to stop the car when we reached our destination), ours was, in fact, a *life* competition. Each of us had considerable ambitions for himself, and each was fighting self-doubt with every weapon in the emotional arsenal; and as time went on, that meant, among many other things, that we were increasingly interested in beating each other. We were friends, all right, and surely devoted in our way—but, as much as the guys who split over the betrayal at the party, we were operating without the safety net of articulated common values.

In retrospect, that began to become explicit only when we went off to college: I to a small California school called Pomona; he to Harvard. *Harvard.* Where else? It is not that I wished anything but the best for the guy—we're talking *consciously* here—merely that I had my own ego to deal with. This proved it: he was smarter, abler than I; and already, at nineteen, better connected.

But if that corrosive feeling was born of less than honorable impulses, I managed to find at least some support for it in the attitudes of my friend himself. We still spoke with some regularity, and exchanged the occasional letter, but now it was hard to miss in him a decided touch of *noblesse oblige.* There was always just this expectation that I ought to be fascinated by what went on in his sphere, without, however, any real interest on his part in what went on in mine.

Some of which, as it happens, was pretty interesting just then. There was, for example, the period when a handful of us at the student paper, out to debunk the administration's claim that the school had an absolutely open policy in regard to student recruitment by outside organizations, had gotten the Communist Party of Northern California to put in for use of the recruitment office. Having had the Reds forward us a duplicate of their written request, we immediately splashed it across our front page, beneath the headline COMMUNISTS TO RECRUIT HERE. The administration, instantly under siege by swarming alumni, hastened to deny it, and presto! we had our issue: if the recruitment office was not wide open after all, why should it remain available to such noxious outfits as Dow Chemical, the manufacturer of napalm, or, for that matter, the U.S. military? For weeks and months the argument raged across the normally serene campus—culminating, one February (which, in Southern California, is not the same as "wintry") morn, when a hundred or so demonstrators packed themselves into the recruitment office, thereby keeping a pair of austere Air Force men from performing their assigned task. The action eventually led to a mass trial, in which we were all convicted and given "suspended suspensions"; which we took to mean, since the place had lately been transformed into a hotbed of liberalism, that the judges had sort of liked the crime.

It was, in brief, an exciting time—but all I ever seemed able to generate in my pal back East was perfunctory interest.

On the other hand, when Harvard had its revolution, more than a year later—and, heh, heh, almost as long after the one at Columbia upon which it was so obviously modeled—my friend expected me to be as hopped up as he was himself, and as conscious of its global significance.

And yet, of course, in objective terms, damn it all, who could argue? The Harvard strike was all over the front pages that week, the lead story on the networks, while our little action had garnered nothing more than an angry editorial in the Pomona *Progress-Bulletin* that, of all things, identified *us* as the Communists.

It is easy to exaggerate all of this. In general, certainly on the face of it, we were pretty much as we had always been; remained, in our own estimation, within the limits of our understanding of the term, the best of friends.

Indeed, the summer after the Harvard disruptions, we traveled together through Europe via Eurailpass, swinging up to Scandinavia and southwest to Barcelona, then eastward again to Switzerland before heading on to England; trying to catch a film or two wherever we went; striking up innumerable fleeting acquaintanceships along the way, sometimes even with females. And if just about every encounter with an even moderately attractive woman seemed to begin the same way— "Where do you go to school?" / "A little place in Southern California called Pomona." / "Oh. How about you?" / "Harvard." / "Ohhh. Do you know someone named . . . ?"—well, I took it with every appearance of good grace.

Indeed, given that the Eurailpass seemed designed to provoke anxiety, leaving one with the incessant feeling of missing out on something else, and the consequent impulse to hop the next train, we got on, that summer, extremely well.

As we would continue to for years afterward. Into our late twenties, we saw each other regularly, caught up by phone at least a couple of times a week. We were both working in New York by then—I at a hip magazine, he in the office of a prominent film producer whose right hand he had become— and in one way or another, most of our conversations had to do with upward mobility: projects we were on, people we had met, what might be happening next. The one-upmanship, though ostentatiously good-natured, was so incessant that sometimes even we ourselves recognized it as comic. He might call to report on a negotiation with a famous writer about the film rights to his latest book, I'd be about to do a piece on a famous athlete; I'd have just reached the newly disgraced Spiro Agnew by phone, he'd have dined the previous evening with then-hot Elliot Gould. I'd often be surprised, and I'm sure it was the same for him, how much his other friends seemed to know about me; and even women he'd dated casually.

Still, eventually, almost imperceptibly, it began to change. In the most obvious sense, work pressures were responsible. His career, in particular, was starting to soar; it now involved regular trips to the Coast and to assorted shooting locations. It made sense that the calls, especially from his end, should become less frequent, the lunches and dinners harder to arrange.

But I recognized from the start that it was not only that. Paul wasn't faking it anymore—he was becoming an important guy himself, one of the people others would brag about having had dinner with the previous evening; and—how else to say it?—my name was slipping lower and lower down his list of people to call back.

By the time his first feature film opened—the first, anyway, on which he got sole producer's credit—he had relocated to Los Angeles. When he came to New York shortly thereafter, we met for a quick lunch at a deli. I'd imagined that I might mention something about it—say that I'd been hurt by the way the friendship had been going, that I even got angry about it sometimes. But it just didn't happen. Face to face, allowing for the difference in stature of acquaintances whose names were bandied about, he was pretty much his old self: bright, full of interesting news and, though guarded in other respects, frankly sentimental about old times.

So I let it pass. And eventually, seeing each other rarely became seeing each other hardly at all; or even talking. More than once I learned afterward that he had been in town for an extended stay and hadn't bothered to call.

And sometimes, even now, without knowing quite why, I find myself dwelling on it, and wondering anew: Does it weigh on him too, this strange loss? Did it have to happen this way?

And yet, finally, there were always clues. Perhaps most memorably of all, there was that late afternoon in London, a week or so before we were to head home from our summer on the rails.

My friend, like seemingly half the Americans in London, had arranged to call the States that day; and so, while he waited for the connection, I hung out at the other end of the bustling telephone exchange off Trafalgar Square, eventually striking up an exceedingly pleasant conversation with some kid our age. A student at a small college in Indiana, he shared my enthusiasm for the Beatles and Stones, and I was very much surprised when he let it drop, in passing, that the year before, during the 1968 presidential campaign, he had worked for George Wallace.

"Isn't that incredible?" I said to Paul afterward, on the street outside the exchange. "I mean, he seemed like such a reasonable guy."

"It's not incredible at all," Paul observed tartly. "Everyone knows that the Wallace movement was very strong at certain colleges in the Midwest."

A foolish subject for a quarrel, to be sure; but it was, above all, the tone that got me. "What the hell are you talking about? It was *not* routine for kids like that to work for Wallace."

"You know, when you don't know what you're talking about, you really ought to keep your mouth shut."

"And you do, I suppose?"

"Yes, I do. The *Crimson*"—the Harvard daily—"did a piece on the subject."

"Well, screw you!" A beat. "And screw the *Crimson!*"

And an instant later we stalked off in different directions. Late that evening, when I arrived at our rooming house, he was already in the room, awake in his bed, but we went to sleep without exchanging a word.

"Harry," he said the next morning, as soon as he saw I was awake.

"Yeah?"

"You okay?"

"Yeah."

"I think," he offered with considerable feeling, "it's really good what happened yesterday."

"So do I."

"We really cleared the air."

"I know we did."

But I remember thinking, even as I spoke the words, *No, we haven't. We haven't even identified the problem.*

IT was in the summer of 1965 that, for the first time, I fell in love with someone I actually knew.

Not, truth be told, that I waited to meet her before falling in love. Spotting her across the lobby of the cheap Left Bank hotel that was to be Paris headquarters of the teen tour for which my parents had signed me up, I was struck, in one of those moments seared into memory, that I probably needed new glasses: no one could really be so pretty. But later that day, unable to dodge an introduction, seeing her close up— the raven hair and high cheekbones, the blue-green eyes and the luminous, lightly freckled skin—I was overcome, more than anything else, by panic.

But the astonishing thing was she was *friendly,* actually wanted to know about *me.* Instantly, if not sooner, I was willing to hand her my life story—my life itself—on a platter.

The problem was, so were five of the other seven boys on the tour—a fact that endeared Christie, for that was her name, to the seven other girls on the tour not at all. But how could it have been otherwise? She was every shy, insecure sixteen-year-old's romantic ideal. At once spunky and sweet, as ready with a laugh as with a look to make one's heart stop, she actually *liked* us. If only, in three years, or five, she would marry us, we'd never want for happiness again.

All right, a case can certainly be made that, as a subsequent decade would have it, we were denying her personhood here. In fact, if we'd known how to look, or cared to, Christie was a highly complex being, if perhaps a less than endlessly fas-

cinating one. As insecure as any of us, far brighter than she
realized, let alone knew how to show—much later, she would
tell me that she was tired of being told how pretty she was,
resented it; but we both knew she also needed to hear it—
she was the product of a broken home: a father who philan-
dered, a mother who'd been briefly institutionalized.

But, then, who ever looked into Cinderella's emotional credentials?

As our group made its way across the Continent, from Paris
to the French Alps and on to Venice, picture-postcard locales
that only heightened the sense of romance, a subtle but intense competition developed among Christie's suitors. Day
after day, always taking care to maintain the gloss of bon-
homie, we'd maneuver to sit beside her on the bus or train,
exultant at our occasional good fortune, stoic in the face of
somebody else's. Each small intimacy offered her and accepted was a milestone, each time she laughed at another's
remark a small setback. Beset by the realization that none of
us had much of a chance anyway, but unwilling to fully accept
the fact, we were, in brief, in a perpetual state of adolescent
angst. And all the while, maddeningly evenhanded, Christie
seemed determined to be friends with us all.

The adults charged with our supervision, a married couple
named Carlson, clearly took it all as amusing. Occasionally,
as the weeks went by, we could even smile at it ourselves.
For in spite of Christie—really, because of her—the six of us
found ourselves becoming fast friends, bound by the intensity
of our feelings and, in a curious way, in self-protection.

Perhaps inevitably, boys—even love-struck ones—being
boys, our blossoming camaraderie began to exercise itself at
Christie's expense. One day in Florence, my best pal in the
group, Petey Alper, the one of us most readily able to distance
himself from emotion via wit, reported that a young desk clerk
he'd made friends with had offered the following assessment
of the adored one: "She is like a beautiful bird—a lot of energy
and a very small brain." That very evening, he was referring
to her, to her face, as "Bird," and so were a couple of the

others. A week after that, in the Italian resort city of Chiavari, the six of us solemnly convened over dinner and made a pact: henceforth, none of us would have anything whatsoever to do with Christie, would not exchange with her so much as a word.

That resolve lasted exactly fourteen hours. The next morning, a bikini-clad Christie was espied upon a rocky precipice overlooking the Mediterranean, having just made her way ashore from an unusually rough sea. Face upward toward the sun, wet hair hanging behind, chest heaving as she struggled to catch her breath, she had never been more wrenchingly appealing. "I'm breaking the pact," shouted Petey, scrambling to his feet and dashing up the beach toward her, and the rest of us instantly followed.

Our group spent the final two weeks of the trip in Avignon, the medieval French town once inhabited by fugitive Popes. There, pairing off, we resided with French families, the larger group coming together only on weekday mornings for instruction in the native tongue.

Obviously, my access to Christie was considerably more limited now, a situation exacerbated by the fact that my housemate was the ever-vigilant Petey and that she was staying outside the town's ancient wall, in the home of an elderly farm couple. Yet it was also the case that our times together were more private—almost, in my willful estimation, like real dates. More than once we met at a small café for peach Melbas. Another time, even more memorably, we spent an afternoon bicycling through the local countryside, Van Gogh country, preposterously ablaze with greens and yellows and reds, before finally laying down our bikes beside a vineyard; there, stretched out side by side between the vines, so close I could feel the warmth of her skin, desperately wanting to make some kind of move but desperately afraid of how it would be met, we began talking more seriously than we ever had before. She had, she told me, always strongly identified with Anne Frank; sometimes, even then, had horrifying dreams in which SS men showed up at night to drag her away. I told her about my dead brother. On the way home, pedaling slowly to make the day last, I sang her the entire score of *Guys and Dolls*.

I did not discuss any of this with Petey or the others; nor were they any more forthcoming about whatever time they passed alone with her. Which, all things considered, was not only better than the alternative, but perfectly okay. We were, all of us, in the midst of the best time of our lives—a fact we fully appreciated even then—and had less use for pettiness and rancor than we would ever have again.

Then, one early afternoon, three days before we were to return home, our host family's nineteen-year-old son invited Petey and me on an overnight camping trip. My friend accepted readily, but I hesitated and finally demurred: there had been some vague talk about getting together with Christie that evening.

We met after dinner, beneath a eucalyptus tree a hundred or so yards from her house, and lay down on the dry summer grass. The light was fading fast as we talked, and after a while a stiff wind came up. And suddenly—I still don't know how it happened, though I am quite certain I didn't initiate it— we were embracing. When we came apart, we smiled, then laughed into each other's faces, then embraced again. After a time, I made a tentative move to kiss her, but at this she turned her face away—"No"—the sense being that, having already staked out so much new territory, we oughtn't to go any further. I understood, even agreed. How long, I asked a moment later, had she felt this way? She shook her head. "I don't know, I just do. How about you?" I laughed, full to bursting. "I always have. Didn't you know that?"

We stayed there, under that tree, for at least an hour and a half; until, to be precise, the skies abruptly opened. We lingered for a moment more, holding each other; then she dashed for the farmhouse and I mounted my bike.

Heading home on the roadway alongside the medieval wall, bearing right onto the main street of the darkened town, the rain plastering my hair against my face and soaking me to the skin as I zoomed past the central square and the Palais des Papes, I was Gene Kelly on wheels. Never had I felt more intense joy; never, ever, had life been so splendid with promise.

The next morning, up early, I was back on my bike, collecting wildflowers on the riverbank near the famous Pont, then dashing back to the farmhouse. From far off I caught sight of her, peering down at me from a third-story window.

"Come down," I called.

"I can't."

Too late. The old farmer, her surrogate father, had emerged from the adjacent barn holding—no joke—a pitchfork.

"Toute la nuit, et maintenant toute la journée aussi!" he bristled, thrusting the implement my way. ("All night, and now all day too!")

"Excusez-moi, Monsieur," I replied, ever the good kid. Still, as I remounted my bike, I tossed the bouquet in Christie's general direction and blew her a kiss.

Petey was waiting for me at home, more sober than usual. "You were with The Bird, weren't you?"

"Yes." I felt joyous and proud and also, suddenly, guilty. "She's my girlfriend."

But how readily, at that age, the emotional climate is subject to violent alteration. *"I miss you terribly,"* she wrote several weeks after our return home, in that loopy filigree so common to girls of a certain bent.

> *Here's hoping it will last, and we will marry and live in New York and go to the theater and have babies after four years and go to Europe and be poor and then be rich when we're old and have you teach me things you know and me teach you how to dance—slow dancing—and move to a farm for a summer where all we'd do is ride horses and sing songs and see people we like.*

And yet already, a month later, she was growing distant. This was for want not of contact—she had passed a weekend at my home and we spoke long distance, New Rochelle to her Delaware home, at least three afternoons a week, staying on as long as we dared, living in dread of the coming phone bill— but of proximity. For, of course, she had suitors on her home turf also, and struggle against it as I might across the miles, I could sense her being drawn back to her prior life.

My most immediate concern was a guy named Eric. "Who cares about old Eric-face?" she had insisted during our first week back in the States; but it was increasingly apparent that she did. One Friday night, when I knew she was with him at a school dance, I stayed up till past 3 A.M., watching that most appropriately maudlin of film romances, *Wuthering Heights;* suffering, but intent upon outlasting them. I had to be sure, by the time I drifted off to bed, that there was no more funny stuff going on down in Wilmington.

On the heels of this came the shattering information that Petey, who lived close to me, had actually taken off a day from school to pass an afternoon with her—and at the station, awaiting his train back to New York, they had *made out!*

Truth be told, it was Christie herself who confessed this, and with genuine regret. It had been a mistake, she insisted, a whim of the moment. But for me, not yet having kissed her myself, that hardly set things right. What she had done was awful enough, but Petey, that sonofabitch, that worm, had violated something even more fundamental than trust: something like decency, duty, honor.

In the years since, it has been hard not to notice that in what hardened souls refer to as "the real world," such things happen all the time. People of both sexes cause their mates all manner of heartache by messing around with assorted others; hell, I would live to do so myself. But—maybe it was because I had so uncompromisingly moral a mother, maybe simply because I'd always taken what passed before me on TV at face value—I believed as absolutely as Donna Reed and

Carl Betz in the sanctity of marriage. And by extension, the sanctity of *all* romantic liaisons. *How could they do it?!*

On the other hand, beginning the very afternoon of her confession, I got to kiss Christie too, and I quickly saw what the fuss was about. She was a great kisser, the sort who would lose herself in the moment, sighing a lot, seeming to struggle against her self-control. Still, it will not take a seer to fathom that my fortunes were on a steep downhill course. Not more than a month and a half afterward, in a cooler, firmer tone than any in which she had ever before addressed me, Christie spoke the dread words "just friends." Our phone conversations continued—most were even pleasurable—but I had the perpetual sense that they had become a good deal more vital to me than they were to her.

And so, one afternoon, surprising even myself, I cut it off. No more chitchat, I told her, no more anything. What was the point?

For the first week things were okay; and reasonably so for the second. But by midway through the third, she was constantly with me, an ache in my chest. I had to hear her voice again, to know that she was still somewhere in my world.

Even my mother noticed. One evening, in a move altogether out of character, she took me to dinner at a local diner and offered some observations from the distaff side. Not just that there were a lot of fish in the sea, but valuable stuff. Like, for instance, that pretty as Christie was, hers were the kind of looks—delicate, predicated on youthful skin—that would not endure past thirty. This had never occurred to me, and it did offer some comfort.

But still I suffered; was, indeed, so nearly at wit's end a few evenings later that after dinner I retreated upstairs and, after wandering aimlessly about for a while, flung myself onto the trundle bed in my father's darkened workroom. Just a few feet away, on the desk, sat a telephone, and staring up into the darkness, I had to resist reaching for it. Then it rang.

"Harry," called my father from below, "it's for you."

"I'm sorry I called,"came her voice, full of urgency. "Sorry, sorry, sorry. But I just had to. You probably don't even remember me anymore."

"I remember you, Christie. Oh, God, what are you talking about?"

But it was in the midst of the glorious ensuing conversation that something very important came to me. So this was how it was! It was indifference she responded to, or at least its appearance.

It is an awful, poisonous lesson, but once learned, it is not easily shaken. "Almost exactly the same thing happened to me," a recent acquaintance told me, after I'd offered him an abbreviated version of the Christie saga. He shook his head. "You learn what works, and pretty soon it begins to take over your whole life. It's the genesis of cynicism."

In fact, in the wake of our reconciliation, I made a point of calling Christie less frequently. And when I did, my manner bespoke control. I'd spin off anecdotes, respond glibly to much of what she told me about herself, offer gentle put-downs posing as wry commentary. I found that I could make her laugh almost at will; that—glory be!—the mere appearance of honesty could pass for charm.

It worked beyond my wildest expectations. By the following summer, she had dumped old Eric-face for good. And one day in August, during a final few days together before we were to depart for our respective colleges, we returned after a visit to a community pool to her empty house, she assumed a languid position on the living-room couch and she allowed me to remove her bikini top; then, to my amazement and vast satisfaction, began writhing and calling my name as I discovered, at long last, how breasts feel and taste.

I set off for school with the conscious determination to find myself a girlfriend before she got a boyfriend, and I did. Immediately thereafter, her letters became even more affectionate. *"Dearest Harry,"* she wrote two days before Halloween, *"you have such a wonderful way with words. It's almost a gift. I'm so used to the way you speak and think and act. It's so special."*

Reading this, I was pleased no end. I adored Christie, didn't I? Except that I also knew, not terribly deep inside, that what she was responding to wasn't really me.

IT is altogether likely that our children, and theirs, growing up post-Reagan and knowing everything there is to know about AIDS, will regard the period during which so many of us came of age with frank stupefaction. *What—you used to have sex with strangers? Grandma did too?!!!!*

Already, in the wake of the heralded comeback of the family, that period is beginning to seem a historical aberration. Back in fashion, along with abstinence, are many of the taboos that just a decade or two ago, when we were in the midst of changing the world, we thought we had banished forever.

Of course, at the outset, as we entered that confused, unsettling, joyous era, few of us were particularly interested in changing anything at all. The shift in attitudes caught us by surprise every bit as much as it did our parents, and we tended to sometimes feel as awkward in the roles we'd been assigned—by the media, by our peers, by our frightened elders—as were all those ridiculous slightly older guys in love beads and bell-bottoms who suddenly believed they had license to hit on women our age.

It is fair to say that that ambivalence about precisely how to behave, and with whom, was greatest among those being most routinely hit upon. Raised, generally speaking, to make the distinction between themselves and girls with "reputations," endowed, by instinct or experience, with enough self-respect to expect some kind of emotional exchange to precede the physical variety, they found themselves in a time in which they were widely deemed unhip if they *didn't* put out.

Afterward, there would come to be a view, propounded by those attached to the we're-all-basically-the-same, some-of-us-are-merely-more-sexist-than-others wing of feminism, that the sexual impulses of women were identical to those of men; that females were not only as regularly horny, but just as inclined to hop into the sack with people they hardly knew.

Though such a proposition jibed with the experience of almost no one, including most of those propounding it most vigorously, it tended at the time to go only lightly challenged. During those angry years—we're talking the early to mid Seventies here—the sexes already had more than enough to argue about; and in any case, for many of us men it was a useful fiction. It is not for nothing that in such short order, swinging coed sex clubs would be so dramatically in ascendancy.

Yep, suddenly we men looked to have it made. As ready as guys our age had always been to have our judgment overruled by our gonads—younger versions, in other words, of the guys in love beads and bell-bottoms—it seemed we had been born at precisely the right moment. The word was out: all at once females were available as never before, tantalizingly so. Not just the ones in heavy makeup and stretch pants who sashayed by in the streets, but hitherto untouchable ones, the ones who sat beside us in class.

And yet, and yet, even for us it wasn't remotely so simple. For starters, some of us didn't even know how to meet women, let alone practice free love with them. "For a long time," one guy I spoke to recalled, "I thought I was the only member of my generation who couldn't get laid. I grew my hair long. I picked up an old greatcoat at the Army-Navy store. I even started wearing granny glasses. But when you're shy, you're shy, period."

"I did manage to get laid occasionally," observed someone else, now a suburban father of three, "but more than anything else, I recall the missed opportunities—girls I could have gotten to bed if I'd only known what to do or say." He shakes his head, still obviously full of self-reproach. "The truth is, I spent a helluva lot more time in my room jerking off than I did with real females."

But just as vitally, many of us, too, sort of wanted it both ways. Kids who'd been brought up not only on the values of the Playboy Philosophy but on those embodied by Ozzie and Harriet Nelson, we found the impulse to be part of a couple, to know one person intimately and be intimately known, as compelling as it had been in our parents' day. The lyric might have been by The Jefferson Airplane, but the message was vintage Jolson: Gotta Find Somebody to Love.

It was a confusing line to walk, and many of us never really got it right; indeed, continued to have problems with it for years afterward.

That I had a girlfriend soon after my arrival at college was due in no small measure to a bit of advice imparted by a friend one year older. "Don't make the same mistake I did," he counseled, on the eve of my departure for college in far-off Southern California. "Meet a girl first, before she has a chance to meet anyone else."

"But how? I'm no good at meeting girls I don't already know."

"I'll tell you the big secret." He paused meaningfully. "Say *anything*."

With this in mind—this plus the conviction that I had to beat Christie, 2,500 miles to the east in Indiana, to the romantic punch—I glommed onto a pretty, demure girl at the very first freshman mixer and engaged her in what passed for conversation; after five minutes, aware both that I was making little headway and that I was perspiring uncontrollably, I excused myself, dashed up to my dorm room, doused my underarms with Old Spice, found a new shirt, dashed back down and located her in the crowd.

She was, thank God, kind, and so registered only passing surprise at my altered appearance. She remained, however, less than encouraging. "I really want to mingle," she said. "I think I ought to meet as many people as I can."

Fine. That made sense.

The next day, I called to ask her to the movies.

She had plans.

A couple of days later, I called to ask again.

She had plans.

Pragmatism, at this point, was warring with self-respect. There could no longer be any question about it: she saw me for the loser I was.

All right, I told myself, I'd give it one last try—but from a safe distance.

"To the nicest person I've met at school so far," said the note accompanying the bouquet of carnations that showed up at her dorm. *"(Of course, I haven't met all the guys on my floor yet.)"*

That did it. At a time when virtually no one our age said thank you, let alone practiced chivalry, it proved a masterstroke; so much so that in subsequent years I would grossly overuse it, more than once sending flowers to the same woman repeatedly. In any case, late that afternoon, *she* called *me*, gushing, overcome, ready to go out anytime, anywhere.

Just to be on the safe side, I made two dates.

A wise precaution. In the midst of the first, strolling together on the quad following an on-campus performance by the Ballet Folklorico de México, with both of us straining to find things to say, she chanced to ask what I thought of marijuana.

I cleared my throat involuntarily, tried to gauge the tenor of the question. "Oh, well," I replied, "I guess it's pretty dangerous."

She—a San Diego native, to my mind the kind of person Brian Wilson wrote songs about—looked at me as if I were some bizarre kind of bug. "Dangerous? You *believe* that nonsense?"

In fact, I no longer did. The previous summer, in the company of a friend of my older brother, I had actually turned on myself; had, at any rate, taken a few puffs of a stubby joint and instantly begun speculating—for of course, this too was part of the ritual—on whether or not I was feeling anything. But having, in my eagerness to please, revealed myself to both of us as a jackass, I chose not to bring this up at the time.

That I did eventually succeed in winning her over was both a matter of perseverance and a reflection of the fact that, getting right down to it, Alison—let's call her that—was after most of the same things I was. Also very much a child of the middle class, fond of good times but not of risk, someone who in early adolescence had actually been a member of a club called The Disciples of Bullwinkle, she too was looking to pair up.

In that fall of 1966, this is, after all, what we both understood college life to be largely about. And if I remained attached to the unpredictable Christie, all those miles to the east, and Alison had not yet gotten over the grand passion of her senior year in high school, some shmuck named Eddie, we none-theless found ourselves, a few weeks later, walking back to campus after seeing *Elvira Madigan* at the town movie thea-ter, pausing every few steps to kiss. And a few weeks after that—what the hell—we began saying we loved each other.

There were times, moved by the feeling of a particular moment—an intimacy exchanged or even an especially warm look—when I, for one, sort of believed it. But if I was not yet wholly cynical about matters of the heart, neither was I as irredeemably naive as I'd been just a year earlier. Nor, I suppose, getting down to cases, as nice. For the truth is, I loved the idea of having *two* girlfriends, gloried in it both as an abstract proposition and in a purely practical sense. Each knew about the other, and it kept both on their toes. If, as now seemed apparent, this business of romance was largely a question of power, I was going to make damned sure that I'd never get stomped on again.

Not that, as men of the world go, I was quite as sophisticated as I liked to let on. There was, for example, the time that Christie, in a flight of kittenish whimsy, asked me to select a pair of panties and send them to her special delivery; though courted at her new address by new suitors, she had evidently presented me to her girl-chums at school as the real thing, a guy of wit and sensitivity. On the advice of a fellow customer at a local boutique, a female senior who seemed vastly amused by the whole business, I chose a lacy white thing that was wide open at the crotch.

Christie, as she subsequently reported, opening the gift-wrapped package in the company of her roommates, was mortified. But what she did not know was that I'd had no idea those panties were lewd, because I hadn't known where the vagina is located; had, indeed, assumed that it was in exactly the same place as the penis, nestled in the middle of the pubic region.

How would I know? *Playboy* had not yet taken to exposing that particular bit of female anatomy, and my mother had certainly never revealed hers. I mean, sure, I had *heard* the expression "between her legs," but I had always taken it as, I don't know, a sort of euphemism.

In fact, I would not come upon the remarkable truth for a couple of months more—until, one moonlit evening, Alison allowed me to stick a sweaty hand into her pants, and inch after dogged inch, I came upon nothing but crinkly hair. My wrist, straining against the fabric, was starting to ache when at last, to my stupefaction, at the very bottom, I came upon this . . . *thing*.

Alison was very much a virgin too, but after this she became less and less adamant on the subject. A couple of days before the start of Christmas vacation, standing outside her dorm door, chatting between smooches, I happened to remark on a curious dream I'd had a few nights before: flying home for the holidays, I'd abruptly become aware that the plane was bouncing up and down across the landscape, like one of those flimsy contraptions featured in documentaries on early aviation. I was in a panic, I told her, and for some reason started looking for my father to help me out. Alison, a psych major, grew dark. A moment later, without quite saying so, she indicated that the time was at hand.

The following morning found me not where I ought to have been—listening to Mr. Learnihan in History 101—but standing before an elderly pharmacist, playing out a scene that was destined to become a cliché.

"Could I please have a tube of Crest, a small bottle of Anacin, some deodorant—yeah, that stuff up there—and, I don't know . . . how about a dozen Trojans."

Alone in my room, summoning up the impending encounter in every possible permutation, electric with excitement, *practicing*, I had, by afternoon's end, exhausted fully a third of my supply.

It turned out that I had not practiced enough. For if I saw myself as being about to forever leave behind childish things, it was also the case that I had never been much interested in the matter of technique.

We ended up, in brief, not in my pad, a dorm room that always smelled faintly of dirty socks, but in the dark, on a blanket spread out upon what felt like a rock pile; and there, after a couple of perfunctory kisses, she liberated herself from a perverse garment known, I believe, as pettipants, and I plunged in. When I withdrew, after less than a minute, the Trojan, its tip full of liquid, hung half on and half off—which didn't stop me, a moment later, from plunging in again. Another thing no one had ever told me: a change of rubber is, under such circumstances, *de rigueur*.

"Oh, God," she moaned.

I stopped, startled; then relaxed. Of course. *This* I had read about.

"I love you," I said, nuzzling her cheek.

"Oh, God. There's a huge rock digging into my back."

Of course, *any* first experience that is not an unqualified disaster is easy for a guy to take as a success, even a triumph. The important thing, at such a moment, is not the quality of one's sex life, but the fact of its existing at all. "I didn't even ask her how she liked it," one guy told me of his own first time, in the back of an Opel—"not because I was afraid of

the answer, but because I really didn't much care. *I* liked it."
It hardly matters that the physical part often seems (God
knows, no pun intended) an anticlimax. We've *done* it, and
feel, at long last, entitled to bragging rights.

I will never forget the look on Allen Fisher's face when,
back home during that Christmas vacation, I offhandedly told
him. "You *did?*" he exclaimed, mouth literally agape. Then,
recovering, sorry to have so fully revealed himself, he added,
"Well, I'm still working on it, myself."

As it happens, I came down with a serious case of mono
during the break, and was obliged to return to school a week
late; and even then remained under strict instructions not to
exert myself. But Alison and I picked right up where we'd
left off, only making sure, in deference to "the kissing dis-
ease," to keep our mouths to ourselves.

I chose to believe that my friends were as impressed by
this as they were obviously amused.

Thinking back on all of this from a distance of more than
two decades, it is surprising that nature, supposedly governed
by a certain self-serving logic, enables those as lacking as I
was in rudimentary sense to engage in reproductive behavior
at all; and to realize that in fact, for centuries men of that age
had been expected to mate and have families and function as
fully responsible beings.

At the time, for us, such a fate would have been greeted
as living death. Oh, we played hard at maturity, all right, in
assorted incidental ways. A lot of us took up smoking. We
thought a lot about the big issues. In relationships we often
mimicked grown-up behavior, sometimes right down to the
endearments. ("Fuck you, dear," I once actually heard a guy
I knew tell his girlfriend, mildly, during a spat over what
movie to see, to which she replied, "Fuck *you*, darling.") But
perhaps more fully than any group of chronological young
adults who had come before, those millions of us who came
of age in that era—largely products of comfortable homes,
unburdened by responsibilities that once had been deemed
routine—remained children.

Not, of course, that we felt we had a thing to apologize for. We were in the vanguard of something new, something that would render all that had come before antique. With the mounting disillusionment over government policy in Southeast Asia, with all the old values under attack, with moral rigor increasingly associated only with the narrowest of fuddy-duddies, restraint had never been more out of fashion.

Nor, for that matter, activism more of a turn-on. On my own campus, the weekly silent vigil for peace—dozens of souls sitting around in front of the student union for fifteen minutes of sorrow and reflection—quickly acquired a reputation as a terrific pickup spot, the contemporary equivalent of the wild frat party.

As it happens, Alison and I would remain together, on and off, throughout our four years at the place. But the "on and off" part is not to be passed over lightly. For like just about everyone else back then—well, just about every man, anyway—I was often itchy. Sex was simply in the air, increasingly so as the antiwar fervor intensified and hemlines rose, and it seemed only just—to me, anyway—that I get my share.

It wouldn't take much more to set my mind racing than a pleasant lunchtime chat with someone who never wore a bra. Hell, fleeting eye contact with a woman in the street could do it. Yet all the while, there was Alison, faithful in every respect; so much so that I began to darkly suspect that she was looking for things between us to continue right into happily-ever-after. Several times I caught her getting sentimental about children; once, actually heard her wonder how *ours* might look.

Yeah, *right*. After that I was too busy to call her for five days.

I did not, of course, discuss with her my furtive yearnings, let alone my periodic flirtations. What to say? Come right out with it? Admit that I'm a filthy slime who wants to jump on fifty women a day? Observe that Sure, sure, we're great together, but is this all there is? The fact is, I was a little bit ashamed of what was percolating within.

And so, in that curious way many of us behave in such circumstances, what I'd do instead when I was feeling put upon was pick at her, and needle, and attack by indirection— try, in brief, to get her to take some kind of initiative.

"Well," I asked one evening, "what did you think of it?" We were sitting in my '62 Pontiac Tempest Le Mans convertible, having just emerged from a film entitled *Alice's Restaurant.*

"It was good."

"*Good?* That's it—'good'?"

I had found it powerful, insightful, moving, thrilling.

"Yes," she replied, already sensing what was to come. "I liked it a lot."

"Why? Why did you like it?"

And at that, I lit into her, savagely attacking her intellect, her worldview, her right to hold an opinion at all, eventually reducing her to tears.

The tears always got to me, of course. I'd apologize profusely, tell her she deserved better, wonder aloud what it was that made me act that way; and then, by way of making up, we'd have a round of terrific sex—which, on some level, was surely part of the reason I'd touched off the gruesome scene in the first place.

But only part. For the frustration was very real, and so, too, were the expressions of self-contempt. In recent years, a variation of the phenomenon has been assigned a snappy name: the Peter Pan Syndrome. But the ballyhooed male flight from commitment involves more than simply a fear of being pinned down; it reflects, too, a profound reluctance to abandon aspects of one's own being that have come to seem fundamental—especially at someone else's behest.

"Even now women occasionally tell me that they feel exactly the same way about sex that I do," one guy, thirty-eight and still unmarried, puts it. "Well, then, why is it *I've* never found it necessary to ask anyone if she's only interested in me for my body?"

Why, for that matter, is it that women, though on hand in equal number at the moment of truth, seem to get so little after-the-fact *intellectual* satisfaction from, say, surreptitious sex in a public place? And why is it not presumed appropriate behavior for women who hardly know each other to inquire—as Richard Nixon, in his desperation to be one of the boys, so intriguingly put it to interviewer David Frost, just before they went on camera—"Did you do any fornicating this weekend?" And why do we so routinely divide along sexual lines in the great cuddling controversy, women tending to regard pre and post behaviors as essential to a fully satisfactory experience, while men, even those who concede that snuggling can be *nice*, just as often, after the act itself, want nothing more than exemption from obligation of any kind? "Let's put it this way," one guy offers in explanation: "when that penis is hard, or about to be, I'm a wonderful guy, I'll do anything she wants. When it's soft again, I'm beholden to no one."

In fact, getting back to those idyllic days of youth, what many of us slowly came to grips with is how irreconcilable with our own are many of the values that govern those of the opposite sex; and given the fact that they are certainly not about to be transformed into us, how dramatic are the alterations, emotional and behavioral, expected on our end. And yet, recognizing that what women tend to value—fidelity, communication, mutual support—comes off as so much nobler than some of the stuff we're after, we guiltily hold our peace.

Still, it is also the case that many of us had no idea what to do with the independence we were always craving. In practice, sex with relative strangers—assuming it could be arranged—turned out to be a highly problematic proposition. For the relative strangers invariably had not only the parts featured in the skin books but, inconveniently, things like feelings and expectations—and if there was zilch between us, sex just didn't seem sufficient justification for going through the preliminary motions, let alone the excruciating aftermath.

Then too, in my case, as time went along and Alison began to wise up, there suddenly arose the alarming possibility that she would step out also. I tried my damnedest to enforce the double standard, but there were times, a couple of them, when she'd simply been pushed too far. At which point, all hint of swagger vanished and I had to beg her to please, *please* come back and be mine alone. It was lucky, she coolly informed me in the wake of one of these episodes, that the suitor in question had shown himself to be an even bigger jerk than I.

That all the while I had managed to maintain a parallel relationship with another woman will indicate just how big a jerk that other guy must have been. The fact is, in my modest way, I had become a bit of an operator; found myself able to say to each of my woman friends pretty much what it took to get what I wanted. There were, indeed, moments of clarity when I wondered why in the world either of them put up with it.

And then one evening, all at once, it was over with Christie. Dining in a cut-rate Chinese restaurant in Northern California, having been reunited over our respective semester breaks, we began bickering over a slighting reference to her father I'd made in a letter, and then, with no premeditation whatsoever, I heard the words coming out of my mouth: "Ah, hell, this relationship doesn't make sense, anyhow. We should have split up long ago."

I wasn't at all sure I meant it, but as I pressed on, enumerating the reasons we were no longer good for each other, her eyes went moist and the scene took on a momentum all its own. In a way, I even enjoyed it. It was a kind of vengeance, and I played it to the hilt, moving from belligerence to regret to a fulsome nostalgia for what we'd once had.

Typically, by the following morning I'd thought better of it, and called to suggest a reconciliation. I was as relieved as I was disappointed, though, when she turned me down flat.

What to do? What else? I rushed back to school, where Alison had remained, laboring over an important term paper, and over the next week pressed myself upon her so insistently that she was unable to finish the thing.

And yet, a bit more than two years later, upon graduation, we parted fondly but with nary a backward glance. She had a nice job up in San Francisco. I'd be attending graduate school in New York—where I already had a prospective girl-friend on tap.

The next time I saw Alison, four years later when she visited New York, she had recently broken up with her subsequent boyfriend. We had a terrific time together, reminiscing over dinner, visiting museums, commiserating over personal problems. I heard with particular solicitude her complaints about the former boyfriend, evidently a pretty scummy character. And when she imparted the most damaging detail of all—that he had induced her to participate in a threesome involving another woman—I registered positive shock. But all the while, I was thinking something else: *My God, who'd have suspected she'd have been up for that?*

Little of the above is noted with pride. But then, there is considerable consolation in the fact that my experience back then was the opposite of unique. By the hundreds of thousands, perhaps the millions, people my age—and particularly men—developed in a matter of a year or two from wide-eyed innocents into quite casual manipulators, always up for involvement but shy of commitment.

The era, overripe with options, woefully short on rigor, the age of do-your-own-thing, certainly had something to do with that. But, too, the times merely enabled us to give full expression to impulses that had been there all along. It is hardly a coincidence that as the restless young systematically engaged in behavior that a decade and a half earlier would have been labeled wantonly amoral, innumerable men of middle age and older found it within themselves to depart longtime mates for younger women.

In any case, for many of us a pattern was set during that time, one that would regularly assert itself in the years thereafter.

ODDLY enough, given the specifics of my own life, I think I can honestly say that I was never one of those men who felt threatened by the women's movement. To the contrary, from the first I was pleased to sympathize with it in virtually every particular. In part (malcontent that I have always been), this was certainly due to my being favorably impressed with any social trend that plays havoc with the status quo. But, too, it seemed clear that there might be some real insights afoot here, that society might even be dragged, kicking and screaming, toward a more equitable future.

Not, of course, that any of those insights had much to do with me. Well into my twenties, I had only the dimmest notion that I might have a problem at all. I was living with someone by then, someone at least as bright as I, and immensely capable, someone who reflected marvelously on both me and my politics. And if I remained subject to mood swings and inexplicable irritability, if I remained chronically detached even from the soul beside whom I slept, well, that just seemed the natural order of things.

But, oh, yeah, I could certainly see how some of the things women were saying applied to other guys.

On the other hand, it was hard not to note that other guys, even the ones I had in mind, tended to feel exactly the same way. Indeed, when I gathered with my male friends and the talk turned to women—and these were men who counted themselves progressive—the attitude often was largely defensive. *Why are they so upset? What have we done that's so terrible?*

What we had done, went the consensus, was simply be ourselves—and that was no longer okay.

"My girlfriend's always telling me that I don't understand how it *feels* to be a woman," noted one guy, over lunch in an

Upper West Side Manhattan restaurant, midway into the Seventies. The gathering, of five male writers, was supposed to have been a celebration—someone's first novel had just been published, and we were all doing nicely in our careers—but the boozy talk was so glum, so characteristic of men of that era, that a couple of us laughingly began taking notes. "Now, don't get me wrong," the guy continued. "I'm all for equal rights and equal pay for equal work and all that crap. But what I want to know is what *she* knows about having an erect cock."

"For a world that's supposedly getting better," agreed someone else, also in trouble at home, "it sure feels like it's getting worse."

Which led, in the roundabout way these things do, to a discussion of the perplexing new feature in the magazine that had been so instrumental in shaping all of our sexual attitudes: the Playmate Data Sheet, in which the centerfold model listed her favorite books, movies, musicians and the like. The strong feeling around our table was that the Data Sheet was a mistake for *Playboy* and, more to the point, a tragedy for ourselves.

"It's so obviously a sop to the women's movement," noted the new novelist irritably. "What they're trying to do is show that Playmates are people. Well, we don't *want* them to be people. People I've got at home. How am I expected to get it up for someone who brags that her favorite book is *Love Story?*"

The guy beside him nodded. "You know what gets me? The way they all say they can't stand 'rude people.' That's always the Pet Peeve—'rude people.' And every time I read that, I'm certain they're talking about me."

"Me too."

"Me too."

"What they've done is taken away the fantasy side of it," summed up the novelist. "That's supposed to be degrading, being reduced to a masturbatory fantasy, and I suppose it is. But men thrive on fantasy, and that can't be legislated out of existence."

There was a long pause. Well, the guy beside me, a magazine sportswriter, finally chimed in, speaking of that, he hadn't been sure he should bring it up, but what the hell: only last week, while on assignment, he had had a fling with a famous woman tennis player.

We were agog, insisted on knowing every significant detail. How had he managed it? What, exactly, had he done with her? How, precisely, had she responded? How large or round or firm had been her pertinent parts?

He answered everything with high good humor until, abruptly, someone dropped the big one. "Does Marianne know?"

"No," he replied, his voice dropping. "I'm such a shmuck, I really am."

I suspect that each of us knew exactly how he felt. The impulse toward such behavior had, for some of us, so long seemed second nature that we rarely even questioned it. And yet, much as we delighted in it on one level—confirming as it did our best hopes for ourselves, and playing spectacularly at gatherings like this—we also knew that it showed us at our most base, thoughtless, irredeemably selfish.

As it happened, I was in the midst of a fling of my own just then—though, under the circumstances, I was hardly about to mention it. As a personality type, I was given to *mea culpas* at least as heartfelt as the one we had just endured. Yet I managed, most of the time, to justify my behavior on probably the same basis on which the sportswriter justified his. Life with my girlfriend was comfortable—to the naked eye, we remained a matched set—but it lacked the edge, the unpredictability, that I had come to expect as my due.

My affair, with a woman I'd known platonically back in college, was, to be sure, a long-distance one. Some months before, when I'd been on a magazine assignment in San Francisco, we had found ourselves sharing a joint, and then a hotel bathtub, and ever since, on occasional nights when my girlfriend wasn't around, we had been titillating each other by telephone. There had, for example, been the evening she'd advised me of the fact that an excellent way for a horny man—

say, me—to replicate the sex act on his own was to get a hold
of a grossly overripe banana, one that was already going brown,
remove most of its mushy contents, insert himself within, and
make love to that. It was past midnight when I was told this,
and it took me a good forty-five minutes prowling the markets
of Upper Broadway before I discovered a suitably revolting
piece of fruit—and the following morning, before my girlfriend's return from her business trip, it took two washings
of the sheets to get rid of the banana stench; but I'll be damned
if she wasn't right!

Several weeks after that, I dared to write her a letter, in
form not unlike those that appeared in the "Forum" section
of *Penthouse*, imagining the two of us in a group scene, screwing like demented bunnies while all around us other couples
did the same. Less than a week later, I received her reply:
she had, she wrote, been *shocked* by my missive, having never
been much attracted to the notion of orgies herself. While in
my fevered imagination, we jaded New Yorkers were humping
away en masse,

> *it's spring in Sonoma County, and in between the
> depressing rainstorms the sun shines on wildflowers
> and lush green meadows, cows cuddle and redwing
> blackbirds dip and glide overhead. You and I are
> tromping through soft spongy fields to the crest of a
> hill overlooking Napa Valley vineyards. We fall onto
> our Japanese silk comforter and roll into each other's
> arms laughing that thank God we don't have to go
> another step and let's have some wine and cheese and
> fruit while it's still cold. As we unpack the picnic
> basket our hands brush, our eyes meet, an electric
> hum is set up between us. The Château St.-Jean Jo-
> hannisberger Riesling is tingly and cold on my tongue.
> I hold the wine in my mouth until my tongue is very
> cold and then I lick up the side of your neck and run
> little kisses along your lower lip. Your lip is sweet—
> you have been nibbling a peach. I am distracted—
> where's my peach? You share yours. It tastes so good,*

*the juice runs between our fingers, you lick my palm
and suck the peach juice off my fingers. As I watch
my finger disappear into your mouth, you suddenly
suck hard on the tip and I feel an electric impulse
travel up my arm and spread into my breasts. My
nipples are tingling—they are like peaches—will
you suck them? I take off my blouse, then unbutton
your shirt and spread it open. I kiss the hairs on your
chest, rub my cheeks against you, smell the musky
scent of your skin. You are kissing my sensitive hol-
low at the base of my neck, caressing my back, my
breasts, running your fingers through my hair—
very tender.*

*My clothes suddenly feel two sizes too small. We
pull away from each other and disrobe quickly and
awkwardly, then roll together with a sigh of relief . . .*

And on and on, ever more explicit, for another two pages.
I showed the letter to no one, told no one about it, but for a
while I read it almost every day: my own, personal piece of
erotica.

What a woman! How fortunate to have stumbled upon her.
True, her aesthetic sensibility was different from mine—all
that stuff about flowers and blackbirds, where I tended to go
straight for the raunchy—and, true, nicely as we got along in
small doses, we likely hadn't enough in common to make it
through a couple of actual weeks in each other's company.
But who cared? Given what we did have—the occasional sex,
the long-distance fun and games, the absolute absence of expectations—there was no reason we shouldn't be able to go
on this way for decades!

It was a couple of weeks later that I arrived at the magazine
office where I was then working to find another letter addressed in her distinctive hand. Delighted, I momentarily
considered putting off reading it till the right time and place;
but the flesh is weak, and I opened it on the spot.

Hi Harry.

Something I've got to tell you . . . How do I say this? . . . I'm feeling funny about what's going on. A little used, I guess. What I'm looking for is someone to hold me, and love me, and make me feel better. Don't get me wrong, this other thing has been very nice, but, well—you get the idea. Sorry. Maybe women are just different.

Six months after that, my girlfriend and I decided it was best to split apart. The evening we finally faced up to it was as emotionally exhausting as any I'd ever lived. By its end, she was outside on the fire escape, sobbing, the sounds coming from her wholly alien to what she had always been. Sitting on a frayed couch in the living room, listening, I was numb.

Maybe she was right. Maybe it was something to think about, this pattern of mine, this business of persistent emotional retreat. On the other hand, undeniably, somewhere deep inside, I was relieved.

It was true, I wasn't a kid anymore. Eventually, I'd have to settle down, stop screwing around, stop screwing things up.

But . . . later.

IN the midst of what might fairly be called a belated, protracted adolescent rebellion—it began in my late twenties and endured a truly embarrassing number of years—one episode came to sum it all up for me: all that had been off between my father and me from the start, the extent to which I'd been undermined by it, how deeply, when I allowed it to, it continued to hurt.

It was early in my senior year in high school that my father decided I should go to Oberlin College, in Ohio. He had had a conversation on the subject with his brother, an academic of some note, and after that it had to be Oberlin.

Now, to be fair here, this sort of thing was rather out of character for my father. He had rarely involved himself in grand planning before—had never been pushy about grades, or made a big deal of whether we were in the right clubs at school; his attitude seemed to be that as long as the kids seemed happy, and were functioning reasonably well, they had a right to lead their own lives.

Then, again, the distinction between laissez-faire and indifference can, from the perspective of a child, be so terribly fine; and when a parent, particularly a father, becomes suddenly, uncharacteristically caught up in the child's affairs, it is easy for said child to feel, without identifying quite what it is he is feeling, that the parent is caught up, above all, in his own needs.

But to hell with this parent-child stuff. The only characters in the drama at hand were my father and me.

I made no objection at all to my father's interest in the

college process. In fact, I was at least as grateful for his help as I would subsequently be wounded by its character. He simply seemed persuaded that so vital a matter shouldn't be left to chance—or, for that matter, me—and I, for one, couldn't argue.

The truth is, I'd had no idea how to approach the college question—was more than a little intimidated by the frenzied activity of so many of my contemporaries that fall, even as I professed amusement at it; and persuaded, more to the point, in spite of good grades, that there was no chance of my getting accepted at any of the better schools they were shooting for. Oberlin, Class of '70, sounded just fine: a terrific reputation, and far enough away that they'd probably have to let me in just for geographical diversity.

And so, we applied for early admission to Oberlin, the two of us collaborating on the application essays, my father putting them into final shape at the typewriter.

Only, the thing was, we—no, suddenly I saw it as *I*—didn't get in.

Those sonsofbitches! Well, screw them! Their loss! I'll go someplace else.

But, no, taking aim at the regular admissions process, my father decided we should head out to Ohio for an interview. So two weeks later, there we sat, face to face for fifteen excruciating minutes with some smug young jerk in the admissions office who made it clear we were wasting his valuable time. Indeed, it was only my father who kept the conversation going that long. A couple of months later, I was not surprised when they turned me down again.

Fine. All right. Lots of people were having their egos bruised just then. I ended up going to college in Southern California instead, and that looked to be that.

Except that three years later, during spring break of my junior year, I was sitting on a grassy hillside in Central Park, leafing through the Sunday *Times,* when at the back of the second news section I spotted an arresting headline: OBERLIN TEST OF STUDENT POWER DASHED BY ADMISSIONS DISPUTE.

It seemed that a couple of student representatives on the college admissions committee, having run across embarrassingly small-minded notations made upon certain admissions applications, had gone out, as was the fashion among student radicals, and leaked them to the press.

My heart was filled with gladness—but then, as I skimmed down the page, looking for specific bits of dirt, it suddenly went cold. Among the more prominently featured revelations was that one especially geeky kid, having been dragged to the interview by his pushy father, had prompted an admissions officer to smirk, in writing, "We can't do this to our girls."

We can't do this to our girls.

Oh, God!

Hell, I hadn't even wanted to apply to the damn place to start with; certainly not a second time. Damn them! Damn my father!!

Quickly, though, within a matter of hours, I had buried it away. I had always been a pretty compliant kid, and certainly remained so; indeed, would not even begin to face what had so long been working at me—the sense of inadequacy and insignificance, the need to ceaselessly prove myself—until early into my professional life.

It was not that I was walking around wholly unaware; only as unaware as the next guy. After all, things seemed all right. I was doing okay with women, okay with my peers, even better than okay on the job.

Indeed, professionally, more than in other ways, I was proving more and more explicitly my father's son. Aside from the doggedness with which I went about my work, there were the subject areas to which I was drawn: politics, sports, show business—all of them inherited interests. Every bit as starstruck as he, I often returned from assignments with anecdotes about my subjects that, recounted around crowded dinner tables, made both of us proud.

The pride is not to be lightly passed over. In fact, at the outset I had sensed in him no small surprise that I was beginning to appear in some heavyweight publications, that people were taking my stuff seriously, that—hey!—I was making a living at it.

I'll never forget the sheer joy in his eyes, the way they quite literally shone, when, following the appearance as the cover piece in *The New York Times Magazine* of a profile I'd done of John Lindsay, he reported that his friend Joseph Heller, the novelist, had told him that it read like good fiction.

By then, the magazines in which I was appearing could be found strategically placed around his house. When I began to write books, those too went on display.

All of which, I recognize, sounds incredibly nice; and, yeah, in a way, especially at the start, it was. Having come of age as the middle child, I'd been surprised to learn that each of my surviving brothers, the older and the younger, had grown up certain that he was our parents' favorite; such a thing had never for a moment occurred to me. Now, however, especially with both my siblings out of mind in the Midwest, I seemed to be making up for lost time.

Still, it was by no means happenstance that it was at this very moment that I embarked upon my shadow career as an angry young man. For what was occurring between my father and me just then prompted questions that, as the months passed, only grew more insistent: Why had it taken *this* to elicit from him the sense that I was valued? Why were the successes only fleetingly satisfying, while the self-doubts remained so persistent? What would have happened if Heller had dismissed the piece as drivel? What *will* happen if the next book stinks?

My father, who is the opposite of dense, began to grasp that something was up. There were, for one thing, the couple of lunches during which, out of the blue, in defiance of all past behaviors, I'd begin laboring, as the newspaper psychologists so insistently urge, to *communicate*—a process that left us both tongue-tied and a bit embarrassed; for another, and far more often, there were the silences with which I'd now greet remarks he meant to be amusing.

Once, years before, when I'd returned from my freshman year at college horribly upset over the D-plus I'd gotten in geology, his reaction had struck me as hilarious. "Jeez, couldn't you have made it a plain D? Then I could have told people you weren't trying." Now, as I looked back over a lifetime of what I suddenly saw as incessant minimization, it seemed to reflect, more than anything else, indifference. Always, I'd simply taken my father as he was. Now, if I ran across him on the telephone line sounding preoccupied or detached, clearly indifferent to something I cared about, an otherwise fine day would abruptly go sour; and I'd sometimes let it work at me for hours, a character out of a nineteenth-century Russian novel brooding over a burger in a Greek coffee shop.

It was, in a sense, no mean feat, painting him in such somber shades. There was so much I had to ignore or, at the very least, misinterpret.

For starters, there was my father's considerable largesse. Never having been much impressed with money, his own or anyone else's, he had never given a second thought to helping out his children in substantial ways; indeed, he had financed the fourth-floor walk-up in which I was doing a lot of my brooding. But this I now saw simply as blood money—he gave bucks because there was so much else he couldn't give, or wouldn't—and so actually managed to read it as another count in the indictment.

Nor, as I rummaged about in the past, examining events long buried away, did I have much trouble shrugging off his other obvious qualities.

The fact is, in the role-model department, we Stein boys had, in vital respects, been quite fortunate. When, for example, during the height of the McCarthy period, so many others had run for cover, our father, then at CBS, had managed to lose each copy of the loyalty oath the network legal department periodically sent down for his signature. "I knew they wouldn't fire me," he told us, "because they were happy with my work. It was my own little protest." Yet it is also the case that at about the same time, a colleague of his trying to avoid a House subpoena—and the almost certain loss of his job that went with it—was invited to take refuge at our home.

Then too, in the realm of life lessons, there had been his experience with *Fiddler on the Roof,* a property that at the outset only he and his musical collaborators, Jerry Bock and Sheldon Harnick, believed could ever find an audience. *It's too ethnic,* they were told again and again. *Who cares about a bunch of shabby Jews in a shtetl?* The moral—that one's best work is invariably that to which one brings the fullest passion and most abiding commitment—is one I'd always tried to bear in mind in my own professional life.

Other lessons he had helped impart, however inadvertently, had proved no less significant. For instance—and in light of the values that have come to pervade this culture, this is hardly incidental—he never gave a particular damn about clothes. It struck him as a ludicrous, trivial concern, and he tended to throw on whatever was close at hand, or choose whichever of two items appeared, on cursory inspection, to be less soiled or crumpled. Consequently, my mother's best efforts notwithstanding, so did his sons. Thus it was that when we'd appear as a family at any eatery more grandiose than a truck stop, we'd invariably be instantly stuck in some dimly lit back room. I'm not even sure my father noticed. But what in another household might have been something of an embarrassment was for me, even as a child, virtually a source of pride; and, I am afraid, the start of a family tradition.

Along the way, he offered regular instruction by example in other public behaviors that, while hardly without their downside, at least evidenced a healthy contempt toward certain kinds of passivity and timidity. During family trips on lightly traveled highways, for instance, he'd declare himself "king of the road," regarding every car spotted ahead as a personal challenge, an affront to the royal authority. Once, when we children were still very young, he insisted, to our

stupefaction, that he could make the car go "a mile a minute."
And squeezing, in those pre-seat-belt days, ever closer to the
odometer as the needle edged toward sixty, cheering wildly,
we watched him make good on the boast.

Our mother, for her part, handled these occasions as grace-
fully as she knew how, frequently admonishing him to slow
down, but working to hold the involuntary shrieks—"Joey,
watch out!"—to a minimum. Her skittishness in the face of
even the illusion of risk was a matter of temperament, something that had certainly predated the accident, and we males,
a veritable band of Errol Flynns, responded to it with appropriate disdain. "Don't worry, will you?" would come his exasperated reply. "We're fine."

But of course, when there are scores to be settled, memory
is curiously selective. Within six months, I was in therapy;
the recollections were coming at me from all angles, indis-
criminately, and the case against my father was growing ever
stronger.

It no longer struck me as insignificant even that when, in
my eighth year, we got a dog—the wise and soulful Buttons—
only my mother seemed to earn his full respect. This was, it
seemed to me, not simply because she was the only one who
could be counted on to feed him, but also a matter of dignity
and bearing.

And a matter, too, of temperamental consistency. For if
our father could be the best of company when he chose to
be, amusing and easily amused, he was at other times quickly
impatient, even petulant. Graciously detached as he generally
was in response to a stranger's praise, he hated even mild
criticism of a work-in-progress, especially my mother's, and
would continue to mutter his defiance even as he stormed off
to his office to try out her suggestions.

He was, in brief, though at the time my view was far less
tempered by understanding or perspective, much in need of
confirmation; as insecure in his way as I was in mine.

"I only asked my father to help me with my homework
once," recalled a friend of mine recently. "Once was enough.

It was geometry, and he got completely wrapped up in it—figured out all the answers, but never bothered to tell me how he'd arrived at them. 'Well,' he asked the next evening, with a big grin, 'how'd I do?' He did fine, but I almost flunked the course."

That story, even now, rings bells and pushes buttons. One time, in tenth grade, assigned to compose a humorous essay, I showed my father a rough draft; and somehow, over the course of the next hour, the beginning got changed, then the end, then, finally, the subject itself—from "Exciting Bedtime Reading" to "Baa Baa Black Sheep Reconsidered." I ended up poring over the day's sports page while he dashed out an entirely new manuscript. (". . . What's this guy doing talking to a sheep, anyway? And look what he asks. Of course it's got wool. What does it look like—Dacron?") Later on, accepting congratulations upon its appearance in the school literary magazine, I had managed to obscure the full truth even from myself.

In contrast, there had been my mother, dead now already four or five years. I—we kids—had at least always known *she* was there for us, loving us for what we were. Hadn't she made a big deal of every crummy piece of art we hauled home from kindergarten? Wasn't she sitting there at every single class play—I'm talking about the ones in the classroom, not just those in the auditorium—applauding as if we were the Barrymores?

But then, that was the catch—she was *too* easy. Her approval came so cheaply, so often lacked a critical edge, that it seemed to carry no weight at all.

It was our father's we so desperately craved. And from him we got only the veneer of involvement.

By that time, my ball playing was pretty much limited to an occasional appearance in a slow-pitch softball league, and even those had become worrisome; I was no longer quite as quick to my left on batted balls, had lost half a step on the base paths, sometimes found myself wondering, as I was about to slide, whether I'd remembered to remove the keys from my pocket.

One cool spring Sunday in Central Park, in about the third inning, my father unaccountably appeared at the diamond and took a seat in the rickety stand. We were playing the fearsome Kings that day, and up till then I'd been having a terrific game—a diving stab of a liner that I'd turned into a twin killing, a long double into the gap. But the very next inning, the roof caved in. They got a couple of hits, our shortstop booted a ball, our third baseman threw another away and then their grotesquely large first baseman, in his other life a piano mover, brought everyone in with a clout to the adjoining diamond. My own error at second base—a routine grounder, somehow bobbled—caused no additional damage, but it did little for my spirits.

"Whoo, boy," exclaimed my father as we trotted in, having finally engineered the third out, "for this I paid good money? I could have stayed home and watched the Mets."

"Why didn't you, then?" I snapped, with a vehemence that surprised even me. "It doesn't make us feel any better to hear crap like that."

Almost instantly, I was sorry. Shit, I thought, stalking off toward the bench, he hadn't meant anything by it.

On the other hand, screw that. *I've been putting up with that kind of crap my whole life!* Why can't you make me feel good for a change? This is *my* team, *my* life, and I don't give a damn what you think. I'm not that scared little kid anymore, the one who went so pliantly along to be humiliated at Oberlin!

For five minutes, I avoided looking his way. When, at last, I glanced toward the stands, he was gone.

It was less than a week later that, lost in research at the library, flipping through the *Times* Index for 1969, I suddenly came upon it:

> OBERLIN COLLEGE: discovery by students recently added to faculty com on student admissions that counselor in admissions office wrote sexual, religious and

> pol inclinations of prospective students on application
> forms . . . Mr. 16, 58:4.

Well, why not? Casting aside better judgment, a well-armored psychic warrior, I ordered up the offending reel of microfilm, threaded the machine and rolled it toward the date and page. Yep, there it was, that gruesome artifact out of the past. It looked almost benign now, no more unsettling than a Dear John letter unearthed years afterward, when one is happily married.

Still, as I began reading, the old feelings returned with a rush. Skimming two-thirds of the way down the first column, I found the very words: "Well, this kid certainly won't help the male image on campus. It's too late even for hormones. Nothing against him, but I'm not sure I want to take responsibility for sending our girls another one of these."

Oh, God!

Slowly, despite myself, I began rereading the story from the top. And, there, at the end of the third paragraph, it was: the detail that, in my shock and shame, had passed me by entirely the first time around. The files in question had been for students applying for the Class of *1973.*

I stopped, read the paragraph again.

How in the world could I have gotten it so wrong?

It hadn't been me at all!

It hadn't been us!

THE notion of an English-language magazine in Paris was hatched, as such schemes often are, at a greasy-spoon. The establishment in question was around the corner from *New Times* magazine, where I was then working as an editor, and that afternoon, having run out of chitchat on sports, politics, women and recalcitrant writers, my colleague Tom Moore and I drifted onto the subject of what, in the best of all worlds, we'd like to be doing—and discovered, to our considerable surprise, that we shared the identical pipe dream. Instantly, ideas began flying across the table. What would be in the thing? How would it look? What tone should we work for?

As to the plausibility of such a venture, we expressed not a moment's doubt. Tom had a live-in French girlfriend. I was a francophile from way back. What other credentials did we need to make it as press barons in the City of Light?

It was with even more than the usual reluctance that we at last dragged ourselves back to the office.

But less than six months later, an odd thing happened. Tom, having unexpectedly come into a tidy, if not quite spectacular, sum—an article he'd co-written for *Life* magazine years before was about to be made into *Dog Day Afternoon*—immediately quit his job, and he and the girlfriend packed off for Paris.

Good old Tom!

Several months after that, while I was on a two-week European vacation, he sat me down in his apartment—a place that might have passed as a stage set, full of that special Parisian light, with billowy lace curtains framing windows that looked out on a bustling marketplace—and put it to me directly: "Look, do you want to do this or not?"

"C'mon, Tom, starting a magazine costs a ton of money."

"I have some money left. We can start with that."

"That'll last two months, tops."

"Well, at that point we'll just have to look at how it's going. If it's going lousy, we'll fold it."

The guy had brass balls, I had to give him that; mine, in contrast, were more like soap bubbles. But my skepticism was more than simply a matter of faintheartedness. By now, I had left *New Times* and had agreed to do a book, as well as a bunch of magazine pieces.

"Look," I offered, "why don't you get started here—make some preliminary contacts, maybe do some market research—and I'll come back in a couple of months? We can talk about it then."

"I've already dealt with a market researcher. He told me it'll never work because no one's done it before." He grinned. "What do you expect from the French?"

By the time I returned, seven months later, Tom was minus his girlfriend—that's a long and very private story—but he had already assembled the beginnings of a staff: a French art director; a Dutch-Indonesian guy who, on the basis of his experience running a small print shop, was to be in charge of the business side; and an accountant named Jean-Pierre, the ex-girlfriend's sober-sided younger brother.

A week after that, following the appearance of our classified ad in the *International Herald Tribune*, we also had one hundred and forty-five potential writers—each of whom, over a frantic two days, we actually interviewed, according each five minutes of our not very valuable time. Not one left Tom's apartment without an assignment. True, the vast majority had no journalistic experience, and some spoke only halting English. But in our desperate estimation, any one of them was apt to turn out to be the next Tom Wolfe; even the elderly Rumanian gentleman who referred to himself as "The Boulevardier" and swept about the place, in a cape very much like Count Dracula's declaiming "The Boulevardier like theeese idea, he *like* it!"

Still, at least fleetingly realistic, we eventually set about gathering publishable material on our own. Tom began researching what would become our first cover story, on the gentrification (though the term had not yet been coined) of Les Halles, formerly the city's vibrant central market, while I assigned myself a couple of lesser pieces. The principal one of these was an interview with the actress Jean Seberg. A longtime resident of Paris, a face to be reckoned with around town since her memorable appearance in Jean-Luc Godard's *Breathless* back in 1959, Seberg seemed the prototypical American expatriate, a natural for our inaugural issue.

When I arrived at her airy apartment on the Rue du Bac, I was a bit jittery—a dozen years before, Seberg had been the object of one of my older brother's fiercest crushes—but when she at last appeared, after half an hour of putting herself together, it was evident that she was even more so. Gentle-mannered, obviously shy, still handsome if no longer ingenue-pretty, Jean conveyed extreme fragility; when she sat down on the beige couch opposite mine—everything in the room was in pastels—her latest husband, French-American and a decade her junior, seated himself at her side, hovering protectively. He interrupted the conversation frequently, ostentatiously making sure that nothing was being misinterpreted, that Jean would come out all right.

Which is perhaps why it was only afterward, transcribing the tape of our talk back at Tom's, that I was struck by what had been her surprising lack of reserve. Though the voice was soft and the tone virtually without inflection—a vestige of an Iowa past that was oddly evident even in her grammatically flawless French—she had wonderful things to tell about the luminaries, literary, political, cinematic, with whom, particularly in the early years, she had been on intimate terms: André Malraux, friend and patron of her second husband, the gifted writer Romain Gary; De Gaulle himself; Truffaut, Belmondo and, of course, Godard.

To an interviewer more than willing to embrace Paris as a kind of ideal, it was thrilling stuff; and if, along the way, she also dropped a few cautionary notes—"You're never truly integrated here," she noted at one point, "because they won't let you be"—I managed to not catch them.

But then, who had time then for reflection of any kind? I slapped the Seberg piece down and was done with it. With publication date approaching, there were other matters to contend with, far more pressing ones.

Indeed, most we never quite got around to at all. Our first issue was a full-scale disaster—not so much because we were weak editorially but because we had neglected to provide for the small matter of distribution; more precisely, our distribution consisted of the Dutch-Indonesian guy slowly pedaling out of our courtyard on a bicycle, a pile of papers stacked up behind him. Astonishingly enough, it turned out he had an even more tenuous grasp of business than we did.

Nor did we have an advertising department, a circumstance that, we were rapidly coming to understand, was of greater consequence even than the fact that with the second issue of *The Metro*—we'd named the thing after a café in the square below Tom's window—due out in two weeks, only four of our vast horde of free-lance writers had bothered to turn in pieces at all, and of these but one was remotely usable.

On the advertising question, it was Tom who came up with a quick fix. "Why don't we get those two women who came by the other day to sell space?"

The pair in question—one English, one American—had happened by the office looking for work. They were gorgeous. *Great idea,* I enthused; *they'll do great.* "Why not get Françoise to join them?"

"Françoise?"

"You know, the architecture student I met on the subway. She's looking for a summer job."

"Yeah, right."

Tom stood there a long moment, chuckling over the thought.

"What an ad staff! They may not sell any space, but I guarantee, they'll beat everyone else's for sex appeal."

Which, to finally sidle up to the point of all this, suggests the spirit in which our adventure was undertaken. It is not that we were unserious about our fledgling publication; we had worked awfully hard to get even this far, had, between the two of us, written most of that doomed first issue and rewritten all of the rest. But this was, after all, *Paris*—and the allure of the project all along had, in large measure, been what the place itself had to offer. The razzle-dazzle. The comfortable cafés and tree-lined boulevards. The wine and the pastries. And hardly incidentally, as long as we're counting clichés, the women—seeming *objets d'art* in their own right; women who to us were all the more attractive for their imperiousness and apparent inaccessibility. Ten, twenty times a day, one of them would stride past on the street—slim, chic, skirt swaying in gentle syncopation, but staring rigidly ahead exactly as she'd been taught in French-person school—and one would marvel at her cool perfection.

And there, quite simply, we both were—unattached and hoping to live out our own version of the *Playboy* fantasy.

Indeed, all around us, every day, opportunity not only beckoned, it seemed to shout. Already, with the aforementioned Françoise, I had revealed myself as more adventuresome, as more swashbucklingly rash, than I'd ever dared to be on native soil. Having spotted her on the subway while on my way to a Saturday flea market, a willowy blonde in tight jeans and cowboy boots, with a jaunty scarf providing just the right note of insouciance, I quickly averted my gaze when she noticed me looking, and experienced the customary pang of regret when she exited at the Pont Marie station; but when, an hour and a half later, en route back home, I glanced up from my paperback copy of *Helter Skelter* and saw, to my surprise, that the same young woman had just taken a seat across the aisle, I spontaneously rose and moved to the seat facing her.

"*C'est le destin*," I heard myself offer. ("It's fate.")

She went crimson; then, haltingly: "*Oui.*"

I had no idea where to take it from there, so I simply babbled on—about the flea market, about the city itself, about our odd little publishing venture—until she quietly noted that the next stop was hers.

Mine too, I announced with alacrity, in French, though we'd in fact passed through mine five minutes before.

And so, exiting together, we repaired—against her every instinct, I expect—to a café. It was there that I ascertained her name—"Frani" for short—her student status and the fact that she was looking for temporary work.

In fact, she turned out to be a decent salesperson, certainly the best of our winsome trio, and had we only thought to have them sell not one-shot ads but contracts to appear, say, in five issues, the scheme might have worked. Faced, however, with the prospect of knocking on the same doors she'd pried open two weeks earlier, Françoise resigned, having landed a job in the Air France information booth at Orly Airport.

No matter. By then we were already enough of a couple that when Tom began hinting it was time I depart his living room, she invited me to temporarily share her tiny studio.

Ah, what an experience! We had almost nothing in common—not language, nor culture, nor personal tastes; but in a bizarre way, that was precisely the mutual appeal. *"Ooof, vous Américains!"* she would exclaim about twelve times a day, blowing out her lips in that uniquely French expression of disdain, reacting to something I'd said, or laughed at, or happened to be wearing. But though the exasperation was convincing, it was not entirely heartfelt. She was as intrigued by my assorted oddities—my habit of whistling in the street, the fact that I had carted my baseball glove all the way across the ocean—as I was by her Gallic version of normality.

"Normal" for the French, and it's the same word, conveys more than simply routine; it also has to do with propriety; what one does, and ought to do, for the reason that everyone else does it. Thus, smoking smelly cigarettes was *"normal"* and abstinence was *"pas normal."* Wearing extraordinarily flattering but physically disabling clothes was *"normal."* So,

even among the young, was complaining of constipation; and, at least in Françoise's circle, talking a lot about philosophy and reading fashionably leftist publications like *Le Nouvel Observateur* (known, affectionately, as *"Le Nouvel Obs"*).

Thus it was that my friend and I spent a fair amount of time, seriously at first but with increasing good humor, playing cultural one-upmanship. *You French are so rigid*, I'd tell her, offering a caustic commentary on another astonishingly pretentious conversation I'd been obliged to endure that evening on some obscure point of political theory; *you're so tight. Haven't you ever heard the expression "full of shit"?* (She hadn't, so I coined my own French version, and thereafter used it often.) *And YOU*, she would reply, *you are all so . . . loose. Everything about you is loose. Your clothes are loose, your morals, your standards, even your bowels!*

But then too, even as we parried, we were learning more about each another's culture than we'd ever fathomed we would, and along the way, were becoming surprisingly comfortable in an alien tongue. I mean, it was *fun*, as happening upon new parts of oneself invariably is. There was, for example, the day I came down with *une grippe*, a truly awful one, and could hardly catch my breath for coughing; but instead of a funk, I found myself in an impromptu language lesson. *Tousser*—to cough. *Le mucus*—mucus. *La morve* (colloquial)—snot. *Morveux, morveuse*—snotty, stuck-up.

Prior to meeting her, my French had been only serviceable, occasionally giving rise to frustration, even embarrassment. Once, interviewing the French general who had directed military operations in Algeria—he'd just written a sensational memoir, admitting, among other things, that he'd authorized widespread torture as an instrument of policy—I sat listening to a series of outrageously self-serving answers to the questions I'd carefully written out beforehand, unable to frame any of the follow-up questions that rushed, in English, to mind. Another time, at a party, I was surprised to find a modest little anecdote—it had to do with greeting my mother at an airport with artificial flowers and a kiss—met with shock and horror. It was only afterward that I learned that the word I'd used for "kiss," recalled from my French III textbook, meant, colloquially, "fuck."

Then, of course, there were the *other* aspects of the relationship. Françoise's body was prototypically French—slim and tight, with a round little tush and smallish breasts—and she was possessed of mournful brown eyes to go with her mane of blond hair. I *admired* the way she looked, held herself, moved; recognized that objectively, especially by American standards, she was a dish. (Eventually, and it was a gesture that meant something, she introduced me to her parents. Her introduction to *my* father, played out only in my head, had the three of us strolling down West Fifty-seventh Street, my father not only much impressed by her himself, but keenly aware of the reaction she inspired in male passersby.)

More than one morning, awakening on the Japanese futon that served as our bed to find her putting herself together for work, applying just the right amount of subtle eye shadow and then slipping into her powder blue Air France uniform, I'd ask her to come over and straddle me. *"Ooof, vous Américains!"* she'd exclaim, but she'd do it, and seemed pleased by my pleasure as I ran my hands up her long stockinged legs and under the remarkable uniform.

In point of fact, however, actual sex between us tended to be pretty bloodless—a circumstance that also had more than passingly to do with our respective cultural backgrounds. Even in bed, in the midst of lovemaking, I was American and she was French. Which meant, getting down to cases, that certain behaviors I deemed perfectly normal, mainly having to do with the mouth and tongue but also including verbal expressions of enthusiasm, she considered *"pas normal."* Quite simply, what was at work here was a life circumstance I had yet to fully comprehend but that my time in Paris would make manifest: that one's personality does not change simply because one takes off one's clothes.

The sexual issue—if, indeed, she even perceived it as one—was something Françoise and I discussed only indirectly. Anyway, of course, it was less the problem between us than its most evident expression. The real one had to do with the fact that beyond our public selves—the ones that, had we been from the same country, we'd have gotten past within the first day or two—we knew each other hardly at all.

It had become my custom, as it is with many men, to lay the blame for such failures of communication on myself. In most cases, there was at least some justification for this, and anyway, there was a whiff of saving nobility in the act. *I may be a shmuck, and a pathetic one at that, who will never know a moment's happiness, but, hey, I'm big enough to admit it.* And even—as, in retrospect, was usually the case—when responsibility had somewhat cut both ways, it at least got it over with, sparing the aggrieved party cause to become even more aggrieved.

But in this instance, and it was truly an eye-opener, Françoise was even more wanting in the sharing-of-self department than was I; was, at any rate, more *overtly* reluctant to open up.

One Sunday afternoon, strolling through the Luxembourg Gardens together in silence, we passed a young woman sitting alone on a bench, sobbing. "I wonder what's wrong," I piped up in English. *"Je déteste les gens qui pleurent,"* replied my friend curtly. ("I can't stand people who cry.")

Which, for some reason, set me off. Why, I demanded, was she so uncomfortable with emotion, anyway? Didn't she know that either things came out or they festered? What were we, goddamn mannequins?

For a long while she said nothing. But as we exited the park and turned onto the Boulevard St.-Michel, I was aware that her own eyes had gone moist.

I took her hand. "I'm sorry."

"No, you're right." She shook her head slowly. "I don't know why, but sometimes I just feel so terribly sad. Sometimes"—she paused—"I feel so . . . empty."

A short while later we reached her place, and safely within, sitting at the kitchen table, back to me, she began sobbing;

and continued, absolutely beyond consolation, for more than half an hour. But when she was done, she was *different*—more relaxed than I had ever seen her, very nearly light-hearted—a condition that persisted until the following morning.

One evening years later, as a father, I told my daughter a bit about Françoise—not the specifics of our association, but about that offhand remark in the park, *"Je déteste les gens qui pleurent,"* and all this person had evidently kept locked up inside. Naturally, there was an object lesson intended in this, one that my child needed not at all; never in my life had I encountered anyone more unapologetically forthcoming emotionally than that curly-headed four-year-old. But she was fascinated by the tale, kept coming back to it for days afterward. "Tell me about Françoise Guérin," she would beseech. "Why didn't she think people should cry? *Why?*"

Thus pressed, I eventually offered up my broad theory about the French in general, which is, in essence, that they behave as they do as adults because of the way they were treated as children. Obliged to perform virtually from the outset as miniature adults—to remain silent unless addressed, and mind their every manner, and keep their clothes spotless; forbidden, even, by municipal decree, to romp on the inviting grass of Parisian parks—by age eight or ten, they tend to have had much that ought to come naturally, including spontaneity, knocked out of them. Americans living in Paris grow almost used to witnessing variations on the scene: you're in the subway or aboard a bus and smile at a small child, who smiles back—and the child instantly receives a sharp slap for his temerity. *"Ne regarde pas monsieur!"* ("Don't look at the man!")

Indeed, the case can be made that it is because they are so rarely allowed to act their age as children that they are not only emotionally blunted as adults but so frequently childish in their behavior; so prone to tantrums, so unready to laugh at themselves, so fond of *pipi* and *caca* jokes and pie-in-the-face humor.

Not, of course, that the French themselves cast any of it in any but the most rigorously intellectual terms. "For us," a leading French film critic actually put it to me, when I was investigating the Jerry Lewis phenomenon for *The Metro,* "Jerry represents the Jewish-American inferiority complex, the man smothered by his mother, resulting in aggressive, anarchic behavior toward society. He is the lost clown in society. His films are like the plays of Molière."

Oddly enough—or, as we came to better understand the locals, not oddly at all—our publication's skepticism about French society actually began to make its reputation; outsiders looking in, saying things no one else thought to say, we found ourselves the very epitome of chic. So much so that a mere five or six months into publication, though our operation still lacked a credible business side, we were regularly being congratulated for our supposed success.

The magazine was, at any rate, keeping us busier than we'd ever been in our lives. Between co-editing the thing and regularly writing for it—I was now doing a humor column—many nights I would not fall into bed until well past midnight.

By then I had a place of my own, Françoise and I having reached the seemingly simultaneous conclusion, without, of course, a word's having been exchanged on the subject, that fun was fun, but enough was also enough. Still, as these things go, we strung out the relationship for a while longer—until, to be precise, the night at her place when even the pretense of plausibility came to an end. Though we were naked, in bed, we had been arguing about clothes. *You know,* she had begun, not unkindly, but hardly for the first time, either, *you really do NOT dress well.* My response might have been programmed. *Again with clothes. What is it with you and clothes? Clothes don't mean a thing!*

Which escalated, in astonishingly short order, into my attacking her priorities in general.

In truth, this was unfair; she was a person of considerable social conscience; had just a month before, in concert with other architecture students, set about reconstructing an aban-

doned building for use by the homeless. But you know how
it is during a good argument.

One thing I had never begrudged her, though: she had
style—more than I could ever imagine having. And on this
occasion, after hearing me out, she eyed me coldly. "I wish
we were at *your* place."

I took the bait. "Why?"

"So I could leave."

"All right, all right," I countered, in a pathetic attempt at
verbal comeback (or—who knows?—maybe the expression
was new to her), "I can take a hint!" And, leaping out of bed,
snatching up my clothes, I was out the door, which is where
I'd wanted to be all along, in thirty seconds.

We saw each other just once after that, at a café in the
Ninth Arrondissement, midway between our two apartments,
for a sort of prisoner exchange in neutral territory. With a
bare minimum of civility, we handed over stuff we'd left at
each other's homes and departed.

She had, however, been right about one thing that last
night—actually, about more than one, but this was the first
I came to agree with her on: my clothes. If it was cold out,
I'd put on more of them; if I was going to a fancy place,
something or other got knotted about my neck. My father's
son, hopefully what I wore was clean, but not necessarily.

But something Paris does to you, if you stick around the
place long enough, is begin to make you self-conscious about
things like that. After a while, you're simply aware that ap-
pearancewise you're several notches below everyone else on
the street, with the possible exception of other Americans;
and aware, too, that everyone else notices. I remember listening to a French cabdriver—a *cabdriver*—on the subject
of backpacks, standard gear just then for thousands of my
compatriots visiting the French capital. "What do they think
this is," he demanded, "Paris National Park? And what do
they have in there, anyway, *another* down jacket?"

That he would say such things to me, of all people, was
undoubtedly occasioned by the fact that already I had begun

to put some distance between myself and the alleged sartorial primitives. A bare six months before, I had allowed myself to be led by Françoise into a large Left Bank jeans emporium only under extreme duress; and had been incredulous when asked by a salesman to *lie on the floor* so that a pair of size zero could be worked, inch by inch, up my lower torso; then, having purchased the infernal things and finding that they impeded not only locomotion but circulation, especially to the genitals, I had loudly speculated that *this* was what must have killed French interest in sex—a notion, by the way, that a subsequent study would actually bear out. But now, here I was, shelling out for French duds with the best of them—not only for those jeans, but for nifty little jackets, and shoes that murdered my toes, and corduroy slacks with lots of tiny pockets in odd places.

The culmination of my new life as a clotheshorse, my symbolic step across the line, was the purchase, one hot summer morning, of a purse. What choice did I have? None of the pockets in my slacks were capable of accommodating even American keys, let alone those to my French apartment, which looked as if they might have been used to unlock the Bastille; and even if they had, the result would have been a bulge, which, of course, was unthinkable.

Not that, even a couple of weeks before, a purse would have been thinkable either. It is simply that having, in the midst of the most brutal heat wave in memory, been obliged to wear a heavy leather jacket, a *winter* jacket, solely because it had huge pockets, I had reached the point where I no longer knew what dignity was.

But I'll be damned if I didn't come to like the thing. More to the point, Paris being Paris, not a soul, male or female, looked at me askance as I scurried along, clutching it close to my body, the way we purse carriers had been taught back in New York. In fact, taking the long way back to the point, I happened to be doing better with women just then than ever before in my life.

Part of this certainly had less to do with me personally than with the faintly unpleasant way the world works. *The Metro* was increasing popular; our offices in a sixteenth-century *hôtel particulier* attracted a steady stream of would-be writers and others, and it was hard not to note that assorted individuals, women among them, were friendlier than might have been the case had I been working in, say, a foundry.

But it was also beyond question that for expatriates in the French capital, it was startlingly easy to make connections; that since most of us were unattached, footloose and unfettered by local convention, things tended to happen to us, and *between* us, that would never have happened back home. For one thing, there was generally little in the way of expectation on either side. Since we were more or less passing through, en route to permanent lives, what would have been the point?

There were times we even acknowledged this social dynamic, men and women together, marveling at how, for the first time, we were truly able to regard each other simultaneously as lovers and friends. Since the Sixties, of course, this had been a kind of ideal, a utopia of emotional/sexual equals, and the notion that we were living it was both pleasing and self-flattering.

But then, there was a dirty little secret: among ourselves, we men tended to discuss women pretty much as we always had—and we couldn't *believe* how lucky we were.

Unexpectedly, at almost any odd moment, one was likely to be privy to an extraordinary tale, old-fashioned locker-room talk with a Gallic twist. One Sunday, between innings of the weekly softball game in the Bois de Boulogne, a youngish American businessman told me how coolly distant had been the French woman he'd been out with the night before— until, parked in the car in front of her apartment, about to drop her off, he'd happened to mutter something in English. "It was unbelievable, but suddenly she was all over me. In French I was a bust, but in English, I was allowed to do *anything* to her I wanted."

"So you talked to her in English?"

"Yeah."

"And you did what you wanted?"

"Of course."

"What'd you say?"

"Oh, you know, whatever came to mind."

"What?"

He hesitated, a bit embarrassed. "Actually, she seemed to like it best when I sounded gruff, so I did Charles Bronson. You know: 'C'mon, baby, I ain't got all day!' That sort of thing." He shrugged. "Thank heaven I was the only one who could understand it."

Then there was the afternoon I passed at a local swimming and tennis club, on assignment with a photographer. Returning from an interview with the owner of the place, I found my colleague lying on the grass, chin cupped in hand, staring in the direction of an attractive young woman sunbathing thirty feet away, wearing only a bikini bottom. "Her name's Monique," he observed. "We met by the pool."

"I've noticed quite a few terrific-looking women around here," I said.

"There are six," he corrected. And he began ticking them off on his fingers. "There's this one here. Right now two are having lunch in the dining room. The redhead, I think her name's Sylvie, is playing mixed doubles on Court Four. And the last two are at the pool."

Most notably, there was the morning I answered a violent pounding at my door to find my good friend Bernie, a sloppy grin across his bearded face. It turned out that Bernie had passed the previous night in bed with *two* women, one American, one Dutch.

"A *ménage à trois?*" Until that moment, I am not sure I had ever uttered the phrase.

He giggled. "I can't believe it myself." And he proceeded to describe the episode in such graphic detail that I felt almost like an interloper. Almost.

Still, if racking up numbers was the goal—and it was certainly part of it—I myself could hardly complain. Working as hard as I ever had, sometimes putting in fourteen-hour days,

seven days a week, at the office, I nonetheless found time to
see a large number of women—"women," as Bernie was wont
to describe them, for between ourselves we kept a running
geographical tally, "of many lands." There were Americans,
of course, and French; a Swedish *au pair*; an Irish law student;
a dogged New Zealander hoping to establish a French beach-
head for her nation's cheese; others. Almost all of them were
seeing other men, of course—in one case, other women—
and that was fine. Easy come, extraordinarily easy go. Indeed,
there was actually a day that I had sex with women of three
different nationalities—waking up beside one, seeing another
during lunch, falling asleep at night beside the third—and
failed even to realize it until the following day.

But then, who am I kidding? Even now, having nearly
persuaded myself that it's all nicely in perspective, I can't lay
off the bragging. For that, of course, had always been of incalculable importance. Giddy as a particular evening might
leave me, and temporarily empowered, it was vital too for
others to know; know that these women, this veritable international parade, had passed on me favorably.

All right, this hardly bespeaks a sturdy self-image, but we're
talking facts here. And the truth is, when I think back on that
period, I recall with nearly as much satisfaction as I do any
of those amorous adventures a lunch, on a visit home to New
York, with a good friend of my father's—a man I knew would
pass along every word—and his rapt attention as I spun out
my tales, and his evident envy. "Hmm," he mused at the
conclusion, only half joking, "any room for me on that paper
of yours?"

Back in Paris the following week, I resumed right where
I'd left off, proceeding, for this is how I would often put it in
subsequent years, "to sow enough wild oats to fill a barn."
Later, too, I would occasionally maintain, doubtless with some
justification, that such a period of sexual abandon reasonably
early in life is useful, satisfying a curiosity that might otherwise
prove corrosive later on.

But what, for years afterward, I failed to mention to anyone was how very often I would lie awake at night, listening to the sound of the traffic on the Rue Gay-Lussac, feeling profoundly, irredeemably alone.

Still, it remains a measure of precisely what I was about just then that when at last I did draw closer to someone, the someone I chose was Arabella Stanley.

I first spotted Arabella at perhaps fifty yards, heading my way on a narrow sidewalk, and as she came closer I became intent on finding a flaw. Without question, her body—encased in a tight leather jacket and tight faded jeans, at once compact and pleasingly full—was extraordinary, its appeal heightened by a walk, one foot crossing slightly ahead of the other, that produced an undulating sway of the hips; this last, indeed, was so hypnotic that it was only when she was within ten yards that I perceived, with a rush of dismay, that her face was perfect too—large blue eyes and full lips, framed by shoulder-length black hair. *Now I was in trouble.* The gauntlet was down. If I didn't at least try to speak to her, I'd loathe myself for the next half-hour.

To make matters worse, I happened to be wearing a snazzy new suit and filthy white sneakers; and under my arm I carried not only my purse but a pair of boots with floppy soles, my destination being a neighborhood shoemaker.

What to say? What to do?

But abruptly, she veered to the left, crossed the street and disappeared into a small grocery. I hesitated only a moment, then followed.

The shop was dimly lit, but I instantly picked her up. She had snatched up a condiment from a back shelf and was heading toward the counter to pay.

"Pardon, Madame," I addressed the proprietress, the plan being hatched even as I spoke, "would you know where I can get these"—I held out the boots—"repaired?"

She gazed at me, as I'd hoped she would, with that peculiarly French look of annoyance and contempt. "Monsieur," she said tartly, "this is not an information bureau."

Bingo!

The young woman, having made her purchase, headed out the door—and I was free to follow her and repeat the question.

"Oh," she said pleasantly, "you can talk to me in English." So she was English—evidently upper-class, at that.

"Is my accent that bad?"

"It's not hard to recognize an American 'r.' "

So, standing there outside the grocery, we fell to chatting. She had been in Paris a couple of years, she said; was currently working as a guide at the Pompidou Center. She asked about me.

"I work on an English-language paper."

"Not *The Metro*?"

"Yes, as a matter of fact."

"I love *The Metro*. What's your name?"

I fairly shuffled my feet; my column was arguably the most popular feature in the magazine. "Harry Stein."

She furrowed her brow—"Hmmm, that sounds a bit familiar"—then brightened. "Do you know Bill Throgmorton? I adore him."

Our film critic, a pretentious artsy-fartsy turd. "Oh, yeah. Sure I know Bill. Nice guy."

And so, eventually, I got around to asking if she was up for a glass of red, and we headed for a nearby café. We talked for a while about feminism—she was reading Germaine Greer—before getting back to the subject at hand, ourselves, and I found myself more than a little surprised to perceive so cool an intelligence emerging from such a package. Nor was this exclusively a matter of her exquisite looks; everything about her manner—the softness of the voice, the too-ready laugh and smile, the way she batted her eyes and licked her lips and passed her hand through her hair—was powerfully seductive.

And then there was her startling candor.

"I don't only work at the museum," she announced at one point, virtually out of the blue. "I also have another job."

"Oh?"

"I'm an escort-service girl. Do you know what that is?"

"Yes."

"It's a euphemism for call girl."

Somehow, by that time, I was not entirely surprised. In fact, in light of the rapidly developing intimacy between us, I was more taken aback to hear, as I walked her home, that she had a boyfriend—a fellow named Simon with whom she evidently had a tempestuous Burton-Taylor kind of relationship.

No matter. I took her number—she scrawled it in red across a full page of the address book I'd been trying hard to keep tidy—and hurried back to *The Metro*, still carrying the boots.

"Tom," I said, bursting into his office, "you're not gonna believe this!"

"A whore?" he asked, incredulous, after hearing me out. "Now you're involved with a whore?"

"She's not a *real* whore. I don't think she does it more than a couple of times a week."

He laughed—a deep, hearty laugh. Tom was laughing a lot like that these days; he had a bona fide girlfriend, a blond Australian who worked in the art department, whom he would eventually marry. "Well, all right, as long as she only does it a *couple* of times a week . . ."

But—how could I explain it?—I was intrigued by Arabella, and no longer simply by the way she looked. When we got together over the following weeks, generally at a sedate wine bar on the Rue de Rivoli, she would go on and on—about her various clients, all of them rich and connected, a few of them well known; about her problems with her boyfriend; about her past—and I never tired of listening. This was partly because I could never quite be sure what would come out of her mouth next. "Have you ever noticed," she might suddenly muse, in that lovely voice, part Lady Astor, part Marilyn Monroe, "how difficult a time French women seem to have moving their bowels? At a public toilet, one is absolutely flabbergasted by the grunts and groans. Tell me, is it the same for men?"

But above all, it was her honesty about herself that was so arresting. Arabella was, beyond question, highly neurotic; in fact, in important ways, she seemed only semifunctional. Once a promising student at the Royal Ballet, more recently a graduate of London's most prestigious art academy, there she nonetheless was, earning her keep by bedding down with Texas oilmen and Arab sheiks. Still, the thing was, she was able, as well as anyone I'd known, to articulate how she'd ended up as she had. She talked not only about the dramatic stuff—her mother's death in a car wreck when Arabella was thirteen, immediately following a fierce mother-daughter quarrel—but the vivid impact of vagrant events out of her childhood; and more and more, she probed for details about mine.

I had never been much interested in this psychology business, had never figured it had anything to do with anything. Nor had anyone ever particularly demanded that I ask questions of myself. For Arabella, however, the link between past and present, between the experiences one has lived and how one functions day to day, was altogether obvious; and slowly, even I began to make a few rudimentary connections.

Not that I let anyone know. Indeed, I tweaked her endlessly about her own astonishing self-absorption—which, to my surprise, since I was evidently the only man who had ever done so, both interested and pleased her.

"Do you really think I talk so much about myself?" she inquired one afternoon, earnestly.

I couldn't keep from laughing. "Yes, I really do."

She reflected on this for a moment. "Tell me, what do other people talk about?"

She had, at any rate, a good idea of what certain men talked about. It was part of her job—that's how she always referred to it, just as she referred to her sexiest dress as her "working clothes" and otherwise refused to wear it—to go to swank clubs and restaurants with the men who rented her, and often she returned from these encounters dripping scorn. "My goodness, when you get them off the subject of petrodollars and deutsche marks, there's absolutely nothing in their heads."

Sometimes she appeared frankly exhausted by the effort expended in having had to be pleasant. That was the work, she suggested, even more than the sex, over which, at least, she could exercise a degree of control. She made it a personal point of pride never to spend the night in a client's bed and would, if at all possible, contrive to be back in her own before midnight.

Yet, as she told it, she was apt to enjoy a working evening even less when, as occasionally happened, the client was sympathetic. For instance, there was the case of the cultivated Dutch businessman, recently widowed, who wanted only to buy her an expensive dinner and ruminate about his departed spouse.

"Sometimes I don't know what I feel anymore," she said afterward. "I spend so much time playing at feelings that sometimes even I have trouble telling what's real and what's pretend." She shook her head. "I can't keep on doing this job."

I thought back on this exchange the evening when we at last moved beyond the platonic stage. "When you kiss me," she offered in a throaty whisper, just as we were getting down to serious business, "you make my knees buckle"—and even now, I have no idea if she was remotely sincere. But I'll tell you, at that moment I didn't give a damn; or even later. Arabella at full throttle, toying with a man, even if the man happened to be oneself, was truly something to behold. In bed, she was not only a technical marvel—before that night, I'd never truly understood all the hoopla about oral sex—but was terrific with sound effects and exclamations. If, for a man, it is always a considerable turn-on when a woman drops the veneer of civility and becomes a primal being, the effect was especially potent here, because both behaviors were so extreme; and afterward, relaxing beneath a down comforter, a cup of tea balanced on her knees, the BBC playing in the background over her shortwave, she made lovely conversation, before we settled down for another round.

And yet, after that it was never quite the same between us. It seemed natural, the obvious next step, for us to draw even closer, but it just didn't happen; nor, finally, I guess, knowing each other as we did, did we want it to. Simon was still very much on the scene, a chap who occasionally answered her phone and seemed to resent me not in the least; and of course, she also had her work. In brief, the role I seemed to have been assigned was that of boyfriend-in-waiting, old reliable, in case things should sour again with number one. Such an arrangement had its pluses, but it was hardly one upon which I wanted to stake my future.

Not, in the end, that that was an option. *The Metro*, by now an established critical success, had secretly been in financial jeopardy for months—playing at big business, we had borrowed a considerable sum, which we couldn't figure out how to repay—and by the late summer of 1978, the jig was just about up. Before the year was over, many of us would be back in the States.

It was just as the end was approaching that I happened to see Jean Seberg again. I had reestablished contact for professional reasons—I wanted her to write a memoir for a special issue marking the tenth anniversary of the worker/student uprising of 1968, a landmark event in recent French history—but when I tracked her down, she was in some sort of clinic; for alcoholism, I think, though this was never made explicit. We agreed to get together on her release.

Several weeks later, we sat at a corner table in an inexpensive restaurant. The proprietor, delighted by her presence, probably, like so many French men of roughly his age, having once included her in his fantasies, lingered a dozen feet away, ready to spring at the merest suggestion of a request. Because she was gracious, and because she was pleased, too, Jean more than once looked his way and offered a smile.

But it did not take long to gauge that she was in distress. If, since our previous encounter, I felt as if I'd aged considerably more than two years, she seemed a decade more fatigued. Her marriage had recently ended, she explained, and though she had seen it coming, that hadn't made it easier; nor was there much in the way of work coming her way.

After a time, she began talking about her previous marriage, the one to Romain Gary, dropping intimacies—about the peculiarities of their sex life, about their respective affairs—which, entertaining as they might have been in another context, now made me acutely uncomfortable. Rarely had I encountered anyone so needy, so desperate to make contact.

In response, to put distance between us, I told her all about my girlfriend, Arabella—neglecting to mention her line of endeavor, her boyfriend, my actual standing in her universe.

That seemed to help. Soon she was reminiscing instead about her career, particularly the period of her great success, the early years with Godard. Suddenly animated, she launched into a story she had told me before, about the time the three of them—Godard, Belmondo, herself—had set out to make a sequel to *Breathless* to be called *The Greatest Swindle in the World*. They had arrived in Marrakesh, she said, and had begun shooting, when Godard abruptly closed down the production. He'd been fighting with his girlfriend by long-distance telephone and decided he wanted to be back in Paris. "Everyone said, 'You can't do that,' " recalled Jean. " 'Why not?' he answered. 'It's just another swindle.' "

The first time she had laughed at the anecdote, but now she offered only a small smile. "I have great affection for Godard. But in many ways it was childish, the way we lived. It's so easy not to grow up here."

When we parted, she offered me a ride; it was also an invitation. I thanked her, said I'd walk and watched her drive off in her white Fiat, the one in which she'd be found a year later, an empty vial of barbiturates on the seat beside her.

Arabella, for her part, at first refused to believe that I would be leaving town. How could I, she seemed to suggest, when it would be inconvenient for her? At last persuaded, however, she consented to a farewell very much in the spirit of our liaison. We went for a weekend to Deauville, the Channel resort, then out of season, dividing our time between the misty beach, the elegant casino and our room in the largest of the imposing Victorian hotels fronting the water. There Arabella told me some of her few remaining secrets and pried a few more from me.

Still, perhaps fittingly, my most persistent memory of that prolonged farewell is of lying contentedly in a hot tub and suddenly hearing, from the adjoining room, a staccato clop-clopping.

"What are you doing out there?" I called out.

"Running around in circles."

"Why?"

At that moment, having worked up a head of steam, she came clopping into the bathroom, entirely nude except for a pair of black heels. These she kicked off and leaped into the tub, sending a couple of gallons of water splashing onto the floor.

"What in the world are you doing?"

"Don't you like it?"

"Well, I mean, I suppose if you're expecting it, it could be kind of sexy."

"Isn't it, though? I do it with Godard. It's his absolute favorite thing."

I do not mean, at this juncture, to get weighty-sounding—anything but—but the fact is, in the lives of a lot of us, there are distinct emotional turning points; recognitions about ourselves and our place in the world that result in a sharp distinction between who we are and who we used to be. And if they are rarely so dramatic as those that turn up in biographies of statesmen and the second acts of made-for-TV movies—if, indeed, we ourselves sometimes come to recognize them for what they were only in retrospect— well, who said insight has to be blinding?

In fact, more often it accompanies the lingering pain associated with a kick to the gut.

Though even now it irks me to credit her with anything positive, and irks my wife, too, my particular introduction to the light had more than something to do with a person named Sally. She was a would-be actress, extraordinarily self-possessed and quick to laugh, and the very evening I met her, sometime after my return from Paris, as I watched her move from the table in an Upper West Side restaurant/bar where we'd been exchanging initial intimacies toward the ladies' room, her tight blue woolen sailor's pants showing off her ass to maximum advantage, the little chains on her boots jingling as she walked, it occurred to me that this was the woman I was going to marry.

Thus began, for me, a sustained ride aboard your average American emotional roller coaster: six months of stratospheric highs and depthless lows, of flaring angers and glorious reconciliations, of—and this was the main thing—never being

entirely sure where I stood. For, especially at the start, she
dictated the terms. Usually she believed we were ideal together, but sometimes she was sure we just weren't; sometimes she found me immensely appealing physically, but
occasionally she didn't want me near her at all. When I withdrew, she would come close; when I approached too eagerly,
she would disappear. Endlessly, week after week, we would
hash it all over. Indeed, the whole business was so consuming,
it involved so much wondering and hoping and calculation,
that often it was hard to concentrate on anything else.

Not, reflecting on it subsequently, that there hadn't been
signs of what was to come from the start, if only I'd begun to
know to look for them. So what if, as she told me that very
first night, she'd lost a whole series of jobs—at an advertising
agency, managing a restaurant, at a television production company—because others were jealous of her? Looking at her, I
could believe that. So what if she made several less-than-
charitable references to people who ostensibly were friends?
Her candor was disarming. So what if, even as we spoke, our
chairs ever closer, there was another guy waiting in an apartment barely three blocks away for her return? *That* was actually kind of nice; I mean, hey, in the glorious game of love,
someone's gotta lose.

As it happened, my time with her would, at least, prove of
value professionally. Shortly after we at last broke off, I was
asked by (talk about ironies) *Playboy* to compose an article
with the intentionally provocative title "Ten Kinds of Women
to Avoid at All Costs"; and on the basis of that single association, I already had four categories firmly in mind: The Tra-
gedienne ("There are a startling number of people in this
world who don't know they're experiencing emotion unless
it's pain"); The Perpetual Noncommitter ("The stigma of evad-
ing enduring commitment has, of course, long been attached
to men. But there are thousands of women out there, and
their numbers are increasing, who have precisely the same
tendency"); The Man's Woman ("The woman with no women
friends. Women see things in other women that we men,

struck insensible by a coy little smile or the purr in a voice, or an appropriate roundness in the right place, rarely spot until panting, with our hearts lying on the floor, it is much too late"); The Victim ("Someone for whom everything has always gone wrong, personally as well as professionally, but it is never her fault").

But then, getting right down to it, who was I trying to kid? What was *I* purporting to be if not a victim? The obvious question, the one I was loath to face, was what had I been doing caught up in such a relationship in the first place?

There were easy answers, of course. Sally *was* nice to look at, and there had been some terrific times; she was someone who was generally up for just about anything, from a spontaneous weekend at a country inn to modeling, for the edification of visitors, the half-dozen dresses lately owned by Tricia Nixon that I'd purchased from an employee of Tricia's building as they were en route to Goodwill. And, too, there had been moments of genuine contact, conversations in which we'd edged toward some acknowledgment of how screwed up we were. I talked a lot at those times about my parents, both of them; she talked almost exclusively, indeed, obsessively, about her father, a wealthy, conservative businessman whose approval was the very essence of conditional—making it crystal-clear, by the by, that he would never approve of me.

This last was, of course, part of the difficulty between the two of us: neither, when it came right down to it, did she. But, too, of course, finally, that was her appeal.

One evening, still early on, we had a tentative dinner date, but for hours I was unable to track her down. When she finally answered the phone at her place, around midnight, she was oddly cool, and got off quickly. The next day, by way of explanation, she let me know, without evident embarrassment, that there'd been a man with her, someone from her office she'd had her eye on for a while; my call had come at just the right moment, she added with that laugh I'd always before taken as charming, because the guy had been shy and the phone was in the bedroom, and she'd been wondering how to get him in there.

But instead of getting out of the thing forthwith, I sulked a couple of days, and avoided her a couple more, and then was back in the middle of it, having accepted her ostensible bewilderment at my anger. Indeed, every time she realized my worst fears by rejecting me, there was a powerful, unrelenting ache, an almost physical need to somehow make her love me again.

And yet, I chose to believe it couldn't be quite so sorry as it seemed. I was, after all, by the end, giving as good as I got; Sally may have been capable of myriad cruelties, direct and offhand, but, dammit, so was I. In fact, I reassured myself, *that* also was part of what had kept me interested. Where in the past, too many women had allowed me to run amok, Sally, at least, was a challenge.

But, then . . . oh, boy, talk about insights!

Could it be? Had I really, all those years, in my pleasant, unobtrusive way, been a male version of *that*?

Less than a week after we split for good, Sally, she let me know herself, had a new boyfriend. I, for my part, had an appointment with a therapist.

The first extended conversation I ever had with the woman who would become my wife, over dinner at an Indian restaurant, eventually worked its way around to the subject of emotional fatigue. There we sat, I a mere thirty years old, this Priscilla person only twenty-nine, yet already, we laughingly acknowledged, we had each been through more social convulsions, attitudinal gyrations, relationships than had several generations of our forebears combined; and we were sick of it.

"I shudder every time I've got to begin laying out my history for another new person," I recall her saying. "I just don't have the energy anymore."

I nodded away. "I know, I know. I hear these things coming

out of my mouth, and even I'm bored by them. It's work trying to sell yourself."

And yet, for all the candor, we parted that evening less than excited about each other.

From my perspective, this was basically a matter of her bearing, demeanor, body language, what people for whom I tended to have a certain contempt described, far more accurately than I could, as the "vibes" she put out. It was one thing to object in principle to the pressure of having to reveal oneself to a new acquaintance; it was quite another to hold back with *me*. I mean, for all my complaining, in recent years I'd gotten *used* to women trotting out pieces of their past over introductory dinners, and I readily did the same for them— not, by the way, bored in the least by what I was saying; in fact, delighted to command their full interest, wholly caught up in the hunt—so that afterward, in bed, we'd both feel a lot less like strangers.

I recall thinking afterward, with both of us at home in our own beds, that maybe I'd put her off with a passing remark I'd made early on—a favorable reference, if one must know, to Plato's Retreat, the famous urban sex resort.

Of course, I found myself concluding, it had to have been that. For all the articles that had lately been appearing about Plato's in the mainstream press, in spite of the fact that it was actually enjoying a kind of vogue just then—and that every man I knew was as intrigued by the place as I—I knew full well that women tended to react to its very existence with reflexive distaste. When, on other occasions, I had raised the subject with women—ones I actually knew—as in "Ha-ha, I wonder what that place is really like," the response, "Ha-ha, forget it," had always seemed more than vaguely accusatory.

Reflecting upon my gaffe with Priscilla, I found some comfort in the recognition that it might have been worse; I had, at least, been alert enough to avoid mentioning to my future wife that I had in fact visited Plato's myself.

It had been nine months before, the weekend of my thirtieth birthday—by point of reference, a few days after the mass suicide at Jonestown—and a Paris friend, a photographer I'd always liked both for her decency and for her uncommon spontaneity, was taking me to dinner. She showed up at my apartment in a striking tuxedo outfit.

"What's the plan?" I inquired.

"Italian food. Then, Plato's! You should see what I'm wearing *under* this."

And three hours later, we were wandering about the place, kneeling to dip our fingers into the pool, playing pinball in the game room, peeking around corners. There were, clearly, a great many other first-timers on hand, but fully half the individuals present were at least partially nude; and all over the place, couples—and the occasional threesome, foursome, fivesome—were going at each other with great and greater abandon.

It would better serve my residual sense of propriety, especially given the sexual climate of the late Eighties, to report that the scene's lack of subtlety, its rawness—on top of the fact that many of the bodies on view would certainly have looked a lot better in clothes—left me ready to bolt the place. In fact, after a time, as I relaxed, I felt almost inclined to join in.

So, it seemed, did my companion. Before long, we found ourselves in a private room in the back, sitting on cushions, backs against the wall, in conversation with two other couples. One pair was nude, the other clad only in towels, and the talk, under the circumstances, was remarkably impersonal. Mayor Koch's recent performance. The declining quality of the club's buffet table. Real estate prices in the neighborhood.

But abruptly I became aware that the woman opposite me, the one without the towel, was sizing me up.

"Why don't we get to know one another?" she proposed a moment later to the group. "Why don't we introduce ourselves, say who we are and how we ended up here?" And—I'm not sure anyone else noticed—she stroked my inside pant leg with a bare big toe.

For three or four minutes we proceeded as suggested, and the ice was beginning to break. Then it was my friend's turn.

"Well," she began, "my name is Jane, and I'm a photographer, and for the past two years I've been living in Guyana."

"Guyana?" It was the woman across from me. "You mean where all those people . . . ?"

She nodded.

"Did you know Jim Jones?"

"Yes, of course. As a matter of fact, I'm a member of the People's Temple myself."

At that, I actually saw an erect penis begin to deflate.

"Really?"

"And I want all of you to know that it's a terrible tragedy, what happened to poor Jimmy Jones. He was a wonderful man."

Five minutes later, after everyone else had fled the room, she offered me a smile that was the very essence of sheepishness. "Sorry. I guess I really just wasn't up for this after all."

But what I am getting to is this: I had it all wrong about Priscilla. She wasn't put off by the Plato's reference in the least. In the years since, she has come to know Jane well, and she occasionally tells the Plato's story herself; had I offered it on our first date, she'd have been at least as interested as by anything I did say. One of the things I would eventually come to love most about Priscilla is that while she is dogmatic on questions of values, she is extraordinarily tolerant of human, even male, nature.

No, what actually gave her such pause about me that evening was something else entirely. Apparently, inadvertently, so subtly that I expect another man would not even have noticed, I let on that I was still in turmoil over Sally; and, worse, offered a couple of clues as to the substance of that harrowing liaison. And her want of interest was as conscious a choice as mine, in reaction, was visceral.

Several days after that dinner with Priscilla, on a softball field in Central Park, between innings, I happened to mention the date to a writer friend of mine.

"Oh, I know her," he said. "She works at Orion Pictures."

"She's nice," I ventured. "And smart."

"Pretty, too." He hesitated. "But there's something about her . . ."

Instantly, I knew exactly what he meant; among men who know each other even reasonably well, basic assumptions on the subject of women tend to be shared.

One of my friend's pet expressions—borrowed from all those D-movies in which, in the last reel, the retiring secretary takes off her glasses and reveals herself as a knockout—is "My God, Miss Jones, you're beautiful!" Well, Priscilla had the physical essentials, all right—might even, if she'd wished, and worked at it, and been lucky, have turned herself into something Helen Gurley Brown would have considered *Cosmo* cover material. But the attitude wasn't there. She was complex instead of pliable; less obviously sweet than problematic; seemingly unaware, in brief, that it was her business to at least strive toward our version of perfection.

And it all showed. Priscilla is possessed of one of those faces that tell everything, mirroring her quicksilver moods with utter reliability; more so, I think, than even she is aware. "I can't get over it," she herself would remark years later, after coming across yet another newspaper story about a rock star's involvement with a blond model, "what is it about blond hair?" Well, the blond hair is certainly part of it, and so are more primal considerations ("There are three very simple secrets to keepin' a man," as Mick Jagger's blonde, Jerri Hall, puts it: "Be a maid in the living room, a cook in the kitchen and a helluva whore in the bedroom"); but as much as anything else, the attraction is in the neutral expressions on those placid, conventionally pretty faces. *That's* what we grew up aspiring to, not full-blooded beings as complicated, as demanding, as ourselves.

It goes without saying that any such judgment on our part was the very pinnacle of presumption. I mean, there we were, a couple of guys who had come of age actively embarrassed by certain aspects of our physical selves; alert to comparisons with Groucho, I *still* hesitated to be seen, in unfamiliar company, with a cigar.

And yet it never would have crossed our minds that there was anything amiss in our thinking. Thinking that way about women is simply something men like us had always done, like shaving, or peeing standing up. "A friend of mine and I," offers one guy with whom I spoke, "even now sometimes compare specific parts of women we've known. Not just tits and ass, but which one has the best lips, the best hair, the best ankles? This guy is convinced no one has ever run across a better pair of *thighs* than the ones on a woman he used to date." "With me," notes someone else, "it was never so much a question of seeking perfection as of being bothered by too-obvious *im*perfections. It's a fine distinction, but a real one. For instance, I remember once being really hot for someone—until we got undressed and I noticed a long hair growing out of one of her nipples."

I myself—how's this for a damaging admission?—more than once imagined a woman I was seeing being turned into wet clay, so that I would have, say, ten minutes to make whatever physical alterations I wished before she dried and reassumed human form; so there I pictured myself, busily lending a bit more roundness to the buttocks, transferring a bit of substance from the thighs to the breasts, perhaps smoothing out a bumpy nose—the fantasy not only pleasant but somewhat anxiety-producing because of the possibility, all too plausible on the basis of my experience in certain art classes, that I would use up my allotted time and my subject's body would be grotesquely out of balance and her face permanently deformed.

The syndrome was, all in all, neatly summed up by Tim McCarver, the baseball player turned announcer, in a recent interview in *Esquire*. "Once," recalled McCarver, "I was walking down the street in Philadelphia with Hank McGraw, Tug's brother. There were two women walking in front of us. Hank pointed to the one on his left and said, 'Parkay.' Then he pointed to the other and said, 'Butter.'"

*   *   *

To this day, I can't say for sure what it was that impelled me, several months hence, to call Priscilla again; I like to think it was something subliminal, but it was also the case that I wanted back the book she'd borrowed that first night.

Anyway, we met for lunch, and it was . . . nice. No fireworks, no sudden moment of revelation, but comfortable. She was out of work by then, I kept writer's hours, so afterward we wandered aimlessly along Upper Broadway, chatting as we window-shopped. "I'd love to see that," I recall her remarking, as we passed beneath the marquee of the Loews on Eighty-third Street, nodding toward a poster for *101 Dalmatians.* "I'm crazy about Disney."

"Oh, yeah?"

She smiled, evidently awaiting more of a reaction. "What I *can't* stand is foreign movies. Talk about pretentious!" She added something about her student days at Berkeley in the late Sixties when an avid enthusiasm for Antonioni was, almost as much as proper leftist politics, *de rigueur.* "God, what a hellish period."

In days to come, this was something I would see far more of. Priscilla loves to sound off against conventional wisdom of all kinds, both because she sincerely believes that most people, and especially her peers, are beholden to fashion, and because she enjoys being contrary.

Well, I averred, I could see her point. I knew what she meant. But I myself liked plenty of foreign pictures, happened to be an especially big fan of Truffaut.

She eyed me skeptically. *Oh, yeah? Why?*

So I told her the plot of my favorite Truffaut film, *Stolen Kisses,* and, to my surprise, she listened closely, finally expressing what seemed to be genuine interest in seeing one of the guy's films for herself. "If," she added, "you'll be willing to sit through the most moving picture ever made: *Old Yeller.*"

It was something that would come to characterize the early

days of our courtship, this good-natured sparring; but it was
also a means of slowly revealing ourselves to each other.

Emphasis here on *slowly*. Quite simply, neither of us was
inclined just then to proceed with the eager alacrity so characteristic of the era. She, for one thing, happened also to be
seeing someone else; and I, rebounding, remained open to
all comers. But it was more than just that. We quickly became
aware that we responded to each other in what seemed an
odd fashion, each so appreciating the way the other viewed
the world that we'd almost certainly have been friends even
if we'd been of the same sex—and that was not something to
be lightly tampered with. Our initial dates, if they can even
be characterized as such, harked back, as much as anything
else, to my days of compulsive Risk playing with boyhood
buddies back in my childhood home. We played game after
game of casino or gin, making reasonably pleasant conversation all the while, but both desperate to win. We played
Initials, allotting ourselves a flat two minutes to see who could
come up with the most names to match the paired letters
gleaned at random from the newspaper. At the local Citibank,
we'd join the lines at adjacent cash machines to see who could
get his money first.

It sounds, I know, like a curious way to breed affection; but
the point is, for all the games we played, there was, for once,
no romantic gamesmanship. For better or for worse, with
minor allowances for the social niceties, we presented ourselves as we were. And slowly, slowly, we began to discern
that we had not only interests in common, but a wide range
of perceptions; and, most vitally, values.

It is safe to assume that my friends and hers believed, to
the extent they gave the matter any thought at all, that we
were spending most of those evenings together in bed. That,
after all, is certainly the way these things more often proceed.
"Partly," as one fellow I spoke with straightforwardly put it,
"it's that you're incredibly horny, especially with a new person; but partly, too, it's a hump that you have to get over.

Once you've had enough sex, *then* you can get to know each other and—who knows?—maybe even hit it off."

That is the way it had generally been for both of us as well. But now even the smooching was minimal, the sort of stuff more readily associated with Archie and Veronica than with a pair of contemporary adults who, *in toto*, had had more lovers than could be counted on eight hands.

If there is any note of self-congratulation in the above, only part of me intends there to be. For another reason so little transpired between us for so long—why, getting right down to it, I failed to jump her bones—is that for me, all the usual signals were skewed. She was so much the opposite of flirtatious or coy, so different from the sort of women who'd aroused my interest in the past, that I found it hard to regard her—and though the term may be objectionable, at the pivotal moment this is what it adds up to—as a sex object. "Morons in love," she observed dryly one afternoon when, channel-hopping, we chanced across a moon-eyed, verbally backward pair trying to express themselves on an afternoon soap; but my appreciative laugh was also just a bit nervous. I mean, the woman was at least my intellectual equal (perhaps, as she herself smirkingly proclaimed, in the wake of one particularly hard-fought triumph, my superior), someone who read more books in a month than I did in two years, a person who liked *opera*, for God's sake. How was I supposed to deal with this in the sack?

But when it finally came to pass, early on the afternoon of her thirtieth birthday, the day the American hostages were seized in Iran, during halftime of the Giants-49ers game, sex was as emotionally effortless as all that had come before. Afterward, holding hands, walking through a crowded street fair on Columbus Avenue, we competed to see who would run into more people he/she knew. She won—but having said "Hi" to lots of passers-by who only looked startled in return, I refused to admit it.

Oddly, at least from my perspective, over succeeding weeks

and months, we drew only closer. Almost always before, as the initial emotional rush gave way to some kind of routine, I would find my interest, if not precisely waning, gradually becoming less intense; but now, week by week, against all odds, it only increased. At once waspish and unabashedly sentimental, she more and more seemed a soulmate, someone to be counted on as an ally in an often hostile universe—and yet more than challenging enough to force upon me even unwelcome truths.

As curious as anything else, for this was so very vivid a break with all that had come before, our sex life became more passionate instead of less; and Priscilla, whose physical short-comings I had long before catalogued mentally—breasts that were a bit too small, knees that were too bony, those furrows in her brow; nothing that couldn't be patched up if she went clay for a few minutes, but hardly perfection—now struck me as appallingly beautiful; I'd not have altered even those features she'd have readily changed herself. Eerily, joyously, for the first time in my adult life I found myself without the slightest interest in any other woman, including those anonymous many passing in the street.

All right, all right, the early days of almost any union—even one that will end badly—tend to seem that way; the American social landscape is littered with emotional casualties who still can't figure out what went wrong between day one and, say, year five.

The obvious truth is that we had some problems—easily glossed over, just then, but very real nonetheless—the sort of problems most people in like circumstances eventually face: the ones having to do with the emotional baggage that both of us had long toted around.

In all the evident ways, Priscilla's background was just about as different from mine as those of two individuals nominally of the same culture can be; indeed, as a couple, we were something of a contemporary cliché, she, of *Mayflower* stock, California born and bred, playing Diane Keaton to my Woody Allen.

But as is invariably the case, on closer inspection the tidy assumptions simply didn't hold. For although, yes, she actually does call her mother "Mother," and there are those in her extended family who respond to "Sis" and "Brother," we had, she and I, in the ways that counted most, been raised in a similar fashion; by intensely devoted mothers and fathers who . . . influenced us in other ways.

I had heard a great deal about Priscilla's father, my future father-in-law, this fellow from Arkansas named Mo Turner, long before I ever met him. Among her childhood friends, he was known as "The Count," a sort of male Auntie Mame—brilliant, erratic, opinionated, aggressively unconventional. A gifted mathematician who had been singled out by the military during the war for advanced training in engineering and physics, he eventually ended up in nuclear-weapons research, and some of the best Mo stories had to do with that. There was, for example, the time during the tense days preceding the Six-Day War that Mo, believing Israel to be in mortal danger, decided to personally give that nation the bomb. "No, Mo, *don't* do it," Priscilla recalls her normally compliant mother beseeching, throwing herself against the door like an anguished heroine in a silent film, "you'll lose your job." "Oh, hell's bells," he is said to have replied irritably, before ditching his plan because he got caught up in a good book, "get out of my way, woman!"

Then there was the time that, having failed to get treatment for a worsening virus because he doesn't trust doctors, he became delirious—wandering through the house in a daze, spouting equations—and eventually had to be rushed to a hospital in critical condition. Believing he was dying, he dictated letters to assorted administrators and colleagues at the Naval Post-Graduate Center in Monterey, where he was then teaching: he was *glad* he was dying, he wrote, because he'd always thought they were stupid and now he'd never have to see them again. Then he recovered and had to go back.

The night Mo blew into town, alighting at the home of Priscilla's sister, Priscilla and I were at a friend's house, play-

ing poker; since Mo flew exclusively by military aircraft—it
was free, on a standby basis—he tended to hop all over the
continent before being deposited in the general vicinity of his
destination, so we'd had no idea when he'd be arriving; in
fact, he had last been sighted fully six days before, heading
from his California home on foot. "If you don't get over here
in ten minutes," he barked into the phone, when he'd tracked
us down, "I'm leaving!"

And half an hour later, there he was, this wizened, rail-
thin guy in woefully mismatched clothes and worn hiking
boots, gray hair wildly askew, dumping the contents of his
duffel bag onto the dining-room table, then picking among
the dirty socks for the gifts earmarked for all and sundry. To
me, he presented a genuine gold pocket watch. "TO F. W.
LEEPER," read the inscription on the back, "IN RECOGNITION
OF HAVING MET THE ANNUAL SALES QUOTA IN THE MONTH
OF OCTOBER. THE PEPSI-COLA CO., 1941."

"Now, I hope you're serious about my daughter," he said,
"or I'll *take it back!*"

Five minutes after that, in the living room, he was offering
opinions, theories, random observations on just about everything—Harry Truman (the last President with guts we had
in this country), the state of American culture (lamentable),
those who purport to be connoisseurs of wine (snobs)—his
Ozark accent so thick, his words coming in such a rush, his
references, ranging from Milton and Shakespeare to something he happened to have read on the plane that morning
in a military handbook, so varied, that sometimes he was a
bit hard to follow. But if he obviously delighted in being
outrageous, he was also joyously, unapologetically human. I
instantly took an immense liking to the guy.

Still, it was easy to figure out that life around his household
had hardly been *Father Knows Best*; not, of course, that in
his wildest dreams he'd have wished it to be. Priscilla's mother
was, is, a gentle and reassuring presence, but Mo is Mo—
and under his tutelage, Priscilla came of age with a conception
of normality even odder than those, on the basis of our own

quirky experiences at home, embraced by most of us. Since, for example, there had been four beds and five children, each had been obliged to dash home from school each afternoon to claim a place to sleep; it was Mo's belief that such an arrangement bred not chronic insecurity but a healthy competitive spirit.

Above all, Mo was controlling. Even now—and he has mellowed considerably—little Sadie, far less inclined than most to brook nonsense, refers to him as "Ordering Grandpa"; we all laugh when she does this, no one with more pleasure than Mo himself. But growing up under innumerable constraints, quiet, studious, shy Priscilla was, by the age of ten, subject to migraines. And in adolescence, she rebelled with even greater ferocity than most, touching off father-daughter battles that remain the stuff of family legend.

At this juncture, by any standard, the two of them are extremely close; aware of their similarities, respectful of their differences; both, for all their sharpness of tongue, are soft as custard within.

But it nonetheless remained, in substantial measure, Mo's legacy with which she continued to contend—and with which I too was now obliged to. For if Priscilla was able to help me begin to face much that was dark and uncertain in myself, it fell upon me to do the same for her.

Not that this was quite so much a matter of benevolence as it might sound. Generous in my admonitions—always ready to remark on her quickness to anger or her vast capacity to take something the wrong way—the fact is, I enjoyed getting a rise out of her, and found it convenient, when she would come snapping at the bait, to retreat, like my father before me, into bewilderment. *"What's the matter—can't you take a joke?"*

Then, likely as not, a short while later I'd be after her again, this time for her tendency, at such times, to draw deep, deep into herself.

This last, however, from my admittedly narrow perspective, was a far more serious matter. I found the trait immensely unsettling, even scary. Though, certainly, I'd wield the issue of opening up and coming clean for my own purposes, and with an abandon she quickly came to regard as the very height of gall—*you*, of all people—it was, at the start, a real problem between us. "I really have no interest," as she Freudian-slipped one day, when I wanted to use a telling incident out of her past to illustrate a point I was making in an "Ethics" piece, "in having my private life made personal." Even she now laughs about the time that, having at last agreed to accompany me to a session with my therapist, having sat still for forty-five minutes of intense give-and-take, she turned on me the moment we'd closed the office door behind us. "Don't you *ever* talk about me that way in front of a stranger again!"

And this, lest it be forgotten, was our idyllic phase.

But then, as one guy with whom I spoke put it, "even in the movies people hardly ever just fall into each other's arms anymore and live happily ever after." And all in all, that's probably good. Things don't go right between people month after month and year after year by magic. The magic is learning to respond to the other person's point of view with grace; and not to be hurtful; and to be able to apologize.

Which, without its ever having been articulated, is precisely the recognition we came to. Quite simply, in each other's company we were—worked at being—more consistently thoughtful and compassionate than we'd ever thought to be before.

"Fiction is fantastic," I happened to be told at the time by a fellow journalist, just then beginning work on his first novel. "I'm writing about my wife, and I can make her everything she isn't but I wish she was." And I remember thinking how awfully sad that was—and how relieved that I would never have to feel that way myself.

But, God, how we are tested! Little more than ten months after we met, just after we moved in together, Priscilla got pregnant.

And, thoughtful and compassionate guy though I was certain I'd become, I still had considerable difficulty sharing her distress over the fact. My attitude was simple: *What's the big deal? Why do you think abortion was invented?*

It was, at last, against every instinct that she went through with it. Already we had talked marriage; but this, I'd made it clear, *this* was definitely not part of the bargain—not yet, anyway.

But for days afterward, there was smoldering resentment on her part, occasionally punctuated by tears; and instead of a return to the status quo, the ensuing weeks brought bickering in a different spirit—angrier, with more of an edge.

Then, four months later, with the acrimony just beginning to fade, she got pregnant again.

There was no way out—not if we were going to survive. All right, I agreed that very day, we'd get married right away; we'd have the baby; we'd be happy forever.

And then, disappearing into the bedroom, lying there, staring up at the ceiling, I very quietly proceeded to go to pieces. *A baby.* The end of life as it had always been. Living death. God, Priscilla, I wish I'd never met you! *All right, let's do it!*

At the time, in my isolation, my chronic sense of alienation heightened by legitimately alienating circumstances, it never occurred to me that mine was an extreme version of a prototypical male reaction; but then, given who we had always been, how could it be otherwise? "The night I found out," a thirty-four-year-old executive reports of his own reaction to impending fatherhood, "I lay awake half the night, unable to sleep. I kept thinking about a conversation I'd had with a woman in my office about her ex-husband, who never seemed to have any time for their child. 'He's not a serious person,' she said. It struck me as an odd choice of words, and I remember thinking, 'Neither am *I!*' " "My overriding reaction," adds a writer I know, "was that there was so much to do and so little time. I'd always been something of a jazz fan, but now I started to go to jazz clubs three or four times a week. By myself. My wife was home in bed."

This last I had especially little trouble identifying with. Following our marriage, in the city hall of a small town upstate, and two days of nominal honeymoon in the region, I retreated to an even better hideout than a smoky downtown club. I had a contract to do a book with a lot of baseball in it, one that needed to be researched at the Baseball Hall of Fame in Cooperstown—a place, especially with the approach of the brutal upstate winter, as seemingly distant from the city to which my bride had to return as Vladivostok.

There is, I confess, nothing admirable in this. But when, after a couple of months, I did emerge from my upstate lair, research completed, it was with equilibrium pretty much restored. I began joining Priscilla in rummaging through friends' hand-me-down baby stuff. I accompanied her to the obstetrician, the only male among numberless pregnant women as I waited for a peek at our sonogram. We took Lamaze together; and together, our old selves, we started cutting classes.

Then, bright one early-spring morning, Priscilla emerged from the shower smiling. "Something's going on. This might be it."

ONE late afternoon three and a half years later, I emerged from a neighborhood grocery store onto Amsterdam Avenue, little Sadie Stein at my side.

"Why did he say that, Papa?" she demanded, a large peach in her hand and pain in her eyes.

"It's very hard to explain, darling."

"Why did he say that? *Why?*"

I knelt down to face her; larger people glanced down at us as they hurried past. "Well, a lot of grown-ups don't think very hard before they do things. And sometimes they make other people feel bad."

"Why do they?"

"I don't think they know why themselves."

I am quite certain that the individual who had provoked this powwow, the owner of the establishment we had just left, had no idea why he had said what he did, and he clearly had no idea that his words were hurtful.

"Is it a boy or a girl?" he had asked me, not unpleasantly, while Sadie was over by the peach bin.

My daughter has tight blond curls, and when she's dressed as she was that day, in blue coveralls, it is conceivable that someone might not have been entirely certain.

"She's a girl."

And yet, a moment later, when we had paid and were about to depart, the fellow thanked us, smiled and said, "Bye-bye, little boy."

"I'm not a boy," spoke up Sadie sharply, "I'm a girl."

He grinned my way and offered a conspiratorial wink. "No, you're not, you're a boy."

"I'm a girl!"

I was at a loss. It wasn't simply that the pointlessness, the futility of speaking up was manifest; I honestly would not have known even how to begin. By pointing out to him that she was a human being, too, with sensitivities and insecurities as pronounced as his own? By remarking that since her hair had taken its time coming in, she had long since tired of people getting her gender wrong even by accident? By noting that with a baby brother on the way, she professed not even to *like* boys?

In retrospect, I am sorry I didn't say something, if only for her benefit. One of the memories I most cherish from my own childhood is of my mother confronting the guy who'd made fun of three-year-old me for wanting to buy her a stick of candy lipstick for her birthday. "Don't you ever do that to my child again," she raged, after I'd exited the shop in tears, bearing the dime gift he deemed more appropriate. "Don't you ever do that to *any* child."

But then, I was only just beginning to learn—about parenthood and a good deal more. The truth is, upset as I was at that moment on my child's behalf, I understood full well what the guy was about. It had, after all, been so short a time since I'd come to realize there was anything wrong with such behavior myself.

In recent years, there has of course been something of a backlash—especially on the part of women—against the sensitive and ostentatiously involved father. "I'm so sick and tired," one old friend, a divorced mother of two, put it to me, "of all you guys who think you deserve a medal for having engaged in the act of procreation. Why do you behave as if no one's ever been a father before?"

The answer, alas, has more than we'd like to do with the fact that as parents, so many of our generation remain what we have always been: hugely self-involved, unalterably fixed in the notion that whatever phase we happen to be in is, by definition, the place to be.

But even so awkward a truth does not diminish the power of the emotions associated with new parenthood, or their legitimacy. It is, in fact, precisely because those emotions tend to seize us so unexpectedly, because the discovery of how dramatically children can alter one's existence for the better remains so fresh, that so many recent parents, particularly fathers, behave so curiously. "It is as if," as one such guy summed it up, "circuits that had been dead for thirty years suddenly kicked in."

It is heartening to believe that such a circumstance arises spontaneously, nature at its most generous and canny. I have heard more than one man describe the surging joy, the love beyond all anticipation, that came with his first sight of his offspring; and even for the most constitutionally blasé among us, such a memory calls up the word "miracle" with surprising regularity.

But, in general, miracles need to be helped along. I was fortunate enough not only to find myself the father of an exceptionally winning child, sunny and curious and responsive right from the start, but just as vitally, married to someone who forced me to fully appreciate the fact.

Indeed, the depth of the feelings triggered by this new presence in our midst came as nearly the shock to Priscilla as it was to me. Prior to Sadie's birth, I had simply assumed— and my wife had seemed more than open to the possibility— that we would both resume our working lives with maximum dispatch; that at six months, or perhaps eight, our child would embark on her own career as a day-care kid and we would make as much "quality time" for her as our own schedules allowed.

This, after all, was what virtually all the fashionable publications were recommending just then; indeed, in large measure what this new world in which we found ourselves was supposed to be about. It was, moreover, the part that I, like most ostentatiously progressive men, liked best of all. Our wives and girlfriends were out there making real dough, picking up tabs, their professional standing (while usually not quite on a par with our own) reflecting as wonderfully on us as on them. And we had been given every reason to assume it would be this way forever, or at least until, together, we reached mandatory-retirement age.

So when, finally, Priscilla decided she just couldn't do it, insisting with considerable vehemence that our child needed her more than did the story department at Columbia Pictures—in fact, that Sadie needed *me* every bit as much as she did her mother—I was terrifically ambivalent. On the one hand, I certainly didn't want anything that would in any way harm my child and was as inclined as most new fathers to defer on child-care issues to the nearest available female. On the other, I found it hard to fully suppress the sense that I'd been duped; that there I was, stuck with one of the few women in the contemporary world who did not care whether she had a career beyond motherhood, at least not enough; someone who probably had been marking time all along.

"I can't believe you have this *traditional* family structure," exclaimed a guy I know whose own child had already been in day care a year. "It's just like our *fathers* and *mothers*." And though I held my tongue, resenting the comment bitterly, part of me agreed with him.

But as the months passed, it was an increasingly small part. For slowly, slowly, never before having given the matter a moment's serious thought, I was being led to accept the seemingly bizarre proposition that unlike, say, probably, chinchillas, small children sense from the outset how they are regarded; that even when they are so tiny as to seem virtually inanimate, objects to be carted around at the whim of others, they are, moment by moment, picking up data about the world and their place in it; that, to get to the point, if they are to become the capable, emotionally functional larger people we profess to want them to be, they must be accorded not only the security of love in overwhelming measure, but considerable respect.

It was, in sum, my wife who early on induced me to become the father, if not exactly the husband, I'd never otherwise have been inclined to be—to not just adore my child, but to take her needs as seriously as I have always taken my own.

We were, to be sure, in one basic sense, luckier than most. For in the roller coaster that is a free-lancer's financial state of affairs, we happened to be at a peak just then, since an article of mine had recently sold to the movies; and later on, when things got far tighter, we squeaked by thanks to the New York real estate boom, which enabled us to sell our apartment, bought on my return from Paris for a virtual pittance as a bachelor pad, at an almost unconscionable profit.

Still, the course we chose was hardly without drawbacks. Aside from the lingering tension between the two of us on the work issue—for eventually, as I myself became a zealot on the kids-needing-parents question, I found myself with the gall to regularly assert that I'd be *thrilled* to spend half my time at home, if only she'd arrange to bring home half the income—there was a frequent sense of isolation from my peers. One might quickly grow accustomed to impatient waitresses and store clerks, to strangers who smile indulgently, or smirk, as one tries to talk turkey to a two-year-old, but sometimes even friends do little to mask their skepticism. A year and a half afterward, a French woman of whom I am extremely fond, herself the mother of two, was still laughing about my having bundled up Sadie, miserably jet-lagged and unable to sleep after our arrival in Paris that day, and taken her on a midnight cab ride to see the Eiffel Tower.

Then again, in the end, who gives a damn? Just recently, out of the blue, my daughter turned to me at the dinner table. "Papa, do you remember that night when I was little that we went in a taxi to see the Eiffel Tower? That was *wonderful.*"

Who could believe that it had been a mere six years since my other life in Paris? Or—what?—only five since that night

at Plato's Retreat? Who, more to the point, would have believed I'd miss the times like that hardly at all?

During my wife's pregnancy, in that period when I was
persuaded that it was to be all downhill from there, I had an
extended conversation on the subject with an old friend, the
first guy in my professional circle to have become a father.
He told me that parenthood, if I went about it properly, would
do nothing less than oblige me to "grow up morally."

Now, yeah, I know, that's precisely the kind of contemporary man-to-man observation, smacking not only of sentiment but also of self-congratulation, that sets so many women
on edge. And it is certainly true that any claim on my part to
have been reborn with the coming of Sadie, morally or otherwise, will sound pretty fishy. Even on the most obvious
level—that having to do with cooking, cleaning, trying to
make order of the chaos a small person leave in her wake—
I am still regularly found wanting, far closer to Dagwood
Bumstead than to anyone's version of the mythic "new man."

And yet there is so much that is invisible to the naked eye;
momentous events experienced in the privacy of one's being
and perceived only by those few to whom one is most intimately known.

On the pavement outside the grocery store, my daughter
refused to let the matter rest. "Why did he say that to me?"
she asked again.

"He was teasing you." I'd caught myself; I'd almost said
"*only* teasing you."

"What's teasing?"

"That's when someone says something they don't mean to
another person."

"Why? Why do they?"

"I don't know. I guess they think it's funny."

She made no response. "Do you understand? Do you understand what teasing is?"

She nodded. "You do that to Mama sometimes."

It is—need any parent be reminded?—among the most

unexpected and jarring aspects of rookie parenthood, this business of suddenly becoming aware there is a truth cop on the premises. Now, in general, this is a glorious phenomenon, one I view less as a threat than as a challenge. This time, however, I met my daughter's observation with a stiff smile.

For virtually all of my life I had managed to effortlessly rationalize away the trait to which she referred. She got it wrong, by the way. I'm not precisely a teaser. Rather, I'm inveterately facetious, the sort of a person who at any odd moment is apt to be flippant; who in the midst of the most earnest conversation finds his head swimming with potential quips; who is given to making light of even the most delicate of concerns. Indeed, the more sober the topic at hand, the more pronounced is my reflex to begin transforming it into something else. Not very long before, after reading an article on how parents react to the loss of a child, my wife expressed the hope that should so unspeakable a tragedy ever befall us, we would somehow manage to draw together and not apart.

"Not a chance," came my reply. "I'd find a way to blame you."

Why do I do this? It is a question to which I was only now beginning to give serious thought, and the conclusions I was coming to were hardly reassuring. Certainly it had to do with self-protection, with the impulse to remain emotionally dis-engaged even from some of those who loved me most. Though my modus operandi was less abrasive than more direct forms of assault, and considerably less likely to provoke a hostile response, the message it conveyed was very nearly identical to the most pointed barb, delivered with a sneer: that the person with whom I was dealing was less valid, less worthy of serious attention than myself.

And, too, like all automatic behavior, it had to do with history, with an emotional agenda that was taking shape before I was consciously aware of much more than shapes and colors.

It was only now, for example, that I was becoming aware how precisely the adult behavior I describe mirrored the stance I so often adopted as a small child in dealing with my brothers;

indeed, how all the emotional weapons I have wielded to such effect in the years since were forged with the family somewhere in mind.

Which is not to suggest that such glimmerings of self-knowledge necessarily, at that juncture, enabled me to behave differently than I ever had—especially in the face of conflict or pressure. Indeed, barely two months later, with the arrival of our second child, I suddenly, unexpectedly found myself in a state of quiet turmoil, laboring merely to put up a mature front.

There, on his very first morning home from the hospital—August 22, 1984—stood my daughter and I, staring balefully at the seven-pounder lying face up on a yellow towel on our bed.

"What's that thing?" demanded Sadie, pointing at the plastic clip affixed to the vestige of the umbilical cord.

"That's the place where the food went into him when he was inside Mama."

We stared for another long moment.

"Why is his penis purple?"

"Well, I guess it's still a little sore."

"Why?"

"They cut off a little piece of it."

"Why?"

Why. The fact is, I'd never known precisely why myself. "For health reasons."

"So it wouldn't get blisters?"

"Yeah. Maybe."

The baby began to stir, working the air with his feet, turning his head this way and that. I wondered, fleetingly, why my wife was taking so long in the damn bath.

"Do you love him?"

"Well, I don't really know him yet. I'm sure I will."

"I won't."

I touched her hair. "That's okay, darling. Maybe later you'll change your mind."

"I won't."

The truth is, I saw her point. There was so very much about this presence in our midst that was unsettling—alarming, even—that suddenly our shared future looked the way the Atlantic must have looked to Columbus's itchy crew: full of peril far more pointedly than of promise. Frankly, at that moment, I don't know which of the participants in that seemingly idyllic tableau was under the greatest strain: the four-day-old, just back from the hospital, who flinched at every sudden sound; the three-and-a-half-year-old, whose serene world was abruptly overpopulated by one; or their father.

To be sure, it was I who had lobbied for a second child; and I had always made it clear, when asked, that this time I preferred a boy. At last, I had routinely said, with the kind of surface honesty that invariably passes for candor, at last I felt prepared to be the father to a son.

Yet now, questions that had always been readily kept at bay—easy to dismiss as ludicrous inanities culled from some volume of pop psychology—bore frighteningly on the task at hand. Would I feel as comfortable clasping a boy to my breast as I would tossing him in the air? or kiss him as reflexively when he was smiling as when he was in tears? Would I be able to love him fully, as he so needed to be loved, without qualm, or qualification, or excessive expectation?

A *boy.* Who the hell knew?

Indeed, all at once it struck me as curiously appropriate that in the book I'd brought home one afternoon the year before—the one that was supposed to help would-be parents determine the sex of their child via pre-conception "girl" or "boy" diets—the "girl" menus seemed to have been formulated by a nutritionist, while the "boy" eats were right out of a slop joint; not snips and snails, exactly, but steak and bacon and just about everything else you can think of loaded with fat, carbohydrates, carcinogens.

And yet, in another sense, all of that had initially made the prospect of helping to raise a son somehow even more appealing. For if many of us, sons of detached fathers, routinely find ourselves on less-than-intimate terms with that which is best within, that which is sensitive and humane—if, in fact, we are as potentially loving as females, but grew up ashamed of our vulnerability—there was something compelling in the possibility of helping someone perhaps not unlike myself come of age stronger, smarter, more secure than I was; and—who knows?—maybe getting a little bit stronger myself in the process.

But all of that had been just theoretical. Now, here he was—and if the pregnancy had been any indication, this kid was showing up at the starting gate as vulnerable as they come. Three months along, my wife had begun bleeding heavily and had to take to bed; the overwhelming majority of miscarriages, we subsequently learned, involved male fetuses. Six months after that—a week before he was due—our baby, who had been in launch position, abruptly turned and clawed his way back into the womb. Our doctor was unable to come up with a plausible explanation for this phenomenon; we guiltily gauged it to be the result of the wrenching fight we'd had several days before. *The little guy just didn't want to come out.*

In fact, when the time had at last arrived—a breech, natch—he'd had to be yanked into the world, screaming bloody murder.

Eight minutes later, swaddled and atop a little table, he was screaming still.

"Don't you think he should be held?" I demanded of the attending nurse.

She distractedly dabbed at him with cotton while trading shoptalk with an intern. "That can wait."

"I think," I said more insistently, "he should be held."

She faced me, hands on hips. "I beg your pardon. I am concerned with the baby's health."

"And I'm concerned with his *emotional* health."

And I was. And yet, throughout those first several days I'd felt not only ambivalence toward the little guy but a curious sense of detachment. Even in the privacy of my wife's hospital room, rocking him to sleep for the very first time, watching his eyeballs roam beneath his lids, and his tiny mouth sucking away at a dream breast, I was also elsewhere: Shea Stadium, to be precise, where Dwight Gooden was on the mound for the Metsies. It was with a start—and a surge of guilt—that I realized that the song I had been singing to my infant son was not "Rockabye Baby" or "All the Pretty Little Horses," or my daughter's old favorite, "Sunrise, Sunset," but a raunchy radio hit out of the late Sixties by someone called Mongo Jerry about picking up lots of women and screwing their brains out.

I, for one, could appreciate why now, at home, his eyes, as yet unfocused, glinted with what seemed to be panic.

"Why did we name him Charlie?" demanded Sadie, looking down on him.

"It was my grandfather's name, and also your mother's grandfather."

"Both of them?"

"Yes. Do you like it?"

She leaned close. "Can I touch him?"

"Sure you can. Of course."

She did, very quickly, on the leg. "He's soft."

"Babies are very soft. Pretty soon you can hold him, too."

"I still don't like him. Do you?"

And then, suddenly, it came, rising in a graceful arc of perhaps two and a half feet before falling—directly upon us. Shrieking, Sadie dashed to the other side of the room. While I, in some ludicrous parody of responsible behavior—or maybe it was an Eighties version of machismo—stood my ground, shielding myself from the geyser with my hands. It was interminable, must have lasted a full five seconds. By the time it ended, it was in my eyes, running down my cheeks, matting my hair.

"Why did he do that?" asked Sadie, quietly, from across the room.

I wiped my glasses on my shirt. "I guess that's what boys do."

* * *

At the beginning, little Charlie seemed to acquire a new nick-name every week. He was Gnarly for a while, then Goofus. For a few days, until my wife put a stop to it, he was Chaz. He was Munchkin and Bronto-face and Leaky Lou. Some-where in the middle of the fourth month he became Charlie Muffin, after some dimly recalled character in an English mystery, and that was soon reduced to Muffin, which managed to stick.

But almost from the first, I had a personal nickname for him: Monster Boy. I coined it deep into one of the many nights Charlie refused to sleep for more than twenty minutes at a stretch, awakening with the shriek of a mortally wounded jungle creature and then, at my appearance, becoming more hysterical still, refusing to be even momentarily consoled. At least by me.

"Monster Boy wants his quarter-pound of flesh," I an-nounced that first night, lowering the thrashing bundle, at arm's length, toward his mother.

She offered a groggy smile and lifted the Berkeley T-shirt in which she'd been fitfully sleeping. "Milk bar open for busi-ness."

Before long, however, my joke—to the extent it had been one—was stale, and she was reacting to the phrase with all the good humor of a mother bear in a Disney nature film facing down an intruder: all snarls and bared claws.

"Stop it," she snapped, one early morning a couple of weeks later, after I'd suggested that we invest in a couple of live-in psychotics to get Monster Boy to shape up. "Can't you see he's suffering?"

I snarled back—maybe that was what I'd been after all along: the opportunity to lash out at someone more or less my own size—but I instantly knew she was right.

In fact, quietly, in my own way, I was suffering for him. Having entered the world affronted by all he saw—a per-spective I could fully understand—he had almost immediately had his bleakest fears confirmed. For at six weeks, just as we seemed to be making a bit of progress in persuading him that there might be such a thing as security outside the womb, Charlie had had the singular misfortune of falling back into the hands of doctors. The procedure, the repair of a hernia that had come with his father's genes, was uneventful, at least from the medical point of view. But then, high among the doctors' concerns was convenience—their own; and so the surgery was performed in the early afternoon—by which time Charlie, awake since 6 A.M. but forbidden to nurse, became so hysterical at being taken from his mother that it took a half-hour longer than usual to administer anesthesia.

I am not a psychologist, and it will be clear from the above that my father's heart is far from impartial; but it strikes me that that day must have felt to my little boy like a couple of years in an Iranian torture cell. For when he at last made it home, he was a different guy; not merely touchier than before, and given to even gaudier exhibitions of ill feeling, but sometimes beyond consolation for hours at a time.

I acknowledge that in a world in which countless children are born with crippling handicaps, physical, emotional, material, this is hardly tragedy on the grand scale. Indeed, even I regard it as a little presumptuous, a reflection of minus-gumption, to make an issue of it at all.

But—what can I tell you?—when the problems are close to home, one's perspective has a funny way of getting narrow. Quite simply, as anyone who has ever found himself in like circumstances will confirm (if, that is, in self-protective wisdom, he has not already blotted out the memory), a home under siege by a willful infant tends to be a forbidding place, characterized by all the pessimism and meanspiritedness that marked the French in 1940 as things were caving in. Otherwise reasonable souls, numbed during daylight hours by incessant squalling, alert for the dread stirring noises throughout the night, are themselves reduced to behavior that begins to rival that of the culprit.

If, for example, I occasionally sympathized with the tribulations of my wife—the circles around her eyes became so pronounced that one evening, studying them during the pan-

demonium that was dinnertime, I thought it might be interesting to measure their depth with a ruler—I nevertheless
made no secret of my belief that of the two of us, she had the
better of it. At least he *liked* her. Usually, eventually, she
could comfort him. When settled, he would nestle in her
arms, sucking and apparently content, for hours at a time.
Me he seemed to have no use for at all, screaming with rage
and arching his back when I changed his diaper, stiffening
every time I lifted him from his crib, learning, as the fabled
fine motor coordination proceeded apace, to go for my eyes
with his little fingers.

I knew, I knew. None of this was to be taken personally.
I knew about how much infants depend on their mothers and,
yes, that boys tend to be particularly needy. But that was
merely my rational side. There was also the rest of me.

"Are you going to be a heartbreaker, Muffin?" cooed the
local Madonna late one night, as child slurped away. "Are you
going to curl up at some woman's breast someday trying to
re-create the good old days?"

And three feet away, I snorted and scrunched down a little
deeper under the covers. If, even at the time, I was fully
aware of what was going on, and even somewhat amused by
it, I could nevertheless not escape the fact that there I was,
cast as the heavy in a psychological cliché.

"How," wrote Dan Greenburg of his own reaction to a
sonogram in which the penis of his son, minus four months
of age, was first visible, "could I possibly feel threatened by
a fetus's penis? Am I in sexual competition with an embryo
or what?"

Boys! It sure as hell hadn't been this way with our daughter.
From the very outset, in almost every way, she had been a
breeze.

But now, suddenly, even that was changing.

We had not, of course, been quite so dumb as to suppose
that our first child would have *no* difficulty adjusting to the
second. It's just that we never for a moment anticipated that
Sadie might abruptly turn into Linda Blair in *The Exorcist*.

Oh, yes, there were extenuating circumstances. Three months into Charlie's career in mayhem, desperate for more space, we abandoned our New York City apartment for a house in the suburbs. Still, as our daughter began letting us know with alarming frequency, her biggest problem was with her brother.

"He's *bad*," she would rasp as she lay on the floor, complaining that her head hurt, that hitherto serene visage screwed up in something unsettlingly like fury.

"No, he's not," I would explain, on my knees beside her, squeezing her hand, "he's just very little. Who knows?—maybe pretty soon you'll like him."

"No, I won't. He wants all the attention. He's *baaad!*"

"We still give you lots of attention, darling. Of course we do."

"Not Mama."

There was, alas, no entirely acceptable response to be made to this. Priscilla wasn't happy about it herself, nor was I—all at once, we seemed to be living out every syndrome associated with "New Baby: Male" in the annals of psychology—but given the exigencies of the moment, there we indeed found ourselves, pretty much divided along father/daughter–mother/son lines.

In brief, as Sadie might have put it, things were rapidly going from bad to *baaaad*.

The nadir was almost certainly the 6 A.M. when, having been raked across the face once too often, muttering oaths, I stalked into the bathroom, emerged with the nail-cutting scissors and went to work. I was going to cut those suckers close, so close that for the next week, every cornea on the premises could rest reasonably secure. Only I was groggy, and the light was dim and . . . oh, hell, on the fourth nail, I also got a bit of fingertip.

Instantly, the blood began to flow.

Oddly, Charlie didn't cry. But then, far, far worse, there was this look he gave me; a look indicating bewilderment, confusion, broken trust.

"Oh, God, I cut off the end of his finger! Oh, God, Priscilla, help him!"

I leaped from the bed, ran to the bathroom, came back with Band-Aids, first-aid cream, a wet washcloth.

"Let's run it under cold water," said my wife calmly. "It doesn't look too bad."

"What's going on?" asked Sadie, running in from her bedroom.

"We had a little accident. I was trimming Charlie's nails, and—"

"Is he hurt?"

"No, darling, he's fine," called Priscilla, over the sound of the water rushing in the sink.

Charlie, past the initial shock, began to scream.

Though she had more than once wished him ill—"I can't help it," she once told me, "when something bad happens to him, a smile just pops out on my face"—Sadie was obviously shaken. She buried her head in a pillow and refused to look up.

Anxious to maintain at least the appearance of parental control, I resisted the impulse to follow suit; instead I just stood beside him in the bathroom as his mother treated the wound, kissing his head and wailing "I'm sorry, Char, I'm sorry."

By late that evening, after an especially long nap, Charlie was fine. No obvious physical discomfort. No apparent psychic scars. But for days afterward, I was a wreck.

Indeed, I was still in guilt's grip a week later, when Priscilla and the kids departed for a two-week stay with her family in Northern California; a condition that was in no way mitigated when I realized how relieved I was to find myself in an empty house.

Still, everything passes. By the third night, if my conscience continued to ache a little, my body, conditioned to bolting upright at the merest stirring from the adjacent bedroom, was starting to feel all right about things; and by the fifth, my mind was right there with it.

Then, too, of course, there were the nightly phone calls,

which kept me somewhat in touch. Sadie assured me that she was having a marvelous time, and offered much supporting detail. Priscilla was as run-down as ever, but was more concerned about Charlie. He evidently became so distraught at even her momentary absences that the grandparents had made it clear that they did not wish to be left alone with him.

"My father's afraid Charlie is going to have a heart attack," she reported that fifth day.

"What are you talking about?"

I could almost see her weary smile. In the background, I *could* hear Charlie. "He says that when I'm not around, his heart starts beating so hard that he's afraid it's going to burst. My mother agrees with him—and she's never known a baby she couldn't master."

From the sanctuary of our bedroom, three thousand miles away, I chuckled. "So what else is new?"

"He misses you, Harry. He misses you terribly."

About this I was more than a little skeptical. From the start, my wife, bless her heart, had been passionately interested in strengthening the bond between us.

"I miss him too. I miss you all."

"Why don't you talk to him?"

"Okay."

And suddenly, across the miles, up close and personal, came Monster Boy's piercing shriek. "It's Papa," intoned his mother in the background. "It's Papa on the telephone."

"Hi, Char," I said cheerily. "Hi, darling. It's Papa."

To my surprise, he quieted down.

"Hi, darling." I paused, then brought up my voice a couple of octaves. "Leaky . . . Leaky Louuu . . ."

Priscilla came back on. "He's stopped crying. Wait a minute, he's reaching for the phone."

"Hi, Leaky. It's Papa. It's Papa, darling."

And I'll be damned if the sound coming from the other end wasn't *cooing*. And stranger still, it was a sound I heard every night for the rest of their visit.

*   *   *

It is truly a kind of magic how the feeling just sort of sneaks up, how a sense of obligation toward a child—and the discomfort over not feeling more—suddenly give way to a love beyond description, something so profound as to approach irrationality.

For over the following weeks and months, my little boy and I drew ever closer, constantly finding new ways to be unexpectedly delighted by each other. It is not that he abruptly mellowed, or that I did, but simply that each had at last come to recognize, in his own unconscious way, how very much the other had to offer, and began reaching out for it.

Every day now there passed wonderful moments between us, imperceptible additions to the accumulating bankroll. Most were so unremarkable as hardly to merit note. And even the one that has remained most vividly with me seems, from this distance, not only trite—big deal; my whole life is trite these days—but revealing in the wrong sort of way.

There I was, late on a spring afternoon, toiling away in my third-floor office, when the door swung open with a creak and Charlie, eight months and attired in T-shirt and diaper, crawled into the room.

"Hi, Char, what's up? Where's Mama and Sadie?"

But he offered only a fleeting smile and headed toward the corner. A moment later, on hands and knees, I joined him there—and noticed that he was holding a tennis ball.

"Where'd you get this, Char? Did you find it in the toy basket downstairs?"

He held it out, offering it for my inspection.

I ran my fingertips over the worn fuzz. "It's nice." A beat. "Lemme show you what you can do with it." And sitting up, I bounced it a couple of times between my legs. "See? It bounces. And it does lots of other things, too."

A moment later he had assumed the same position, and we were gently rolling the ball back and forth across the two feet between us. Our first catch. And—I can't help it—for ten, perhaps even fifteen minutes, both of us were unutterably content.

"Well, well, I can see there's some serious male bonding going on here." There stood my wife in the doorway, her smile as sardonic as they come.

But who, by then, had the wit to bother with a sardonic reply? For Charlie had flung himself into my arms and was getting the hug of his life.

THE guy showed up the evening of the day after the movers had come and gone, and the house was still awash in unopened cartons. I was surprised to see him. We had met only once before, on the day several weeks earlier when we'd dropped by the house to do some measuring and my daughter, catching sight of another little girl on the lawn across the street, had prevailed upon us to head over and introduce ourselves. Face to face, the kids had been mute, and the husbands had been only marginally better; if it had been remotely feasible, we'd have been down there with our daughters, peeking out at each other from behind female thigh. But instead, myself and the guy—roughly my age, bearded, heavyset—had endured the exchange of pleasantries and nodded our goodbyes.

Yet now here he was, apologizing for having taken so long to come by, wondering if he could be of any help. There was a note of obligation in this, but I was still much impressed by the gesture. It's certainly not something I'd have done. Besides, I did need help. For the previous half-hour, intent on hanging a large framed mural that had been in my possession since the Nixon years, I'd been trying to hammer a striated nail purchased expressly for the purpose into brick, a process that thus far had produced only a storm of reddish dust.

"Let me see," he offered, assuming a surprisingly authoritative air, when I'd described the problem, and then his judgment was swift. "No wonder," he said: "you're using a toy hammer."

This was untrue. It was, all right, a small hammer, and a

cheap one, made of something decidedly other than tempered steel, so that when the going got rough, it gave way instead of the thing being hammered; already its head was full of ugly nicks and gashes, while the brick was unscathed. But it was definitely not a toy. Sadie had a toy hammer: *it* was made of *plastic*.

I nodded at the guy, resenting his straightforwardness, yet, grasping that the intent had not entirely been the destruction of my ego, also sort of appreciating it. And when, after he'd hastened back to his place, returned with a powerful electric drill and some lead plugs and proceeded to complete the job in ten minutes, I was unstinting in my gratitude.

He took his stuff and started to leave, but we lingered in the front hallway, chatting.

"What do you do?"

"I'm a writer."

"Oh, yeah? What sort of stuff do you write?"

This is always a tough one for me. "Oh, it's pretty eclectic. Last year I published a novel. But I also do a column for *Esquire* magazine."

"On what?"

"It's called 'Ethics.' It deals with, you know, all the incidental moral dilemmas we come up against day to day. Not that it's as preachy as I suppose that sounds." As always, a conversation stopper. "How about you? What do you do?"

Oddly, the question seemed to make him ill at ease too. "I'm a lawyer." A beat. "But that isn't really what I do. I'm in bricks."

"Bricks?"

"Real estate. In the city. What's the name of your novel?"

"*Hoopla*. Wait. Wait here a second." I dashed up two flights of stairs to the room that was to be my office, burrowed through a carton and came up with a copy of the novel and a collection of the "Ethics" pieces.

"Here," I said. "But please don't feel you have to read them. I'm always being avoided by people I like because they feel guilty about not having read my stuff."

"You don't have to give me these."

"No, I want to." And not merely as a reciprocal gesture, either; call it insecurity—it *is* insecurity—but I often feel called upon to prove to strangers that I'm a real writer.

"Well, thank you," he said, with a depth of feeling altogether out of proportion to the circumstance. "That's very generous."

Later that week, I was told by my wife, who had been told by his—from the outset, the women engaged in casual give-and-take—that Steve was well into the "Ethics" book and seemed to very much identify with my point of view. This I took as further reflection on his character, and remarked enthusiastically on our apparent good fortune in neighbors.

Still, for six months thereafter we remained friends only in the most superficial sense of the term. When we spotted each other across the street, one of us would meander over and we'd briefly shoot the breeze; or, face to face with yet another calamity with the boiler, I'd call him for counsel. Several times the families did get together for dinners set up by the wives, but these were hardly opportunities for real contact either. Given the chaos in our household in the wake of the move to the new house, with Charlie seeming to cry nonstop and Sadie in a fury at him and the changes in her own routine, everyone was generally anxious to have the occasion over with.

The lone exception was the barbecue at their place when, my wife's anatomy being necessary to Charlie and it being a glorious May evening, Priscilla volunteered to take the kids home by herself. Steve and I ended up lingering on the terrace for what must have been two more hours, drinking white wine and, for the first time, telling each other something of our respective pasts; eventually alighting on the odd circumstance that each of us had lost an older brother, and speculating at length on the repercussions that had had on our lives.

Still, though it was an honest conversation—surprisingly so, I recall telling my wife that night in bed—it was not an easy one, nor terribly much fun. I knew by now that Steve tended to be intensely guarded—those meeting him for the first time often characterize him as dour and furtive-seeming—and if some of that had lifted this evening, it was also the case that those two hours had been unleavened by a single wry anecdote or amused self-put-down; and so, oddly, for all the information exchanged, in a real sense the contact had been, once again, superficial. I still didn't know for sure about this neighbor of mine, but I myself just have trouble with unrelieved earnestness. It just isn't the way I am. With my real friends, and I was lucky enough to count several, the vital stuff was always communicated, sometimes soberly, but without the sacrifice of overall tone or context.

Which is a large part of the reason that when, soon afterward, aware that the chaos at home was playing havoc with assorted deadlines, Steve offered me the use of a basement room in one of the buildings he managed, I was reluctant to take him up on it. The rest of the reason was that (a) I didn't particularly like the idea of being away from home all day and (b) for all his persistent generosity, the guy resisted receiving in kind—even if the suggested payback was nothing more than dinner for four at a local restaurant—and so the arrangement struck me as potentially awkward.

But, as these things go, the bottom line managed to supersede pride as an imperative; and so, one September morning, we set off together for the city for the first time.

It is something you hear so routinely these days, it rarely comes as much of a surprise: some guy telling you that his closest friend is a woman.

Indeed, if your view of the world is more or less the same as his—and why else would such a thing even come up?—little explanation is called for. Sure, of course, there are lots of guys out there to get along with—bright, decent, amusing, in many ways even sensitive—but there so often end up being lines that can't be crossed, feelings that will never be broached.

One guy with whom I spoke, someone I've known casually for quite a while and always liked, actually balked, in an

extreme manifestation of the phenomenon, at disclosing a
single detail of his family history.

"Why should I?" He smiled. "Knowledge is power."

Finally, after considerable good-natured cajoling—from his
end, in response, came some arch remarks on my idiotic faith
in the efficacy of openness—he allowed simply that he had
made the decision, at sixteen, to no longer "let them get to
me," and he had stuck to it.

"How many are there in your family?"

He offered the broadest smile yet. "Several."

Not, of course, that the guy himself identifies such a mind-
set as a problem. "I get pretty impatient," as someone else
put it to me, "with this notion that men don't form honest
emotional attachments. Sure, it's easy to take a lot of what
passes between guys as shallow—but, dammit, not every moment of your life has to pass muster as serious or meaningful.
It's a pretty grim world out there."

Still, it is striking how often even such men, after kicking
the subject around for a while, will offhandedly acknowledge
qualms about the content of their relationships with others of
their sex: recalling times when, in the pinch, guys with whom
they thought they were close hadn't been there for them; or
conversations memorable for their candor that, the very next
time they saw the other guy, might as well never have occurred at all; or immensely promising first encounters that
never managed to get followed up; or, most telling of all,
intense friendships of considerable duration, like mine with
Paul, that at some point simply cease to be.

A case can be made—is, indeed, made all the time by those
well or even passingly versed in psychology (often women
who happen to be exasperated with men)—that the problem
is basically terror of what, if we looked closely, we might find
in ourselves. It is, alas, harder to dismiss such an assertion
than we'd like it to be. It is not for nothing that so extraordinarily many of us, including most of us liberal types loath
to admit it, are such rank homophobes; that, gay lib or no gay
lib, in conversation among straight men, even among those

who hardly know one another, gays so often remain "fags," and what they do in the privacy of their own bedrooms, while good for the occasional laugh, is understood to be hugely distasteful; that, in fact, before it was understood to pose a threat to the heterosexual community, even AIDS, far from prompting real anguish, was, in many quarters, regarded with something shamefully like equanimity.

And when we are confronted with what the experts have to say about all of that—well, suddenly there is new depth to the term "defensive." *I mean, c'mon, me?* Indeed, even when such a reaction is sincere—by the literal millions, after all, having grown up dreaming of putting it *there*, we were frankly appalled to learn that, yccch, there exist so many people who prefer putting it *there*—we remain spooked by the very suggestion. *My God, deep down, do I have those impulses too?*

"Isn't it remarkable," as my own wife once put it to me, "how every guy in the world wants to be in a *ménage à trois*, but it always has to be two women?"

All of which, of course, bears hugely not only on the style and content of male friendship but on the comparative ease with which, in contrast, we will confide in women. Aware on some level that opening up necessarily engenders a certain loss of control, ever wary that something might be misconstrued, frankly terrified of the possibility that one's own worst suspicions might one day be even partially confirmed, we find yet another potent reason to regard intimacy itself with unease. It is not coincidence that every sanctioned male social situation—from gatherings on the playing field to those around coffee machines—is so heavy on structure and ritual that even warm moments are rarely tender, and physical contact is always readily identifiable as playful.

Still, even this appears to have been lately in the process of change; not because our insecurities are any less pronounced than they ever were, but simply because we've lately found ourselves with greater license to express them; and so, if they are far from dispelled, they are at least less crippling.

But, more, having gotten some practice in emotional give-and-take from the opposite sex, most of us continue to yearn also for the companionship of those more likely to share our interests, perspective, peculiar history; yearn, in sum, for the old along with the new. We want to talk sports and women as well as movies and how we're feeling about things, or combine them all in whatever ways we damn please.

And the odd, wonderful thing is that all at once, others who feel the same way seem to be all over the place.

Eight or nine months later, as we shot down the Major Deegan through the Bronx,—not our normal route—suddenly, off to the left, loomed Yankee Stadium.

"Hey," Steve piped up, "did you hear that Steinbrenner's planning to give his son control of the Yankees? How'd you like to have that as a toy to play with?"

"Yeah. Except that chances are, the first time they lose two in a row, he'll take them back again."

He chuckled. "Right—and probably also take the kid out of the will." A beat. "And give the team to Billy Martin."

"God, can you imagine what it must be like having *George Steinbrenner* as a father?"

"Oh," he said, "the same old thing. Only more so."

We had, by now, spent—let me see, now: an hour and a half a day, times five, times thirty-six weeks—perhaps two hundred and seventy hours side by side in the damnable Subaru or the even more damnable Peugeot—more than eleven full days—and such a remark called for no elaboration. Over the months, we had often talked about our own fathers, as well as the father-son bond in general; and we'd talked, too, between the lines, about how money tends in this society to distort personal morality, not to mention sundry other aspects of assholedom. So if we had never before talked explicitly about the loathsome Steinbrenner, we knew more than enough about each other to fill in the appropriate blanks.

This is not to suggest that things between us had instantly gone smoothly. At the beginning, we'd kept it light, avoiding subject areas that tend to involve especially tender parts of the psyche; and, too, at least a couple of times a week we'd find ourselves in the same push-pull over who'd get to pay for breakfast or the latest tankful of gas—a bit of classically dumb male behavior that, in this instance, though even then we were able to kid about it, had more to do with our respective struggles to be the good guys we hoped (but secretly doubted) we were than with traditional macho posturing.

Perhaps above all, we'd been cautious around each other's moods.

These, in Steve's case, often had to do with his work. He is a landlord—that is, he manages ten or twelve family-owned buildings, most of which were put up by his father or grandfather—and as such is subject to a great deal more than the average amount of stress and personal abuse. Indeed, being a good liberal, inclined to support The People on every front, I myself had long simply assumed the worst about landlords as a class: this despite the fact that I had never actually had a moment's difficulty with one of my own.

But Steve, as I was learning, while hardly a pushover as a businessman, also totes around a sense of obligation to others that can border on the irrational. Moreover, he loves his buildings the way Reggie Jackson loves old cars. More than once, early on, he insisted that we drive out of our way so that he could show off to me some special feature of one of his places— a striking facade, or a genuine Art Deco mirror in a lobby; and I could not help noticing that even when the surrounding neighborhoods had begun to look shabby, the buildings had not.

That we pass our days doing such different things has, I think, subtly helped the friendship along, not only affording each of us special access to a wholly new area of experience but, by no means incidentally, serving to preclude even the remotest sense of professional competition.

The corrosive effects of which, especially in a business like mine, can hardly be overstated. While researching this book, for example, I passed an entire evening talking for the first time in several years with a onetime colleague and erstwhile friend. As the conversation proceeded, I began to feel glimmers of the old affection, and I suspect he did too. We were more honest with each other than ever before, discussing various writerly insecurities, and at one point he acknowledged how desperately he had always secretly yearned for "something that was my own—a style, a reputation, anything that would separate me from the rest of the world."

My reply—I honestly believed it to be not only candid, but supportive, though who knows all the levels on which these things work?—was that in conversation, he always *had* had a very special voice, full of insight and humor, and I'd never really understood why he seemed reluctant to put more of that into his prose.

It was only later, as I was driving home, that it hit me how devastated he had been by this; how it had altered the evening's dynamic. And I was not entirely surprised when he called a few days later, apropos of nothing in particular, and after a few preliminaries, weighed in with some sharp criticisms of my recent work.

Having come to loathe such ghastly, ego-reducing battles, I found it a source of real wonderment that by virtue of his business, Steve was obliged to fight them almost every day. It was not that he had problems with very many of his tenants: merely that those with whom he did—now that I was more or less seeing things through a landlord's eyes—were often maddeningly unreasonable, if not outright crazy; as, I suppose, are a similar percentage of the New Yorkers with whom one regularly comes into contact. One guy had been refusing to pay his rent for five years, and had filed a legal claim against my friend, because a building that had been erected a block away partially obstructed his downtown view. Someone else, withholding hers, was insisting, with a lawyer's help, that there were dangerous microscopic particles in her apartment air; someone else, because the sink was cracked—and never mind that she had cracked it herself, or that she refused to allow workmen inside to replace it.

My friend is not entirely without a sense of humor about these things. "It takes a worker in an asbestos plant forty years to get asbestos poisoning," as he remarked after some maniac renter who had it in her head that she'd been stricken had ranted at him for an hour; "it takes a tenant forty minutes." In fact, Steve has long insisted that his little office, beset as it constantly is by assorted loonies and shysters, would make a terrific setting for a *Barney Miller*–type sitcom; and if there had been any doubt that he meant it, it was dispelled one morning not long ago by his behavior in court. His adversaries, as it happened, were a husband-wife television producing team, responsible for a hugely successful weekly series; though they had five years before left their rent-controlled New York apartment for a Malibu beach house, they were fighting hard to retain it. And, along the way, lying through their teeth— not only claiming to be residing full time in a building where no one had ever seen them, but producing documents that showed a joint income for the previous year of $8,000. It was, in brief, even as these things go, a tense and ugly confrontation. But in the middle of it, Steve turned toward the woman, standing a few feet away. "Now, tell the truth," he whispered: "wouldn't this make a *great* situation comedy?"

In response, she only stiffened and—this part he imitated— her face assumed an expression of extraordinary sourness. But even in retrospect, Steve wasn't sorry. "Hey, it was my one and only chance to 'take a meeting.'"

All right, it sounds like I'm covering for my friend. I realize that. I only hear his side of things, and obviously it is possible that he's wrong more often than I know. But I don't think so; indeed, would maintain that such a suspicion confirms the point. Frankly, I don't know how the guy takes it, this almost universal presumption that head to head with his landlord, a tenant is automatically right. At least a couple of times every week, Steve heads downtown to Housing Court, invariably to face a hostile judge, only to have whatever case it is postponed yet again; and often as not, back at the office there awaits some new headache—maybe someone yelling on the phone about a backed-up dishwasher, or, worse, an imperious directive from a functionary at some government agency who would never, of course, try to get tough with a Helmsley or a Trump.

I had begun to get used to the fact that, riding home with Steve after a particularly rough day, there were likely to be a lot of silences. But one such late afternoon, a Friday, perhaps two months after we'd started, he surprised me. I'd made some innocuous remark about a dinner party Priscilla and I would be attending that evening, and he replied, evenly, that though he and Susan had lived in the community a good year longer than we had, and actually knew the people in question better, they'd never once been invited to their home. "That's because you're the right stuff. I'm the wrong stuff."

"Oh, c'mon, cut it out. . . ."

"It's true. You're the writer; I'm"—he gave the word a contemptuous, vaguely sinister spin, the way Snidely Whiplash used to speak of himself—"the *landlooord*."

What to say? We both knew the score; there was some truth to it.

"Tell me something," he said: "I'm not a terrible person, am I?"

"No, Steve, you're not a terrible person."

"I don't *think* I am. I *try* not to be. But all these people treat you like shit, and after a while you begin to wonder. . . ."

For a good two minutes we were silent.

"I had a dream the other night," he picked up suddenly. "I was back at my old school, the one I went to before my brother died and we moved away."

I had heard how devastated Steve's parents had been by their older son's death; knew, indeed, that though he had been an exceptionally promising science student, perhaps even a gifted one, my friend had gone into the family business largely to please them.

"Yeah?"

"And it was . . . frustrating. Incredibly frustrating. I wanted so much to be back there."

"I thought you hated that place."

"I did. But it was a good school; it had so much to offer."
He paused. "If I'd stayed there, my whole life would be different."

There was, to be sure, an element of overdramatization in this. But it soon led, as surely in some way it was intended to, to territory we had heretofore conscientiously avoided: the extraordinary depth of our self-doubts. Which, oddly—or perhaps not oddly at all—itself eventually became a discussion, an increasingly upbeat one, about various times during our former lives when we had felt inadequate around a particular woman—and the ways we had managed to obscure, indeed, sometimes even overcome, the fact: which led, in roundabout fashion, to some pertinent observations on the ways we relate to the B.W.'s—a sobriquet borrowed from the late gossip columnist Earl Wilson for our wives.

Nothing of substance was resolved that day. Not a single suggestion on how to deal with future business crises was solicited or offered. Still, something quite remarkable was beginning to work between us, and by the time we turned the corner of our street, I, at least, was feeling terrific.

In subsequent days and weeks, it became ever easier, this remarkable business of coming clean, until, finally, it was a matter of routine. No remark was too revealing or bizarre, no admission would be misconstrued or, more to the point, turned by one against the other. With each other, our egos were safe.

Eventually, as these things go, the common understandings and inside references evolved into a private mode of communication. It was simply understood between us that mimes are an embarrassment to the species, for instance, or that paranoia and cynicism are more frequently justified by the facts than is generally allowed; indeed, that we were both perhaps a bit distorted in this last, and fervently wished it not to be so, and frequently behaved as if it weren't, but, what the hell, it was the sense with which nearly forty years of history and day-to-day experience had left us.

At appropriate moments, for emphasis, Steve was apt to make a point in the growl of *Sesame Street*'s Cookie Monster, or the screech of Charlie Stein at his most desperately needy, or, when the subject was shifting to blame or self-congratulation, in devastating parody of former Mets left fielder George Foster; I, in turn, could move for a word or a sentence into French, or pseudo French, and know that my friend, with his four years of high school French, not only would get it but might embellish it a bit.

It may be taken as evidence of how definitively the barriers had fallen that one morning, in the wake of a contretemps the previous evening with Priscilla, I admitted even before we hit the highway what had touched it off.

He shot me a quizzical glance. "You hid her diaphragm? Why?"

So I got right to the nitty-gritty: that more than once lately, I'd wanted sex and she hadn't; or, more accurately, she'd gone ahead with it but, at least at the start, with a clear absence of enthusiasm.

He smiled, nodded. "I know, I know. You know how it is when people walk a dog—they say they're waiting for him to 'do his business'? Sometimes that seems to be the attitude— 'do your business.' "

I laughed. "*Yeah.* It's so much on her terms. So when it happened a couple of nights ago, I said to myself, 'Screw this; the next time *she* wants to, she's gonna find out how it feels.' " A beat. "And that's when I hid the diaphragm."

And yet, as we talked, it became clearer that what I was actually bothered by was something else, something with which my friend identified even more readily: the sense—irrational, to be sure, but powerful nonetheless—that what we were dealing with here was emotional withdrawal, that she might no longer be there for me as readily as she'd once been.

"That's what I really wanted," I acknowledged: "to provoke a conversation about *that*. Except she got much angrier than I expected. She said, 'You hid my diaphragm? That's the most childish thing I ever heard.' And she stalked out of the room."

"She's wrong. I've seen lots more childish things."

"The point is, I never even got to tell her about it."

He smiled. "So you're telling *me* instead."

Well, yeah. Damn right.

And the following morning, after Priscilla and I had passed much of the night hashing it over—with my coming once again to the realization that her insecurities are as pronounced as my own, and she acknowledging that I had a point as well, and both of us pledging once again to try harder; all of it, not surprisingly, followed by one of those extraordinary sexual interludes that click on all levels—I told him, at least in general terms, about that as well.

Then too, of course, we often discussed our children. Indeed, a shared view of our responsibilities as fathers was at the very center of our friendship. The fact had sort of crept up on me, but suddenly almost every one of my closest friends seemed to be the kind of father who, for all the chaos of recent years, feels considerably more right with the world than ever before. It is not that I have consciously winnowed those who have made other choices from my existence; I have, truth to be told, more often felt, sometimes bitterly, winnowed from theirs. It is simply that I tend to be as lightly engaged by their most fervent preoccupations as they are by mine.

Most generally, Steve and I merely swap the kind of anecdotes about the children for which we might otherwise never find a willing audience. But often, too, we compare notes on our own behavior around them, finding, each in the other, a sympathetic critic; and, as always, a visceral grasp of what it means to have traveled this road, all that has been set aside along the way and all that has been gained.

The depth of our concern about our children has a lot to do with why, when late last summer there appeared an issue of *New York* magazine with a cover story on city dwellers who had recently moved to the suburbs, I was particularly anxious about Steve's reaction. My wife and I had been interviewed for the piece and were presented therein, at some length, as slickers amusingly out of sorts with our new environment.

While this was essentially our own doing, we were also sometimes quoted inaccurately, or entirely out of context. We were
not much upset by Priscilla's supposing to have claimed that
she was the only one in town who ever walked anywhere, or
by my characterization of the community as a spawning ground
for every organism known to produce an allergic reaction. We
weren't even bothered by the suggestion that we wished we'd
never left the city. But we were horrified by the clear impli-
cation—it appeared without quotation marks—that we had
disparaged the local elementary school. Sadie does not go
there. Most of our local friends' children do, including Steve
and Susan's daughter.

I dropped a copy of the offending magazine at Steve's the
evening of the day it appeared, accompanied by some hasty
self-explanation. The phone rang half an hour later.

"This is the Community Betterment Association." A beat.
"And you'd better leave the community."

I relaxed a little. "You read it?"

"Yeah, I read it. You came across as pretty stupid."

"You think anyone will be offended?"

"Do I think anyone will be offended? *I'm* offended."

He was, too, very much so—and over the next week or
two, he let me know it in all kinds of ways.

In fact, those were a gruesome couple of weeks for the
family in general. If no one actually went ahead and burned
a coffee cake on our lawn, as a city friend of Priscilla's had
anticipated, we found ourselves repeatedly snubbed at the
A&P and the stationery store; and a couple of the aggrieved
actually presented themselves at our front door to offer pieces
of their minds. We could do little more than offer what seemed,
even to us, a lame explanation and lamer apology.

It was several days into the ordeal that Steve, who had been
regularly speculating on the impact his being seen with me
might have on whatever reputation he possessed locally, let
it drop that he would shortly have available a sunny, inexpensive three-bedroom apartment in the Washington Heights

section of Manhattan. "It's rent-stabilized, right beside Fort Tryon Park. It's really going to be a terrific deal."

"All right," I bit. "How much?"

"Oh, no. Uh-uh," he said, "not for you." He paused. "I mean, c'mon, what would *I* do if you moved away?"

I felt like hugging the guy.

Not, of course, God knows, that I would.

THE call came a little after 10 A.M., just as I was getting into the day's work.

"Mr. Stein, this is June Diamond, the nurse at Sadie's school."

"Yes?"

"There's been an accident. It's not an emergency, but I'd like you to come down here, if you could."

"What happened?"

"She was in gym class and she got a bit of a bump on her head. She probably ought to be looked at by a doctor. Just as a precaution."

But by the time I arrived at the school, the nurse was no longer being quite so casual. Sadie's teacher was there in her office too, her concern equally evident. My daughter lay on a cot in the corner, a heavy olive-green blanket—it looked to be Army issue—pulled up to her chin. She was pale, her eyes half closed, her breathing labored.

I knelt beside her. "I'm here, darling."

Her eyes fluttered open and she reached out to me with a small hand. "Papa."

"I know, precious." I stroked her head; her forehead was unnaturally cool, her blond curls damp with perspiration. "I'm going to take you to see Dr. Lewis."

"It hurts! Papa, it hurts so much."

I turned toward the nurse. "Should she be moved?"

"We have no X-ray equipment here, and it might take a while to get a doctor."

Gently, I brought Sadie up to a sitting position. "Come, darling, I've got to get on your jacket and shoes."

"No, please let me lie down." She slumped against me, thirty pounds of dead weight.

"Darling, I've got to take you in the car."

"Please, Papa, no."

"Come, Sadie, let me put on your jacket."

"It's the back of the head," the teacher spoke up for the first time. "She was running fast, and collided with another child, and she went down very hard. At first—"

But all at once, Sadie was throwing up, her little body convulsing with the effort. It lasted perhaps five seconds.

"There," I soothed, panic-stricken, "is that better?" The nurse was beside me with a damp towel, dabbing at her dress, the sky-blue one with the big red heart in the middle. "Throwing up always makes you feel better. The idea sounds terrible beforehand, but when—"

But abruptly she pitched forward and began again.

Once inside the car, she immediately curled up on the backseat in the fetal position, the seat belt loose around her.

"Would you like to hear a tape, little one?"

"Uh-huh."

"How about the 'Old Wild West Thinkernik' tape?" Her current favorite.

A barely audible yes.

As we pulled out of the school lot, I rifled through the glove compartment with my free hand, sending half a dozen tapes clattering to the floor.

"Just give me a moment, doll." I glanced back at her and smiled. "Don't fall asleep."

Don't fall asleep. With a start, I realized where that had come from. "Your child must sleep," a nurse had coolly informed my mother that spring afternoon in 1950 when, beside herself, she was insisting on seeing my brother. "He needs to rest." Two decades later, as she quietly described the moment, her acquiescence still haunted her. "I know it's crazy, but maybe, *maybe,* if I'd been able to keep him awake . . ."

I turned up the tape full blast. "Well, here we are, Thinkernik," said Nancy, the narrator, bright as ever, "standing right in the middle of an old Western town . . ."

Shooting down the West Side Highway at close to eighty, ready to enlist any cop who pulled me over as an escort, I rolled down my window; fresh air might help. Then, with the first blast of December air, I rolled it back up, flicking on the heat instead.

"The sheriff's waving us to step inside the stagecoach. Let's run, Thinkernik."

I stole a glance behind me. Her eyes were shut tight, her face serene.

"Sadie. *Sadie,* wake up, darling!"

I popped out the tape so that at least I'd be able to hear her breathing.

My mind raced in all sorts of directions. If she died, how would we break it to Charlie? How could he possibly deal with the enormity, the incomprehensibility, of the loss? Then— my God, was it possible?—I myself had actually been a couple of months older at the time of Genie's death. Of course it affected me! And my father—what words would I use with him? I framed the sentences, could almost hear him respond. But then, all at once, I felt nothing but weary. Oh, God. The truth was, if it did happen, if my little girl never opened her eyes again, I wouldn't want to talk to anyone at all, except those few for whom conversation would be an equal burden; not until so much time had elapsed that people would no longer feel obliged to raise the subject; until, in the intensity of my grief, they would regard me as self-indulgent and choose to avoid me altogether.

Sadie awoke in my arms as I dashed the two blocks through the cold toward her pediatrician's office, and by the time he looked at her, she was very nearly her regular self.

"Papa," she said brightly, looking up from the examining table, "finish the story."

"What story, darling?"

"The one about the wine."

The reference was to a breakfast-table chat on a report in that morning's *Times*, about a two-hundred-year-old bottle of Château Lafitte allegedly once owned by Thomas Jefferson that had sold at auction for more dough than we'd paid for our home.

"That wasn't a story, darling. It really happened. In London." I smiled at the doctor. "Something we were talking about at breakfast."

"What," he inquired, peering into Sadie's left eye with his little light, "did you have for breakfast, Sadie?"

"Rice Krispies."

He peered into her right eye. "Anything else?"

"Umm." She paused. "Orange juice—only I didn't drink it."

"And a vitamin," I added a bit too hastily. "She always has a vitamin."

What is it about certain categories of people—pediatricians, teachers, PTA honchos; *accredited* child lovers—that they leave so many of us with deeper voices and facial hair feeling inadequate? Do they really suspect that our interest in our children is a pose, another of the game faces the contemporary man feels obliged to put on, or is it just that we imagine they feel that way?

"Usually," I heard myself note, "she does have a larger breakfast. It's just that she got a bit of a late start this morning."

"I went to bed late last night," my daughter added helpfully. "Papa and I stayed up late to watch *Cosby*, *Family Ties* and *Cheers*."

"Well," he pronounced, "there's no evidence of neurological damage." I resisted gasping *Thank God, Doctor*, like some pitifully grateful wretch in the movies. "I suggest you get her home for a nice rest."

"I'm *hungry*. I want lunch."

I offered an ingratiating grin. "She threw up her breakfast."

* * *

An hour and a half later, having left a $4.95 hamburger vir-
tually untouched, Sadie was back at school. Half an hour after
that, I was back at my typewriter.

Which is by no means to suggest that I was back at work.
In fact, I ended up producing less than a page and a half that
day—and after a cursory reading, two-thirds of that had to be
junked.

Damn!

Then again, how could I do decent work after what had
happened? How could I even expect myself to?

Nah, no good. Plausible-sounding as it was, solid as it might
have seemed to a reasonable outsider, the rationale offered
little real comfort. The unavoidable fact was that I'd screwed
up, punted away another day.

Damn!

In this sense, let's face it—in the sense of *needing* to achieve
professionally—I had changed less in recent years than in any
other. Almost as vividly as at age twenty-three, when I sold
my first piece to a national magazine, I still sometimes find
myself seized by the notion that twenty-four hours barren
of professional progress is not merely a day wasted; given
the competitive nature of my business, it constitutes an imperceptible step backward. And if I am no longer quite
so impatient with those without comparable hopes for themselves—or, worse, who in Stephen Sondheim's memorable
phrase, have "the dream, yeah, but not the guts"—neither,
finally, do such souls and I fully understand one another.

I recall, way back when, being admonished by a female
acquaintance, a neighbor in my building, to slow down, for
heaven's sake, stop worrying, relax. *But you don't understand,*
I told her. *People my age have written Big Books already,
directed major movies, are running entire corporations.*

And anyway—though I didn't know her well enough to put
it quite so bluntly—what the hell could she know about it?
She made it clear what she was after in life: security—i.e.,
enough money to be comfortable, thank you—and never mind

the quality of the work, let alone the possibility of leaving any kind of mark on the world. Indeed, she already pretty much had what she was after professionally, a pleasant job at a travel agency, which, though it could have paid a bit more, provided decent benefits and fabulous vacation opportunities.

The distinction she failed to make, quite simply, was the one between a job, which one gets essentially to pay the bills, and a career, which is something one embarks upon and nurtures, something that ultimately involves one's very definition of self: you can quit a job; you don't walk away from a state of mind.

More than anything else, it is this understanding that has, for all the lofty talk of recent years, effectively relegated the notion of a new species of American male to that of utopian ideal.

Yeah, sure (in one of those themes that ripple through the culture), we are everywhere encouraged to draw closer to our children, to come to know them in ways in which so often we were never known by our own fathers. All well and good. But we also happen to recognize that when it gets down to cases— how we're regarded by others, what we think of ourselves— our options remain precisely what they've always been.

Norman Podhoretz, the editor of *Commentary* and self-appointed defender of traditional sex roles, in his characterization of those men more involved with their children than with more classic male pursuits, routinely bandies the word about in public: *wimp*. So, for all their support in the abstract, do a staggering number of women. But then, in this most achievement-oriented of societies, at a moment when everyone, to one degree or another, is identified as a winner or a loser, how could it be otherwise? One has heard a lot from women in recent years about emotionally unavailable men, notes California psychologist Warren Farrell wryly, but almost nothing about *unsuccessful* men who are "afraid of commitment."

Not, of course, given their own problems in this regard, that we should have expected such a dilemma to elicit real sympathy from the opposite sex. Once naive enough to believe that their own juggling act would simply be a matter of good organization and lots of pluck, women by the millions have had to face up to the fact that "having it all" rings false even in the beer commercials. "No matter what you're doing," as one career woman I know sums up a constant in so many lives, "you're feeling guilty about not doing something else."

Still, women at least find some solace in seeing their plight regularly getting its public due; indeed, in the very places—on *Donahue*, in the pages of the women's magazines—where only yesterday it was full speed ahead on the career front and no questions asked; and, too, they find support, a sense of community, genuine concern, among friends and acquaintances.

We men, on the other hand, if we dare to make an issue of it at all, are lucky to get even the Podhoretzes of the world to pay attention.

But of course, more than the weight of general opinion, we men who have given even passing thought to seriously shuffling priorities have ourselves to contend with. For all the talk of the diminished work ethic in this country, we grew up, most of us, with a sense of the emotional rewards that come with a job well done; an appreciation of the sense of capability engendered by extending oneself in the wider world. Such an ethic remains part of our collective character as a people, impelling us by the hundreds of thousands and millions—from nascent entrepreneurs to those making old dwellings habitable one room at a time, from aspiring nurses to veteran novelists sweating under deadline—to pull the best from ourselves. An Indian prince, reduced to indigence by his government's seizure of the family holdings, remarked recently that "it is better to be in the grip of death rather than in the grip of a job"—and reading it on this side of the water, we snicker. Hell, most of us would rather be in the grip of a job, assuming it was a good enough one, than *anywhere*.

We are, quite simply, most of us men, though in some quarters the term is regarded with frank contempt, bottom-line types; inclined, by instinct and habit, toward action, progress, results.

Which, as almost any child-care professional will readily volunteer is emphatically *not* the ideal frame of mind in which to approach the business of parenting. Indeed, it is not overstating the case by much to assert that as a practical matter, given the contradictory demands of work and family, and the differing temperaments they call for, it is close to impossible to devote oneself simultaneously to both with full effectiveness.

Not, of course, that this will come as news to anyone obliged to constantly try to make the mental and emotional leap from one to the other; screwing up miserably at home with behavior that on the job would mark one as a comer.

There was, for example, the Saturday not long ago that my daughter got it into her head to put on a play called *The Princess and the Duke,* and before I knew what I was about, I was urging editorial advice upon her.

"Is that what the Duke's going to wear?" I asked, pointing at Charlie. "His clown suit and red pants and a Pittsburgh Pirates cap?"

"Yes. He's a duke *and* a clown."

"Fine." I reined myself in. "You're the boss."

She had also, I noted, mobilized her dolls to serve as extras in the production. Barbie had been changed into her wedding gown. Her demented cousin, obtained in a thrift shop for a nickel and known around our house, for the odd tufts of short reddish hair dotting her small head, as Chemo Barbie, was, as usual, not only nude but spread-eagled.

"Who's Chemo Barbie playing?"

"The queen, my mother."

"Sadie," I offered, "I have an idea. Just a suggestion. Why don't we make a movie instead? I could get the video camera, and we could shoot scenes in different rooms. And that way we'll have a record of it."

"Could we do some of it outside?"

"Sure. Why not?"

"That'll be great!"

Two minutes later, I had the camera in hand. "Okay. Now, before you begin acting, Sadie, it would probably be a good idea for you to explain to the camera what's going to happen. That way the audience will understand it better."

"Okay."

"Good. Ready?"

She was sitting demurely on a little chair, which she had set before her playhouse. "Yes."

"Okay. Lights. Camera. Action!"

She sat there, staring.

"It's on, precious. Go ahead."

She rose, walked slowly across the room, picked up a drawing she'd been working on the previous evening and studied it. Charlie wandered over beside her.

"Cut!" I snapped off the camera. "Kids, you've got to *do* something. What's the story going to be about?"

"I don't know," replied Sadie testily. "I'm thinking."

"Listen, maybe what we ought to do is write it down. We'll write what's going to happen in each scene and then we can film them one at a time. All right?"

Silence.

"Well, why don't we have you sitting in front of the castle, and then Charlie, the Duke, will come by, and you can ask his permission to go inside. That'll be the first scene."

"No, I don't like that. Anyway, I want Little Leon to play the Duke." Little Leon was another of her odder dolls, a rubber being with a vacant stare and a realistic penis.

"Maybe that's not a bad idea," I agreed. "Maybe we should just let Charlie do the stuff he likes to do anyway—like ride his rocking horse and throw balls and look at books—and try to make *that* part of the story."

To this she made no reply.

"Anyway, darling, the important thing is to decide what's going to happen. We haven't written down a single thing yet."

"Papa . . ."

"What?"

"I think I want to color instead."

"Why, Sadie? C'mon—it'll be fun."

Too late. Already, I realized guiltily, my insistence that even fun must have purpose had transformed the enterprise into something remarkably like a chore.

It was, to be sure, an innocuous enough episode, quickly set aside by all concerned. But it is the sort of thing that over the years and decades is insidious and profoundly damaging— this message, conveyed from parent to child, that the capacity to achieve on the world's terms is all-important; that, indeed, the child too can expect to be judged, even within his own home, on that basis.

But then, of course, we judge ourselves the same way. And that, as increasing numbers of us are at last coming to grasp, is the real pity; that at our best—our most selfless and open and humane—we are so often at war with ourselves.

One of the men with whom I spoke, someone who longs for more time with his children, glumly recalled that during John Lennon's househusband period, "people could not *believe* that he'd actually given up work to raise a kid. I mean, this was *John Lennon* they were talking about, someone who presumably had *earned* some time off."

Indeed, Lennon himself had to contend with the same attitude. "People ask me," he remarked at the time, in evident consternation, " 'What are you doing?' and I say, 'I'm baking bread.' And they say, 'Ha, ha, ha, what are you really doing?' I say, 'I'm looking after the baby.' And they say, 'No, no, no, no, what *else* are you doing?' I say, 'Are you *kidding?*' "

So wholly bound up do our egos tend to be with our professional selves that to even seriously question the pervading value system, let alone reject it, constitutes a kind of risk. If we do so, we generally keep it pretty much to ourselves. Among the most startling discoveries I happened upon in the course of researching this book was that someone I've seen on and off since college—an *economist*, for God's sake, and by reputation a good one—is more interested in the work his sons are doing in the first and third grades than in his own on the fortieth floor of the World Trade Center. Typically, that remarkable bit of information emerged by extreme indirection; when, one wintry afternoon, in his den, between halves of the Giants game, in the course of a conversation about problems with a superior, he made a very small joke. "It's terrible, the way my work keeps interfering with my real life."

"I know," I overcommiserated, keeping things light: *"terrible."*

But thus begun, the conversation continued along its intriguing way until, a few minutes later, he dashed out of the room, and returned with a thin maroon children's book. Entitled *Story Number 2*, it was by Eugène Ionesco, the celebrated French playwright of the absurd. "I want you to hear something," said my friend, and finding the page he was after, he began to read: " 'Josette goes to see her papa at his office. Papa is on the telephone. He smokes, and speaks into the telephone. He says: 'Hello, sir, hello. Is that you? I told you never to call me again. Sir, you bore me. Sir, I haven't a second to lose.' "

My friend grinned. "My six-year-old *loves* that. He says that's how I sound when I'm working. And I'll tell you, I'm not at all sure he's wrong."

That is a wonderful thing to know about oneself, as potentially liberating in its way as vast sudden wealth. But of course, that has always been one of the things most often overlooked about profound involvement with children, especially by those incapable of it themselves—that the bonus is self-knowledge. Over and over, in conversation after conversation, men who short years ago regarded themselves as free agents talked insistently of the self-insight that had come with parenthood and, almost as often, about how it had forced them to examine with new eyes elements of the world around them that hitherto they'd simply taken for granted. Reproduced on the printed page, a lot of what they said would come off as corny, even banal—more than one guy reported he is no longer able to listen to "Cat's in the Cradle," Harry Chapin's lament to a fatherhood of missed opportunities, without getting choked up—but then, in a culture where it is generally alienation that passes for hip, such a confession comes off as oddly refreshing.

"Sweetest Goose," noted a friend of mine, a writer and art historian named Nick Weber, in a letter to his year-old daughter on his own thirty-fifth birthday,

> Picasso has always been one of Daddy's heroes—alive, perceptive, *inventive*. Dad always thinks of him as someone who really did something, and, lucky fellow, had recognition, which Dad knows one isn't supposed to want, but has to admit he can't help wanting . . . Goosiest, when I was an adolescent, I thought that his painting *Child's First Steps* said it all about life and children and growth and all that mattered, but now that I'm a parent I can see that it was painted by someone who didn't really know. It's an observer's painting. Picasso was too caught up by the idea of the cuteness. He probably didn't stay around to watch his kids begin to walk. We know from you that a baby doesn't look so tortured, so much as if he's consciously making an effort to learn something new: it's all much more gradual and natural, spontaneous the way nursing is, not like a lesson. Picasso noticed children, but he didn't have time for his own, the patience to be there and be there again. "Oh, yes, how marvelous," he must have said as he looked at his children and then went off, even if to make something for them. I know how easy it is to be alone, thinking about a baby or buying something beautiful for her; to be with her hour after hour is something else. True, he was painting a Picasso, not just out shopping, but from the baby's point of view it's all time without Dad . . .

There are, of course, lots of times when we all wish we could pull a Picasso—convey every appearance of involvement with family while fully investing ourselves elsewhere. Still, even if we could, few of us would be able to keep the guilt wholly at bay. For it is no longer a secret how dramatically a father's absence, physical or emotional, is likely to affect his children. The stories come at us in the popular media ceaselessly, their cautionary subtext sometimes spelled right out for the benefit of slow learners.

"I'm going to devote exactly five minutes to my father," Kitty Kelley had Frank Sinatra, Jr., telling his nightclub audience the evening Frank Senior married twenty-year-old Mia Farrow, "because, as he once confided in a moment of weakness, that's exactly how much time he devoted to me."

"If you choose to spend your time making money and being on the fast track," *The New York Times* quoted psychologist Bernice Berk, following the killing of teenager Jennifer Levin by a boy from her own tony social set during an early-morning tryst, "that's a choice. And the children know that. When parents spend ninety percent of their time making more money than they could possibly spend and five percent of their time with the family, those values are passed on to the kids."

"They loved him and wanted his love and approval right to the end," one insider summed up the relationship between Seward Johnson, the Johnson & Johnson heir whose death touched off a vicious estate battle, and his pitiable brood. "I'll never know why. They wanted something he was incapable of giving."

Then too, along the same lines but with happier endings, there come all the tales of fathers who manage to salvage relationships with the kids after years of neglect; emotional reawakenings as dramatic, in their way, as that of Scrooge in the final act of *A Christmas Carol*. In a textbook example of the genre, doubtless already optioned as a movie of the week, there was *People* magazine's recent story about Dick Hoyt, a career military man who'd had virtually nothing to do with his twenty-four-year-old son, a victim of severe cerebral palsy, until the two of them began competing together in marathons and triathlons, the father pushing the son in his wheelchair or lugging him through the water by a towline attached to a boat. Hitherto as aloof as they come, the very model of the

male stoic, Hoyt has emerged as a figure of such sensitivity
that he now "toilets Rick, feeds him, changes his clothes and
almost every night cradles him in his beefy arms, laying him
down on his waterbed."

I, for one, always find myself embarrassingly moved by this
kind of thing—taking it, of course, in addition to all the ways
it was meant to be taken, as support for the course I have
taken.

Indeed, sometimes, overhearing a snatch of conversation
in a Midtown Manhattan elevator or on a commuter train, or
just listening as an outsider to the chitchat around someone
else's office, I am frankly taken aback at the subjects that seem
so fully to engage others. For whether the topic at hand is
basketball, or what company might be ripe for a takeover, or
someone in the business who is getting ahead or falling behind, it invariably seems to be about winning and losing, or
making an impression, and almost never about anyone's internal life. And sometimes the thought occurs even consciously: Do these people really believe this stuff is *important?*

It is, needless to say, an immensely satisfying thing to wonder about; and it is only when I am under intense pressure
myself, or involved in a project that demands my sustained
presence in one of those offices, that the self-righteousness
begins to ebb. Quite simply, the character of the process at
hand—the incessant grind, the dogged emphasis on results—
makes the question of priorities pretty much moot. If the
project is to be carried through to a satisfactory conclusion,
if the deal on the table is to come together, it *must* be of
overriding importance. Almost no one, after a long day at the
office, with a briefcase of papers yet to be worked over, is
humanly able to regard the business of piling blocks atop one
another or listening to a halting account of a day at nursery
school as anything but a chore, something to be gotten through
with maximum dispatch.

Yes, naturally, excuses are made, rationalizations snatched
at. It is among life's melancholy certainties that people will
find ways to justify themselves. And in this case, it's hardly

even a challenge, so fully is the careerist ethic supported by the culture. *I mean, c'mon, what does some guy with a crippled kid have to do with me?*

In our own lives, in any case, the absences are so much less dramatic, their immediate consequences so subtle. "My daddy's a doo-doo," I chanced to overhear a friend of my daughter's remark, with that edge of meanspiritedness that so often finds its way into the character of even small children who have been persistently slighted.

"Why?" asked Sadie.

"Because whenever I ask him to read to me, he says he has to make a doo-doo."

Indeed, in a culture ever more reliant on the quick fix, the impulse, for many of us, when there is no $5.95 paperback available offering painless solutions, is often not to acknowledge an issue at all. *At this point, career just has to come first*, we tell ourselves. *The kids will be fine.*

And when, at long last, the agonizing questions present themselves—Why can't I reach my kids? Why do they treat me this way?—well, most of those will soon enough be dispatched in the same way. *Hey, lots of kids are acting the same crazy way. They couldn't ALL have had rotten parents.*

There is, of course, in the end, no fully satisfactory solution. We're all in a bind—those who have determined to do things dramatically differently too. Having made themselves available to their children in such substantial measure, these very often find themselves uncomfortably at odds with the surrounding world; their satisfactions mostly private ones; the incidental slights, in a land where strangers begin conversations with "What do you do?," so often public.

"As far as I'm concerned," one such man told me early on in our conversation, "we've gone bonkers in this country to think that it's natural to be away from your kids ten hours a day. Why should anyone—mothers *or* fathers—have to make that sort of compromise? Why should children be denied their parents?"

An attorney with once-limitless prospects, this guy would

a decade ago have been a candidate for canonization on the pages of *Ms:* after the birth of his first child, he quit his job to stay at home with the baby, while his wife pursued a highly successful career of her own. But in fact, as he continued talking, it became clear he was far more ambivalent about his role in any perceived revolution than self-congratulatory. "We're all victims of historical circumstance," as he put it. "Before the Industrial Revolution, no one questioned a father spending his days alongside his children. In many parts of the world, it still works that way. It's just that if you want to participate in a Western market economy, you've got to make this horrible choice. Well, I've made it. But there's still a part of me that asks, 'Is this just one big narcissistic binge I'm on?' " He paused. "What I'd really like is not having to choose at all— to find a way to participate in the marketplace without worrying about sacrificing the emotional lives of my children."

Though few make the point quite so well, either verbally or in the content of their lives, it is a sentiment shared by an increasing number of American men. If, through our children, we have at last, on some level, come to understand that the only thing truly worth envying is peace of mind, we also cannot help who we have always been. It is no coincidence that on the very day Nick Weber set down his ruminations on Picasso, he dashed off another letter, one he intended never to send:

> *Dear Dicky,*
>
> *You lucky bastard. I see your second novel is on the stands, and I read Lehmann-Haupt's review in the* Times *this morning. Easy enough for you, of course; I might have done it too by now with a million-dollar trust fund and no wife or kids . . .*

But then, I suppose, that is what it will never stop being about. If one's needs and those of one's children were always in sync, if there were no rewards for shucking off emotional responsibility, everyone would be a terrific parent. In the end, growing up is a matter not merely of acknowledging the hard choices, but of making them for the right reasons.

Like Nick, I have acquaintances I envy, occasionally nakedly. But the individual I've lately found myself envying as much as anyone, in every particular except the one having to do with physical well-being, is, strangely enough, Charles Dickens. See, not long ago I ran across an article about Dickens that happened to note, in passing, that even as he was writing all that terrific stuff—not only earning himself a place among the alltime bigs and what Jewish comics used to refer to as "a fortune in money," but giving new dimension to the notion of social conscience—he was simultaneously cultivating a reputation among acquaintances as a peerless family man. But then, as the article, whose author appeared to be a feminist, also pointed out, what was the trick? Dickens had an army of servants to do his bidding, as well as an endlessly devoted wife, and when, at day's end, he emerged from his studio, his adoring kids were plopped into his lap for precisely the dose of fatherly affection he felt like administering.

On the other hand, there's me.

Fully two and a half years after the birth of a son who remains an unreliable sleeper, still in the midst of what ought to be known as Second Child Syndrome—moist eyeballs in sunken sockets, a mind that trails off in mid-sentence, chronic spasms of irritability—I found myself sitting at lunch with a longtime colleague and on-again–off-again friend who had, it became apparent even before I'd dumped the ketchup on my burger, something weighty on his chest.

"Listen," he put it to me, this guy without a single kid to his not insubstantial name, "when are you going to get back on track?"

By this he meant several things, but foremost among them was this: when was I going to recapture the old fire; when was I going to resume producing copy about things that mattered?

But, I assured him, I *was* writing about things that mat-

tered. In my *Esquire* column, almost every month, there had
been something on relationships, or children, or—

"Children!" He fairly spat out the word. "That's what I
mean. Let me ask you something: Is there one political figure,
anyone, who you'd kill to get access to? I mean, full access,
so that you could write the definitive piece?"

I thought about it. "Not offhand."

"How about Castro?"

"Oh, yeah, that'd be nice." A beat. "How long do you
suppose I'd have to be away from home?"

He threw up his hands in a dismay that was not entirely
mock. "See? You're lobotomized!"

Maybe. But the truth is, looking into the life of yet another
politician truly does strike me at this point as less interesting
than trying to fathom, for instance, what is going on in the
heart and mind of a two-year-old during one of those terrible,
inexplicable tantrums; and, more to the point, in the broad
sweep of things, ultimately as less important. Now, getting
Fidel and Raúl to come clean about the specifics of their
relationship with their father—*that* would interest me.

The fact is, pretty much inadvertently, almost in spite of myself, I seem to have made my choice. I am by no means as
good a father as I might be—I am often short of patience; I
shudder to think that on matters as diverse as tidiness, TV
watching and self-control, I may be offering instruction by
example—but my children know that they have gotten about
the best that I have to give. And I have come to know, in
turn, as a matter of absolute certainty, that both day to day
and over the long haul, the bargain is overwhelmingly to my
advantage; that these two extraordinary people, open, secure,
capable, will be friends for life.

Which is not to suggest that it is not an ongoing struggle;
even that I am above a bit of backsliding. For let's face it, the
point the guy made that day over lunch is not blithely set
aside. Far better than he, I know what the trade-off has involved; know, indeed, though the fact would probably leave

him cold, that I have done my best work these past several
years not at the typewriter, but by the light of a globe lamp,
in the bedroom of a preschooler. In fact, having generally
devoted myself on a professional basis to nonfiction, I've sometimes surprised even myself with the turns my bedtime stories
often take, and with their variety.

There is the "Chase and Nicky" series, featuring an older
sister and younger brother who have the capacity, via her
tricks in a basement lab, to make themselves anything they
wish—huge as behemoths or tiny enough to ride the backs
of bees, weightless or all-powerful—according to the specifics
of the adventure they have in mind. (My daughter, when it
is her turn, often opts to have them reduced to infinitesimal
specks, so as to explore various human orifices; I like to send
them back in time to hobnob with Abraham Lincoln and Ty
Cobb.)

There is the "Hogam, Acham and Eeecham" series, starring
three Indians—a wise one, an astonishingly swift one and one
with an insatiable appetite—who live in the woods not far
from our home.

There is Prince Andrew, a medieval prince who has followed his beloved Princess Sally to the modern world, only
to discover that she has enrolled as a student at Columbia
Law School and is seeing someone else; hopelessly trapped
in an age he will never understand, he is a character at once
sympathetic and faintly ridiculous. "Heigh-ho, Sally, what
news?" he is forever shouting, with desperate good cheer, as
he clops through the streets of New York on his nag, heading
toward the brownstone she shares with the new guy.

Lately—in deference to Charlie—there has been a revival
of the "Baby Harry" stories, a highly speculative and idealized
version of my own infancy in which Baby Harry, terribly
curious but with a pathetically limited frame of reference,
misinterprets everything he sees.

It has occurred to me, and Priscilla has more than once
suggested, that we should endeavor to capture some of these
for posterity, if not for profit; that at the very least, we might

leave a tape recorder running some evening and see how it plays the morning after. But, well, you know how it is, when it gets to be around bedtime, who wants to bother? But more than that, who wants to mess with the very best time of the day, a spontaneous half-hour that has made for some of the most memorable moments of my daughter's five years on the planet, and of my own nearly four decades?

None of which, however, stopped me from damning the individuals responsible for *Back to the Future,* a bunch of Hollywood snot-noses who, in the wake of the picture's release, kept turning up in interviews admitting to their own cleverness: as everyone in our household knew full well, that was *our* story, the only difference being that in the original it had been Sadie Stein (with an assist from Chase and Nicky) journeying back to the Fifties, there to cavort through old-time New Rochelle with her future father, Little Harry.

Nor, for that matter, when, a month or so after my erstwhile colleague's lunchtime lecture, perhaps six after Sadie's gym-class scare, a number of professional obligations simultaneously came due, did I resist cutting back on the leisurely evening ritual; first making the stories more perfunctory, then less whimsical, then, finally, refusing to tell them at all. I was too tired, I'd explain. I had work to do upstairs in my office. *Listen, I already READ you a story, darling. Sadie, when are you going to learn to go to sleep without this incredible ritual? When are you going to . . . ?*

It is remarkable how readily that kind of thing begins to tell. On both ends. By the time the work pressures peaked, my little girl was asking—not without some calculation, to be sure, but also not without some concern; and for the very first time in her life—"Do you love me, Papa?"

"Of course I do," I'd reply. "How can you ask such a thing?"

But five minutes later, I'd be impatient again. I had to resolve not to get involved, at least for the time being, in helping her with her letters; I became too easily annoyed by what I took to be a lack of follow-through. Charlie had lately become obsessed with puzzles, but I decided I'd better stay away from them too; the temptation was too great to simply do them for him and be done with it. *Turn it the other way, Char. Have you ever seen a cow with its feet in the AIR?*

Sadie's wistful sorrow was bad enough, but it was easier to take than the frequent withdrawal of Charlie, normally so sweet these days, and full of beans, into petulance or sullen defiance; not only because it was a more direct response to what even I recognized as a provocation, but because it so vividly recalled long-ago reactions of my own.

Still, where was the need for excuses? Work was going better than it had in a long time. It was almost fun again. Hell, I'd make it up to them later. And hey, if I didn't—that is, if I couldn't quite manage it—would it really matter? I mean, already I was dickering to do another monthly column, and there was a nice book contract in prospect, and someone had mentioned the possibility of occasional work on the Coast . . . Suddenly, in more ways than one, I found myself feeling almost as if it were the old days.

But, too, in this sense as in others, given the nature of what I do, I am luckier than most. Almost always, there is time to pull back and reflect and reconsider. Just the other week, in the midst of my work frenzy, finding new life in ambitions that had been unquietly dormant, very nearly persuaded that things at home were under control, I ran across a piece in *Esquire* by Bob Greene, a self-confessed workaholic, presenting the view of priorities offered up these days by many hard-driving but humanistic types. He loves his family, Greene wrote, and often fantasizes about slowing down to spend more time with them. But he guesses that will never happen—not only because of all he suspects he'd be missing out on, but finally, because his identity is so bound up with his work. He recalls the time years before that he spotted George Harrison at a restaurant in Jamaica, blandly identifying himself to inquisitive strangers as "Mr. Blatchford." Greene finds this sadly appropriate. "What do you do that will satisfy you," he concludes, "after your job has been to be a Beatle?"

It was a nice piece, honest in its way, and I clipped it for the files. But that very afternoon, I happened to come upon the John Lennon quotation, a portion of which I cited earlier. In essence, Lennon went on to observe, in what might have been a direct response to Greene, that his crowning achievement of the post-Beatles period was to "rediscover that I was John Lennon before the Beatles, and after the Beatles. I rediscovered the feelings I used to have as a youngster."

There was more, and despite myself, as I lingered over it, it began to get to me. Momentarily, I set aside the page to regain my professional bearing. No good; the concluding words of the passage were a blur, read through damp eyes: " . . . If I can't deal with a child, I can't deal with anything. No matter what artistic gains I may get, or how many gold records, if I can't make a success of the relationship with the people I supposedly love, everything else is bullshit."

"KIDS," I announced one eve-
ning at dinner, "I'm not going to be able to put anyone to
bed tonight. I've got to go into the city to watch the ball game
with Grandpa Joe."

"Why do you?"

"Well, your grandpa is feeling a little sad right now and I
want to keep him company."

"Is it because of *Rags*?" Sadie had seen the show in previews
a couple of days before the official opening, a week or so
before it closed.

"Yeah, it is. This period has been very hard on him. He's
very, very disappointed."

It was true, every word. But then, one also makes a point
of packaging such things for small-person consumption with
the care that used to be shown by Disney Studios.

The fact is, since the demise of his show, my father and I
had been on far more tenuous terms than usual, and my visit
this October evening was motivated more by a self-conscious
sense of responsibility than by anything like altruism or
empathy.

But there was something more going on. Though neither
of us knew it yet, we were approaching an emotional crossroads; indeed, had been over much of the previous year. It
was as if, in our characteristically unconscious fashion, we had
together determined, at long last, to acknowledge what was
wrong between us, even if indirectly; even if neither of us
quite knew what to do about it. And so, for months, things
had been surfacing, sometimes seemingly for no reason at all.

232

"Happy Anniversary!" as my father had greeted me over the phone one morning back in January.

"It's not our anniversary, Dad. Our anniversary was two months ago."

"Oh, well, just thought I'd take a shot."

But over the next hour, I was unable to concentrate on anything else. Boy, that Freud gets smarter all the time; there *are* no accidents, certainly not of that kind. I had, you see, lately made a point of my father's failure to mark, or usually even remember, significant personal occasions, a trait, like his habit of mixing up his sons' names (and never mind that the same thing was beginning to happen to me with Sadie and Charlie), that I took as yet more evidence of his capacity to be at once present and absent. This had been his quirky way of both acknowledging that feeling and laughing it off.

But that was not all. I am quite sure my father was unaware of it himself, but that particular date, January 18, *did* have significance in our lives: it was my mother's birthday.

"Let's face it," came my wife's reaction to the queer exchange that winter morning: "in your father's mind, you're incredibly closely linked with your mother."

"What are you talking about?"

"Are you kidding? Look at the way you're always after him about things he'd rather not deal with. Look at the way you try to hold him to such impossibly high standards. It's like you're her ghost. Think about it—*your* wedding anniversary, *his* wife." She laughed, having surprised even herself with so uncharacteristic a burst of pseudo psychologizing. "On the other hand, I guess that would mean that *I'm* him."

But in fact, the observation stopped me cold. It was true—my mother had been extraordinarily demanding. It was among the qualities in her I had come to remember most fondly, an adherence to a private sense of right and wrong, just and unjust, decent and indecent, that had been all but unshakable.

"Your mother," an old friend of my parents observed not long ago, "was the best friend and ally in the world, full of warmth and humor and sound advice. But, boy, if she disa-

greed with you on what she regarded as a matter of principle—
and she had a *lot* of principles—boy, could she be a royal
pain!"

And so, often, as my wife knows, am I.

The difference is that my mother had always been straight-
forward about it, while I, especially with my father, traded
mainly in unresponsiveness and gentle sarcasm; if not precisely weaseling around the tough issues, hardly doing much
to resolve them.

Indeed, a lot of what I needed to say to my father had lately
been heard instead—or at best, also—by hundreds of thousands of strangers. "Isn't it extraordinary," a TV producer of
my acquaintance once observed, "how much easier intimacy
is in public than one to one?" and he had it exactly. My
mandate in writing the *Esquire* column was to deal with dilemmas that all of us face: conflicts between right and expe-
diency, global responsibility and self-interest—but, too, whether
the subject at hand was brown-nosing, or infidelity, or the
merits of ethnic humor, I was also often dealing with my
parents' competing views of appropriate behavior.

Not that this had been apparent at the outset, even to me.
But by now, there could no longer be any denying it.

Most pointedly, there was a column entitled "The Blood
Connection," in which I used a book out of the Sixties, unearthed
at a garage sale and dealing with the era's famous "generation
gap," as an excuse to go on about our continuing unresolved
business with parents, especially our fathers. "Still unable to
find the uncritical love and support we have craved from the
start," it mourned, "still unable to readily make things different, we find ourselves bereft of alternatives."

On the basis of the mail response to it, the piece seemed
to have struck a chord out there, and even my father's initial
reaction to it, in a casual remark over the phone, was positive.
But when I next saw him, two weeks later, he suddenly let
it drop over dessert: "I'm becoming better known as a rotten
father than as the author of *Fiddler on the Roof*." He grinned—

but then, that was his way. "Don't you think I did *anything* right?"

In fact, in writing the piece, I'd worried about having to face just such a moment. I certainly had no interest in affiliating myself even glancingly with the *Mommie Dearest* school of contemporary literature. And yet, as I thought the matter through—nosing around for some plausible self-justification—it had seemed, above all, that the point had to be made; that indeed, the authors of the sad nonfictions in question, so routinely denounced as callous moneygrubbers and constitutional ingrates, tended to have a lot more in common with the rest of us than was generally acknowledged. Indeed, it was impossible not to note on the page the depth of their uncertainty and pain; impossible, finally, not to regard most of the books themselves as anything other than pleas for belated recognition and emotional sustenance.

And discomforting as such volumes are, there is far, far too much of the opposite going around—anger directed everywhere but at its source. One hears even the elderly, people in their eighties, griping about "Mama" and "Papa," still, in the most fundamental sense, children themselves; never having managed, when it counted, to clear the air.

Not that there was anything like satisfaction in that exchange with my father. Suddenly I was aware of the depth of his hurt, and my heart went out to him. "Of course, Dad," I replied. "You did lots of things right."

He was still smiling. "Damn right I did."

For, it was beyond denying, I also deeply cared for—all right, *loved* —the man. And even as I found myself cautiously moving to challenge him in dangerous new ways, I was beginning to face the responsibilities that ought to come with that.

Deep into research for this book, interviewing regularly, I was newly conscious especially of what in any realm but the interpersonal would have been groan-inducingly obvious: that for all his vitality, my father was no longer a young man.

Indeed, talking with others much troubled by their failure to have made some move toward mutual understanding when they had the chance, noting how the element of regret, of opportunity squandered, was sometimes evident even when the relationship seemed to have been reasonably sound, I found it hard not to feel that I was one of the lucky ones.

"My father always told me not to mourn him, that death is part of life," as a writer friend of mine, whose father had died a decade before, put it, "and at first I didn't. But for the past two or three years, I've been missing him terribly—first for my children's sake, but more recently for myself. Because I realized he was someone I could really have shared things with. He'd be almost eighty now—pretty much out of the game—so the competitiveness would've diminished. And there's so much I'd like to have asked him.

"Also, now, finally, I would've been able to do things for him. He'd have loved videotape machines, and compact discs, and since I have more money than he ever had, I'd have been able to get them for him.

"And books, of course. That would've been the main thing. He taught English, and loved writers, but he never met any. That was his dream, to sit with a real writer at the kitchen table and ask him about the process of searching out the right language or creating a sense of time and place. *Now I could introduce him to writers.*"

His wife, entering the room, overhearing this last, laughed. "Oh, c'mon, don't overdo it. You were plenty angry at your father."

"Yes, but I was just about to get over it." My friend smiled. "Let's put it this way: I could've rubbed his face in the fact of having what he'd always wanted."

"The truth is," said the wife, "you'd never have brought your friends there. You were embarrassed by him."

"No, I wasn't." He paused. "Why was I embarrassed by him?"

"Because he was always blowing his own horn."

"I always blow my own horn too." He stopped again, thinking it over. "Yeah, it's true. He was a wise guy—in both senses of the word. The difference is that now I wouldn't have minded."

That, of course, it should not take a genius to grasp, is at the very heart of any reconciliation—coming to accept attitudes and behaviors that once seemed beyond understanding, let alone forgiving.

This is by no means to minimize the impediments to altering any long-standing status quo. Resentments between fathers and sons in particular, lifetimes in the making, tend—as a matter of pride and psychic self-interest—to be jealously guarded on both ends.

But of course, getting down to cases, usually guarded far more jealously—and who knows it better?—by sons. "It's amazing," noted one guy I spoke to, someone who'd taken more than a decade getting to the bottom of things with his own father, "how many people expect their fathers to come to them with apologies. It's as if we're still five years old, still smarting from all those times we feel we were slapped down, still thinking of ourselves as helpless and our fathers as omnipotent. We extend a pinky and expect them to respond with an open hand. Well, sorry, it just doesn't work that way."

Then too, as I went about my professional labors, I found myself in the curious position of identifying, for the first time, as often with confused and anxious fathers as with petulant sons. "I resented my father for years," one man told me, in what I was sure was going to be another rendition of the familiar refrain, "and when my kids were born, I always made a big point in front of him of how much better I was with them than he'd been with us. How reasonable, and low-key. Then my eight-year-old joined a local soccer team, and he *stunk*—I mean, he just stands there, waiting for the ball to come to *him*—and there was I on the sidelines, yelling like a maniac, 'Attack, attack!' " He paused. "That's genetics for you. Like it or not"—he patted his chest—"he's in there, lurking around."

Sitting there sipping the guy's orange juice, I found myself reflecting on the times when, pitching a whiffle ball underhand to two-year-old Charlie, I have had to restrain myself from, just once, winding up and whipping that sucker right by him. (And frankly, given the way things tend to proceed between sons and fathers, I am already shuddering to think what he might one day do with that admission.)

But even that is not all. For slowly, slowly—based on a study here and a report there, certainly, but just as much on what I'd picked up in others and confirmed within myself— I found increasingly plausible the conjecture that for people like my father, for men in general, holding back is not necessarily a choice at all; or even principally a matter of the way the culture happens to work. "Men and women," as Dr. John Gettman of the University of Illinois noted in a recent *New York Times* piece on the differing views of the sexes on conflict, "have different goals when they disagree. The wife wants to resolve the disagreement so that she feels closer to her husband and respected by him. The husband, though, just wants to avoid a blowup. The husband doesn't see the disagreement as an opportunity for closeness, but for trouble."

The suggestion here, implicit also in much other contemporary investigation, is as striking as it is ideologically dicey: that if we men are not precisely more fragile than women, we are less able to deal with turbulence or pain; that stoicism, in its many guises, is so reflexive a male tendency because it strikes us virtually as an imperative. "My father was a bottomless pit of need," one especially perceptive woman summed up a private circumstance that rings true to so astonishingly many of us. "And it breaks my heart; because the need is so great, he has always pushed everyone away."

Which is part of why, for sons like me as well as for our fathers, the prospect of bridging the gap between generations is almost always so daunting.

But there is, finally, no escaping it: deny it as we may, if we are to be emotionally whole, we need each other. If only in self-interest, we must not only look for openings, but begin creating a few of our own.

One frigid day shortly after that odd congratulatory call from my father, I met him for lunch at a Greek coffee shop on West Fifty-seventh Street, two doors down from his office. He was waiting for me at a back table, sipping tomato juice.

"How are you, Har?"

I hung my down jacket on a hook and took a seat. "Fine. You?"

"Not bad. Not good, but not bad."

"Oh, yeah? What's the problem?"

"Oh, it's that damn show. I feel like I've been working on the thing forever."

He meant *Rags*. A musical about Jewish immigrants in New York at the turn of the century, in the half-dozen years since it had been conceived, it had been through innumerable re-writes; major characters had been added and dropped, plot lines changed, the entire direction of the show often debated and several times redefined. Now, with a leading lady having been courted and signed, my father and his collaborators were moving to beef up her character.

"Stephen and Charles want to make it a tour de force for Teresa Stratas. There hasn't been a dominant woman's role in a musical since *Gypsy*, thirty years ago, so that's what we've decided to go for here."

It flashed through my mind that *Hello, Dolly!* was after *Gypsy*, and so was *Funny Girl*; but uncharacteristically, I kept my mouth shut. This was unsettling, coming from my father. Almost always, in the midst of a new project, he was upbeat, usually relentlessly so. I could recall a dozen times as a child, listening over dinner as he'd wax ecstatic about a just-completed song for one of his shows-in-progress, or a dance number, or some new bit of comic business. I am not sure whether what I felt for my father at these moments was exactly love—who thought about such things?—but I was always immensely pleased for him and, by extension, for us; and I'd always be mystified, *shocked,* when, as sometimes happened, the show failed.

I myself have always been the opposite of my father in this regard; often doubtful about the quality of my work; always pessimistic about its commercial possibilities. More than once, in conversation with my wife—who herself regards the trait as demoralizing, if not self-destructive—he has referred to me, laughingly, as Mr. Bad News.

But on this particular afternoon, I found myself in the un-accustomed role of trying to lighten things up; not, with my father, that that proved much of a challenge. I asked about the shows he'd seen recently, and the new films, and pretty soon he was talking animatedly about *Hannah and Her Sisters*, which, he maintained, included the single most hilarious mo-ment he had ever seen on film.

"Don't tell me what it is," I interjected, since I was planning to see the picture myself, but he was unable to contain himself. It was the moment when the Woody Allen character, looking into Catholicism as part of his ongoing search for the meaning of existence, returns home from a shopping expedition and slowly withdraws items from a paper bag: a crucifix . . . a Bible . . . mayonnaise . . . a loaf of Wonder Bread.

It didn't sound so great to me—*this* was funnier than "Springtime for Hitler" in *The Producers?*—but he was having a major laugh just recalling it, so I more or less played along.

But then, abruptly, unaccountably, he was low again. "I don't know," he offered, softly. "All at once I'm feeling tired. Maybe I'm getting too old for this nonsense."

"Then what are you knocking yourself out for? You don't need the money, do you? Why don't you retire?"

"Maybe I will." He paused for a long moment. "As soon as I'm done with this damn show, maybe I will."

But oh, God, why can't these things ever be simple? Six months later, *Rags* finally opened—and almost immediately, closed: a circumstance that very quickly seemed to set my relationship with my father back a full decade.

In a situation like this, you see, the wagons tend to circle quickly. One is readily marked as either friend or foe, mensch or shmuck. Among the *Rags* contingent—many of whom had been laboring on the show for months and whose enthusiasm for it was wholehearted—certain of the critics were now regarded with cold contempt; and none more so than the man at the all-powerful *New York Times,* Frank Rich—suddenly known, in my presence, for we'd known each other for years, as "your friend Frank."

It wasn't that I had disliked the show—I merely hadn't liked it nearly so much as my father thought I ought to. That is, his work had seemed to me fine; I'd always been a fan of my father's dialogue, and isolated moments here were as effective as his work in *Fiddler.* But much of what went on on that stage struck me as lacking coherence and focus, crying out for the hand of the strong director they had never managed to find.

And when asked, that is pretty much what I'd said: gently, but without particular equivocation.

For all the depth of his anger, disappointment, bitterness, my father was less intemperate than some of those around him. His position was not that the show had been without serious flaws; merely that it had aimed high; had addressed meaningful issues; was as entertainment superior to several currently successful musicals.

Who knows?—in retrospect, my father may have had more of a point than I allowed. The following spring, after only modest revisions, the show would open at a theater in Chicago to quite enthusiastic reviews. And producers in London, Miami, Los Angeles would be talking about mounting other productions still.

Still, for two or three months, every conversation with him had ended up being about *Rags,* and this, after a while, I had not handled well. My attitude, even when unarticulated, was evident: the bad news ain't *all* the messenger's fault, so why don't we just drop it?

But of course, for me the real issue was not *Rags* at all. *So what?* I felt like screaming more than once. *So the thing flopped. It's not the end of the world!* And even more than that: *God, I wish you had the same—hell, HALF—the intensity of interest in your grandchildren!*

It was this part of it that I neglected to mention to my kids that October evening. And later on, as I sat with my father in front of the television set watching Mike Scott, the Houston scuffballer, fire zeroes at our Mets in the opening game of the playoffs, the silences between us were interminable, broken only by bland observations on the action. It was during a commercial break—specifically, a public-service spot featuring Phillies third baseman Mike Schmidt on the evils of cocaine—that we at last began talking. *Only losers use drugs,* Schmidt was saying. *If you're secure, you don't NEED drugs.*

"Big news," I addressed the screen. "The problem is that most people *aren't* secure."

"Maybe *I* should be using drugs," said my father, with a kind of half-grin.

I looked his way; never, in all the years I'd been listening, had I heard him say anything remotely of the kind. "C'mon, Dad, you don't mean that."

"Sure I do."

But by now the ball game was back on, Dwight Gooden facing Bill Doran. I lit a cigar and turned back toward the screen, thinking about it.

Doran grounded out hard to second.

"I'm sorry, Dad, about some of the things I've said about the show."

"Ah, that's all right. It doesn't matter."

"Well, anyway, I'm sorry if it made you feel bad."

A beat. "It *was* insensitive of you."

"I'm sorry."

"*Very* insensitive."

"I said I was sorry—all right?"

We were silent for the remainder of the half-inning.

"Sorry," he spoke up finally. "I didn't mean to make *you* feel bad."

"That's all right." I lit a new cigar with the butt of the old one.

"What do you do, chain-smoke those things? It's very bad for you."

"I got the habit from *you*."

"I never chain-smoked in my life. You remind me of your mother, for Chrissakes."

"What's that supposed to mean?"

"When we had a fight, she used to go into a dark room and smoke cigarette after cigarette, thinking all kinds of black thoughts. It used to drive me crazy."

I laughed. "I remember. She'd be in the living room. Only I didn't know you were fighting."

He nodded. "I thought she was so miserable, I'd keep apologizing just to get it over with. Not that the apologies necessarily worked. She usually had to go through at least a short period of being self-righteous."

"Why'd you apologize if you didn't think you were wrong?"

He laughed. "Who says I wasn't wrong?"

I've never run across a truly satisfactory definition of "breakthrough." But my father and I have gotten together more and more frequently since that evening, and we've found ourselves talking far more easily than ever before. Sadie has a dance class in the city Tuesdays at 4—Duncan Dancing, as in Isadora, wherein she puts on a pink silk tunic and prances around like a nymph—and the family is getting into the habit of congregating at my father and stepmother's afterward for an early dinner. His delight in the children is ever more apparent.

I do not for a moment discount the element of timing. For the first time since the mid-1930s my father is not fully engaged in work; and surprisingly, instead of being perpetually restless, he has grown progressively more relaxed. "Joe Heller is worried about me," he announced the other week, with a smile. "He wants me to go back to work. But you know what? I don't wanna."

As it happens, the evening in question was my birthday, thirty-three years to the day—my God, a third of a century; halfway back to Woodrow Wilson!—since our little chat about excessive crying. I was pleased by the cake that appeared after dinner, chocolate on chocolate, and delighted with my presents: a blue tie spotted with yellow mammoths from Charlie and a portfolio of original art from his sister; an array of cassette tapes from Priscilla and a handsome sweater from my father and stepmother. But frankly, what floored me was the fact that for the first time in memory, perhaps the first time ever, my father had actually gone out and bought a gift uniquely his own, something from the heart.

It was, of all things, a Frank Sinatra album. Could it be, I wondered as I unwrapped it, trying hard to look convincingly enthusiastic, that he finds the man any less loathsome than do I? But he hastened to explain that he wanted me to have it for a single song, one he found deeply affecting. It was titled "There Used to Be a Ballpark," and he wanted us to hear it right away.

> And there used to be a ballpark
> where the field was warm and green,
> and the people played their crazy game
> with a joy I've never seen.
> And the air was such a wonder
> from the hot dogs and the beer.
> Yes, there used to be a ballpark right here. . . .
>
> Now the children try to find it
> and they can't believe their eyes,
> cause the old team just isn't playing
> and the new team hardly tries.
> And the sky has got so cloudy

> when it used to be so clear,
> And the summer went so quickly this year.
> Yes, there used to be a ballpark, right here.

"You remember the first time you ever took me to a ball game?" I asked him, when the song was through.

"Where was it—the Polo Grounds?"

In fact, it was Ebbets Field—a brilliant Saturday afternoon, the Dodgers and the Milwaukee Braves, Erskine vs. Burdette; and I wished he'd remembered. But somehow I am no longer inclined to make an issue of things like that.

Indeed, driving home that evening, my brand-new *Abbey Road* tape in the tape deck, I found myself recalling something else that had happened that long-ago Saturday, something I hadn't thought about literally in decades.

Just as we'd been about to head out to the Chrysler for the trip to Brooklyn, my father, my brother, my brother's friend and six-year-old me, the mailman showed up and deposited several letters in our mailbox. One of them, amazingly enough, was for me; but when I ripped it open, my joy instantly dissipated: it was from the company from whom a month earlier, after studying their ad in the back of a comic book, I'd ordered a set of imitation classic stamps. If they did not receive their $2.49 forthwith, the letter advised, or if the stamps were not returned in mint condition, appropriate *legal action will be taken against you or your legal guardian.*

Oh, God! This was the end. I *had* no money. And I had already licked the stamps, most of them bearing Adolf Hitler's face, and pasted them in a scrapbook.

Abruptly, letter in hand, I bolted out the front door, around the side of the house, into the backyard and through the bushes. I was in a neighbor's yard, weeping uncontrollably, when my father caught up with me.

"Harry, darling, what's wrong?"

"They're going to arrest you. You're going to jail."

"What are you talking about?"

I thrust the letter his way. "They are."

As he held me close, I felt his frame begin to shake with laughter. Soon after, we would become awkward in each other's embrace, and on those occasions when we were obliged to go through the motions, would always come apart gratefully. But on that day, at that moment, there seemed no safer place in the world. "Don't worry, darling," he said gently; "Daddy's not going to let anything bad happen to either of us."

JENNY GRAY, rust-laden, her transmission about to give, shot up Interstate 87, bound for a fun weekend in the Catskills.

"You're sure it's Route 17 we want?" I asked my wife, in the backseat, wedged between a pair of car seats bearing sleeping children.

"Yes."

"You're sure? The exit is coming up in six miles."

"I already told you. Why don't you listen for a change?"

"Don't yell at me, will you?"

"I'm not yelling."

"You're *certain* it's Route 17? It doesn't sound right to me."

"It's Route 17! It's Route 17! It's Route 17!"

This was not the first exchange of the kind we'd had this afternoon. Shaking my head, I struck back. "Goddammit, why don't you learn to drive yourself instead of bugging me?" Always a nice weapon, but never more so than since our move to the suburbs. "I mean, *why don't you?* What does it say that you're the only person in the last fifty years who grew up in California without learning to drive?"

"And why don't *you* fill in some of the blanks between your ears? Try to think of it as sixteen plus one. Or if that's too hard, sixteen plus one."

I snorted. "Forget it. Just leave me alone."

And yet even then, pissed off as I was, I knew, and not far from consciousness, that I wouldn't want it any other way.

* * *

There was a survey a couple of years back—it appeared first in the *Chicago Sun-Times*—that caught a lot of women by surprise. There it was in cold black-and-white: of 2,301 married men polled, fully 77 percent said that if given the chance, they would again marry the same woman.

What made the numbers especially revealing was that they stood in such marked contrast to those in a survey that had appeared just a month earlier in *Woman's Day*. Asked the same question, merely half of married women polled said they would choose to marry the same man.

Though not one woman with whom I spoke expressed any doubt about the accuracy of the *Woman's Day* poll, most tended to regard the one in the *Sun-Times* with at least some skepticism. "Listen," as one of them put it, "if all these guys are so happy, why don't *we* know it? I get complaints all the time—so do most of my friends—but praise? You gotta be kidding."

"Would you marry Stan again?" I put it to her.

There was a long pause. "Probably. But this time it'd be without illusions. This time I'd know in advance what a baby he is."

Something else the *Sun-Times* poll turned up, though, is that relatively few men harbor reservations even of that kind about their wives. In fact, according to Judy Markey, who sifted through the ballots that poured into the paper's offices, many accompanied by poems and letters, "they didn't just love her, they were mad about her."

"*She is my better half,*" one guy rhapsodized, not uncharacteristically. "*She is my partner, my mistress, my best friend.*"

"*The most understanding, trusting, loving, supportive woman I've ever met,*" noted another.

"*Without her,*" summed up someone else, "*I'd be a bum.*"

This last is perhaps most revealing of all. To be sure, there were some correspondents who were less than enchanted with their mates—"*a despicable woman,*" one older man characterized his—but even many of these acknowledged a stark truth. Yes, as one such man noted, he supposed he'd have to marry his wife again—*"because no one else would put up with me."*

Quite simply, reluctant as we may be to share the information with those to whom we are ostensibly closest, most of us are acutely aware of the depth of our emotional dependence on the women in our lives; aware that they are our anchor, our surest ally, often our only link to the world beyond ourselves. It is not for nothing that studies of newly divorced men, many of whom—this falls in the death-and-taxes category—hungered for their freedom while married, have repeatedly found them to be lonely and isolated, longing now for nothing so much as a welcoming home to return to; that indeed, as of the mid Seventies, the mortality rate of recently divorced men was 3.16 times that of recently divorced women.

"The whole thing's my fault," one such guy told me flatly, a year or so after his wife caught him playing around and threw him out. "I messed up and now I'm paying the fucking piper."

"Listen," I heard from another man, someone who, horny as he offers he regularly is, would never in a million years risk thus jeopardizing his marriage. "I don't mean to sound melodramatic, but she's my only friend. I've got tons of acquaintances, but who else can I count on? Who else cares enough to call me on the bullshit and try to set me straight?"

"You want to hear how much I need her?" laughed someone else, just then in the midst of a prolonged professional crisis. "A couple of mornings ago I woke up in the fetal position, sucking on her tit."

There is, true enough, little reason to suppose that such devotion, in depth or character, is unique to our age. The occasional man in a nightshirt—hell, in the skin of a saber-toothed tiger—undoubtedly used to wake up exactly the same way.

Still, in the never-ending drama of the sexes, equal parts irresistible attraction and chronic misunderstanding, things are very different these days than they've ever been before.

Though our own needs remain largely unchanged, we men find ourselves challenged to regard women with new eyes and, far more, to take on vast new emotional responsibilities. It has become all but impossible to find a presentable woman who does not pay at least lip service to the essentials of feminist doctrine, one who will not at least occasionally chafe at being regarded only through the prism of male wants and needs.

But the point is, for all our griping, fewer and fewer of us would even want to be matched with a woman who felt otherwise; indeed, have some trouble with those men who are.

"Let's face it," one old friend, someone I met shortly after college, noted: "guys have always made judgments about other guys according to the women they're with, and assuming she wasn't outright embarrassing in other ways, that used to be basically a matter of looks and/or sex appeal. Well, these days, I have almost contempt for a guy if he's with someone who's clearly not his equal—no matter how good-looking she is. And my opinion of him rises if he's with someone decent and thoughtful and strong, someone who makes him *work*."

It is this last that is perhaps most pertinent of all.

"Who wants a pushover?" another guy sums it up. "You've spent years, decades, trying to sort things out, screwing up, and what you finally come to is that you don't just want to make demands, you need someone who'll make them on you, someone who'll force you to cut the crap. That's what every guy ought to be after, someone to help him be what he wishes he were."

As indeed, they should be looking for the same thing in us.

Still, if the journey from one mind-set to the other is arduous for those of both sexes, it is perhaps even more so for men. Steeped in a culture that celebrates superficials, inclined by experience toward the wrong choices, many of us have to pass through an endless round of mistakes and blown opportunities before finding ourselves even remotely capable of such a view.

"The truth is," one guy put it to me, "without even knowing it, I had just about hit rock bottom. I was so sick of always holding back and jockeying for power in relationships and faking things I didn't feel. And then I met my wife." He paused. "I feel like an alcoholic who got on the wagon just in the nick of time."

Few of us will go quite that far, at least for the record. Melodramatics aside, there remains the issue of power, and who wants to blithely hand over so much of it to someone who must be contended with on a daily basis?

Still, we know the score; know, above all, the astonishing depth of contentment that can come, at long last, with finding oneself challenged, rooted, known.

Over the years, there have been times when, engaging, as the postsummit communiqués have it, in "a frank exchange of views" in the presence of relative strangers, or relative friends, my wife and I have found ourselves misperceived. In fact, we are at least as quick to forgive as to anger; the sort of people who stay upset only when obliged—as we'd both been in prior relationships—to hold strong feelings inside.

Above all, during our years together we have come to realize, though at times the admission still comes grudgingly, that our arguments are only rarely about the subject at hand. Each of us has emotional turf to defend, and each is wont to defend it well past the point of rationality. But we understand, finally—recognize it as our strength and foundation—that each is also the other's surest ally.

The unavoidable fact is, while we arrived in each other's lives relatively free of the constraints our forebears took for granted, we remained bound by our respective pasts; wiser, certainly, than we once were, but by no means wise; beneficiaries of this heralded new relationship between the sexes but also, each in his own way, threatened by it.

Not that we were, particularly in this last, anything like unique. Caught up as our generation may have been in the rhetoric of the early feminist years, we seem by the millions to have simultaneously arrived at a quiet consensus: in the ongoing humanistic revolution at hand, the formal changes—

in the laws on the books, even in the structure of the work-place—are, incredibly enough, the easy part; the heavy labor, the day-to-day dirty work, is in the effort to alter what we are deep inside.

Nor, let's face it, were many of us helped along, especially early on, by some of the stuff that was passing as critical thought. The notion, most directly to the point, that the sexes are identical emotionally any more than physically was always basically hogwash, a triumph of dogma and a curious kind of wishful thinking over honesty and judgment; indeed, a bit of palaver that, in its way, bred enormous anger, alienation, misunderstanding.

So here we find ourselves, in a quieter time, left to sort things out on our own, two by two; trying, though we don't think of it in such grandiose terms, to find ways of remaining true to the spirit of that earlier age while also allowing our-selves our fundamental differences.

Where for women, at the beginning, the revolution had everything to do with being taken seriously on traditionally male terms, it has increasingly come to mean the possibility of being taken seriously on the terms with which one is most comfortable; indeed, the recognition, at long last, that the capacity to nurture and make enduring connections is also an achievement worthy of vast respect. The challenge, often, is melding the two in the same life.

So is it for an increasing number of men—though, so starkly put, the fact remains unrecognizable to some. Moreover, if this past decade has finally yielded up the possibility of ad-mitting to who we are, weaknesses and all, without feeling we're letting down the home team, we must still contend with the sense that we're letting down the *other* team.

"My wife's always telling me she wants me to be vulnerable, to show her my neediness," as a writer friend puts it, "and in theory, she does. But the truth is, she hates it when I'm weak, resists it tooth and nail every time I try to alter the terms of the relationship to where we're mutually dependent and independent. Her head and her heart are at war with each other"—he pauses, offering a wan smile—"and I'm the civilian population."

It is, in the end, tough going for everyone, this business of redetermining who we are and who we ought to be, of re-learning how to operate in the world and, alone at night, with one another. Indeed, that should probably be one of the morals of the chaotic era through which we have been moving: things are simple only in the abstract. Change is less a destination than a state of mind, the restless understanding that things not what they should be can be made better. The key, and a large part of the reward itself, is in the commitment to the effort.

I do not mean to convey the impression that the verbal interplay between my wife and me necessarily involves even passing antagonism. It is simply part of the way we communicate. Both of us grew up in homes where words strung together to interesting, preferably amusing, effect were far more highly regarded than those directly from the heart, and so are inclined to give the conversation a lot of edge—and, this is not to be minimized, keep it reassuringly cerebral, even when the *subject* is emotion.

"Hey, did you see this?" Priscilla exclaimed one evening not long ago: " 'Volatile Men Are Cancer Candidates.' "

I glanced up from the box scores. "How do they mean 'volatile'?"

She studied the article. "These are the traits. 'One—a negative view of life. Two—stormy relationships. Three—ambivalent feelings about themselves and others. Four—an inability to compromise and accept other views.' " She paused. "Sound like anyone you know?"

"Hey," was all I could come up with in response, "it takes two to make a stormy relationship. Anyway, I've changed. Hell, I'm the one who's *really* changed."

"I don't think you've changed nearly as much as you pretend you have."

"I've changed more than you."

"Oh, no, not *this* argument again." But then she couldn't resist. "Anyway, you had a lot further to go."

But that afternoon in the car, heading upstate, in the midst of the same old argument but with neither of us yet ready to acknowledge the fact, the mutual irritation was very much in earnest; for it had been not only a long day, but one that had set off the pertinent issues in stark relief.

She, for her part, had passed the morning in the city, working with a friend on an idea for a children's show for cable; the first time Priscilla, who had been out of action professionally for nearly five years, had ever tried anything of the kind. I, for mine, had been with the Gang of Two from shortly after dawn until just an hour before, when we'd fetched her at the train station and hit the road.

On the face of it, the scene was almost ludicrously contemporary, something out of a grown-up *Free to Be You and Me:* the hip wife and mother, easing her way back into professional life—and television, yet—after a long hiatus home with the little ones, encouraged and supported by the modern husband and father.

And there were, in fact, elements of that. Enormously fulfilling as she continued to find her time with the kids, Priscilla certainly, and increasingly, imagined herself in other realms. And I had always made a point, to her and others, of my high regard for her capabilities, maintaining that she was one of those souls who, with sufficient self-belief, could go as far as she wanted; had, indeed, speculated often on the prospect of a time when the two of us might split the time with the kids and the financial burdens more or less up the middle. Hell, never mind this equality stuff: in my mind's eye, I saw my wife winning so much bread that before long I'd take to lounging around all day in silk pajamas, in an apartment full of deco, like a kept man in one of those Thirties screwball comedies she's so crazy about.

On the other hand, there was reality, part of which involved personal history; in my case, that of a mother who, for all her

brains and energy, for all her generalized ambition, never got
beyond being "the girl with potential"—a circumstance that
did nothing for her standing in her own home; in Priscilla's,
that of a mother, a quite extraordinary one, who never aspired
to any other career and, equally to the point, a father who
has always been characteristically blunt in his view that the
traditional family structure got that way for some very good
reasons; in the existence we had forged together, all the hours
of Sturm und Drang about work and money and division of
responsibilities.

My feeling, and admittedly it came and went unexpectedly,
was that we looked to be stuck. The family dynamic having
somehow ended up nearly identical to the one we'd both
known in our childhood homes, there seemed a harrowing
inevitability to things: I'd do my work, if perhaps no longer
as dominated by it as had been our fathers; she, though certainly more independent than had been our mothers, and less
concerned with appearances, would take overriding responsibility for the home front, and that would be that.

She just really didn't seem to want it any other way, I
complained more than once, didn't even want it enough to
betray even occasional frustration in her current role.

Priscilla—big surprise—absolutely bristled when I started
in this way. *Dammit, she had worked all her life, all the way
back to college. How dare I?*

And true enough, any effort at arguing the point was bound
to come off as at least a little lame, if not outright nasty. It
was all right there on the résumé. Among the four or five
office jobs she had held down over the years, two or three
had been in the glamorous-sounding movie biz, and a couple
carried classy titles. Story Editor. *Executive* Story Editor.

But she knew as well as I that the work had been pretty
much rote stuff, only sporadically engaging her interest, even
more rarely her enthusiasm, never her imagination. Those
jobs had been more than a paycheck, perhaps—they were
also a convenient identity in a world that demanded one—

but they had never built toward anything in particular, let alone tapped her mind or her heart, and we both knew she was glad to be through with them.

Still . . . home with the kids, fully committed to the task at hand, she regarded it as nothing short of loathsome that I would presume to question her capacity to commit to a project or to persevere. Profoundly competitive—indeed, even more so than I realized early on—having come of age scrapping with her father (and having been pegged by him as the tough one, the daughter possessed of a temperament as distinctly male as female), she felt herself belittled, undermined, victimized. She was smart, dammit; smarter, indeed (this was sometimes expressed with bite, sometimes with irritation or cool hauteur, but usually just insinuated), than a lot of people who were celebrated as such, and how dare I!

And that said, she'd stride off, likely as not to lose herself in a volume of Georgette Heyer or Jane Austen.

Her view was that I picked on her when I was unhappy with my own work; that, in the guise of honesty, I could be a jerk of the first order. Moreover, for all my big talk, I didn't even know what it was to have the kids on my own for more than a dozen hours at a stretch.

Which was at least as true as any of the rest.

But, too, a couple of times, in the cathartic aftermath of a knock-down–drag-out, she came out with it herself: yes, the self-doubts *were* overwhelming, sometimes almost paralyzing; warring, always, with her stronger, more capable self. What good was it to start something, she had always on some level figured, when in her childhood home, things begun so rarely got finished?

And yet—talk about a maddening trait!—the next day it was as if the conversation had never happened.

This television thing had been in the works a couple of months now, and it was becoming a new source of tension. Oddly enough, her follow-through this time had been excellent. The thing was, the producer with whom she and her friend had been dealing, someone she knew slightly from her days at Columbia Pictures, was, quite simply, jerking them around. They had been made to write and rewrite the same proposal, on spec, five times; their phone calls went unreturned for days; they had at last come to understand that they were in competition with untold others for the chance to work on something that in fact had likely been illusory from the start. And if Priscilla continued to profess guarded optimism, I, who'd had to do some serious rearranging of my work schedule to accommodate her needs, was showing even less than my usual patience on the subject.

If one notes a seeming contradiction between such an attitude and my expressed enthusiasm for her professional future, well, one is more perceptive than I was; just then, I had not the slightest difficulty rationalizing the damn thing away. *I'm talking work, real work. This thing is an exercise in humiliation. It's driving her crazy; it's driving me crazy.*

Never had that feeling been more pointed than today. For I had a major magazine piece, barely started, due just five days hence.

All right, granted, I had readily agreed to watch the children—but that had been nearly a week before.

"Dammit," as I had pointed out early that morning, having just been jackhammered out of a gentle sleep by one of Charlie's most piercing shrieks, "I just didn't realize then that I'd have this damn piece hanging over me."

"C'mon," she countered, "you've known about this piece for two months." She offered a cool smile. "I thought this was your dream: unlimited time with the kids." She paused. "Of course, we know what they say—be careful about your dreams; they might come true."

"That's not the point. The point is, I've got an editor expecting the thing, and if it isn't in, I'm screwed."

The rest of the point, though I somehow resisted saying it explicitly, was *My thing is assigned. It will bring in actual cash dollars.*

"You want me to cancel my meeting with Jenny?" she demanded. "Is that what you want?"

I hesitated. "No, I just . . ."

"Well, I'm not going to. We've had it scheduled for a week. So stop trying to make me feel guilty about it."

"Fine. You're right." I got out of bed and stalked toward the bathroom, tossing the line over my shoulder. "Only this project of yours better be for real."

By the time Priscilla's train rolled out of the city, I had already muttered her name in vain at least a couple of times.

"Damn, why doesn't anyone ever replace anything around here?"

With the kids' prefab waffles already working in the toaster, I had just discovered that we were out of syrup. I turned over the bottle and pounded, then got out a butter knife and started trying to extract the dregs with that.

Sadie watched me closely. "I think, Papa," she advised finally, in a tone that a less secure person might have taken as condescending, "that we have another bottle. Mama bought one yesterday."

"No, darling. I looked."

"Maybe she hid it. Sometimes me and Charlie like to use too much syrup."

"I really don't think so."

"I was *joking*, Papa."

Suddenly Charlie was tugging at my pant leg, pain glinting in his eyes. "Mama!" he demanded.

"She had to go to New York, Char," I offered. "We'll see her soon."

"No," he shrieked. "Mama!"

"C'mon, little one." I picked him up gently, carried him to his room and lifted him onto his rocking horse. "You're an old cowhand," I began to croon,

> From the Rio Grande.
> And you ride your horse . . .
> or you walk, of course.

Well, you ride all day
and you ride all night,
but you find some time
to play and fight . . .

Yippee-ay-yo-dee-aa!
Yippee-ay-yo-dee-aa!

It had worked dozens of times before—but not now.

"Off," he implored. "Off! Mama!"

I lifted him off, held him close, rocked him in my arms. But wrenching himself from my grasp, he flung himself onto the floor and started screaming.

At that instant, the phone rang. I picked him up and ran for it.

"Hello."

Over the squalling, I could make out nothing at all, except that the voice was probably female.

"Hello. Speak up."

"Harry?" she fairly yelled.

"Yeah." It was a friend of my wife's, someone with a couple of small children of her own.

"What's going on there?"

"Nothing. Priscilla's not home. I'm playing with the kids."

"Sounds like they're having a real good time."

I managed an imitation of a chuckle. "He's tired." *Hey, you jerk, how often does YOUR husband spend a Friday morning with the kids?* "We're doing fine, really."

"Well," she said, "good luck."

"No problem." I held Charlie tighter, trying to muffle the sound. "No problem."

How, I wondered fleetingly, *how* does she do it every day? It is something I wondered anew almost every time, even if only a few days had passed since the last time I'd had both of them on my own.

As usual, though, within an hour, it began to come back to me.

By then we were at the local Howard Johnson's for a late

second breakfast/very early lunch. The old start-by-getting-'em-out-of-the-house gambit. And sitting there over her macaroni-and-cheese, Sadie suddenly fixed me with her most thoughtful gaze. "Papa, when they send food to the poor children in Africa, do they ever send frozen macaroni-and-cheese?"

"Probably not, darling. Frozen food has to be kept frozen, and Africa is pretty far away. Why do you ask?"

"I just want them to be as happy as I am now." A beat. "Do they send candy?"

God, I adored this child.

"I don't think so. Those children are very, *very* hungry. Taste is important, darling, but they're most concerned with those children getting enough good food to stay alive."

"It's very terrible, isn't it, Papa?"

"Yes, darling, it really is."

She paused another long moment. "Is Africa farther away than California?"

"Much farther. It takes only about five or six hours to travel to California from New York by airplane, but it takes a whole night to reach Africa." I thought about that a moment. "Wait a minute, maybe that's just because of the time change. And the rotation of the earth." I stopped again. "Hmmm. Maybe Africa's just a *little* farther away than California."

"How about Brooklyn?"

"No," I said, reassuming my authoritative air, "Africa's *much* farther than Brooklyn."

She smirked. "I *know* that. It was a joke."

"Row, row, row," intoned Charlie, beside me, through a mouth crammed with macaroni.

"Row, row, row your boat," I complied softly, "gently down the . . ."

" . . . steeen . . ."

"Merrily, merrily, merrily . . ."

" . . . merrrry . . ."

"Life is but a . . ."

" . . . deeen."

The guy who'd just sat down with his wife and small child at the adjoining table grinned our way. "He's very bright."

"Well"—for who wants to be identified as one of those superachievement-oriented parents?—"he does like music a lot."

"How old is he?"

"Seventeen months. And yours?"

"Fifteen months."

"Oh." I smiled. "She'll be doing the same thing any day now."

Her? Fat chance!

Twenty minutes later, we were back on the road, heading in the direction of a restaurant called Cook's.

"Papa," asked Sadie, "why when we're with you do we usually have lunch at one place and dessert at another?"

"I don't know." I shrugged. "We've still got some time to kill before Mama gets back. Anyway, Cook's is a special place. I used to go there with my father when I was little, you know."

"Of course I know."

In fact, my children are on familiar terms with much out of my past, and that of their mother also; as, one day, I am quite certain, their own children will be familiar with theirs. As infants, both had been serenaded to sleep with "We Shall Overcome" and the Streisand version of "Happy Days Are Here Again." Already, Charlie could identify the house, fifteen miles from our own, where I had grown up; and his sister, having a year earlier urged me to "Just *ask* them, Papa," had actually been inside.

"Let's hear a tape," I said now, in the car.

"No. First tell us about the first Marx Brothers movie you ever saw."

"Well, I think it was *Horse Feathers*. I saw it on TV when I was eight or nine."

"What was it about?"

Fortunately, the Marx boys were the opposite of heavy on

plot, and I got through it in three minutes. "Now, then," I said, "a tape. We have, lemme see here, the "Thinkernik" dinosaur tape, *Carmen,* the Beatles . . ."

"The Beatles!"

The ride, one suburban town melting into the next, passed quickly. Charlie stared out the window, occasionally pointing at something and calling out its name: dog, bird, man. I tapped my free foot, occasionally singing along with the music. Sadie asked questions.

"Which one of the Beatles is singing now?"

"George." The song was "As My Guitar Gently Weeps."

"Why is his voice so high?"

"I don't know. I never noticed that before."

"It is. Sometimes he sounds like a woman."

"Hmmm."

She was silent for perhaps a minute and a half.

"Who's that?"

"John. But this one isn't actually a Beatles song. It's called "Imagine." John wrote it after he left the Beatles."

"Why?"

"Why what?"

"Why did he leave the Beatles?"

"Well . . . it's a little complicated. He and Paul weren't getting along as well anymore."

"Why weren't they?"

"They just had disagreements about a lot of things. Darling, I'm trying to listen to the music."

"Were they sorry?"

"Who?"

"John and Paul. Were they sorry later? Or sad?"

"Please, Sadie, let's talk about it later."

"When?"

"After the song is over."

"Were they sorry?" she repeated, the instant it ended.

"Sade, did you listen to the song? It was very beautiful. And interesting, too."

"What's it about?"

"First things first. No, I don't think John and Paul were particularly sorry. They just didn't want to work together anymore. Sometimes people feel that way. It's all right."

"Were they still friends?"

"Sort of. But they didn't see each other much. John lived in New York and Paul lived in England."

She paused. "John was your favorite one, wasn't he, Papa?"

"Yes, darling, he was. I think he was a very good person."

"He was mine too." A beat. "Could you play that song again? But first tell me what it's about."

"Sure." I pushed the rewind button. "Well, what John is saying is that the world could be a wonderful place if only things were a little bit different. He's imagining what it would be like."

"If what?"

"Well, listen to the song."

She did, in rapt silence.

"Did you like it, darling?"

"Yes."

"Did you understand it?"

"You know what I think would make the world better? If candy didn't have any sugar in it. Then you could eat all you want, and you would never get cavities."

"But then it wouldn't taste like candy."

"I'm just *imagining*. Like in the song."

At Cook's, the kids opted for mocha chip, Charlie being allocated a large spoonful in a separate cup. I ordered a chocolate malted, as I always had when I'd gone to the place with my own father, my older brother going for vanilla, my younger brother for strawberry.

Gazing about me, I was, as always, a bit taken aback by how little the place had changed. The same pine walls and solid-wood tables and long Formica counter. The same smells, the same sounds drifting in from the game room in back. Except for prices that had quadrupled, it might have been 1956.

"Papa."

"What?"

"Charlie's making a mess."

Which is a helluva way to snap out of a reverie. The problem was that while he liked the ice cream itself well enough, he had no use for the mocha chips; and so every time one of these happened into his mouth, he allowed the cool liquid within to flow down his chin and onto the powder-blue jacket that I had neglected to remove.

"Oh, no, Char . . ."

I dabbed at the jacket, soaking up the puddles but leaving large brownish wet patches on the material.

"That jacket is *pretty dirty,*" observed his sister, as we got up to leave.

"I think it'll come out, darling."

She nodded. "Mama will clean it."

"What—you don't think *I* can clean a jacket? All you do is put it in the washing machine." It was uncanny how one so young could have so many sexist notions.

"But, Papa, Mama *always* does the wash. You know that."

By the time we fetched Priscilla at the station, I'd decided to hold off mentioning Charlie's jacket, at least for the time being.

"How'd it go?" I asked, as we eased from the curb, heading for the highway and the first leg of the trip north.

"All right."

"Just all right?"

"The proposal needs a lot more work."

"Oh, yeah?"

"We threw out everything we'd done. It just wasn't right."

Abruptly—what can it have been, thirty seconds?—the day's pleasant feelings were giving way to low-grade irritation. For *this* I'd sacrificed my day? Here it was Friday, and I'd surely get no work done this weekend, and that damn piece was due the following Wednesday.

"How much more time will you need?"

"I don't know."

"How much more do you *think?*"

"What is this, an inquisition?" She paused. "We'd like to take at least one day next week. Is that a problem for you?"

"My piece is due next week."

"It's due Wednesday. I made tentative plans with Jenny for Thursday: all right?"

I made no response.

"*All right?*"

"Maybe," I replied sullenly. "I don't know. I might need the extra day if I don't finish in time."

We rode in silence for ten minutes. Charlie, exhausted, conked out. Sadie, lids heavy, showed every sign of doing likewise.

"So how was *your* day?" Priscilla piped up, with exaggerated good cheer.

"Okay."

"And what did *you* do?"

"It was fine. We had a nice time."

"We went to Howard Johnson's for brunch, and Cook's for ice cream . . ." It was Sadie, back with us like Wonderland's dormouse. " . . . And we listened to the Beatles, and Charlie got his jacket filthy, and Papa told us the story of *Horse Feathers.*"

And—no exaggeration—no more than fifteen seconds later she was out.

But oddly enough, in the roundabout way these things work, it was Sadie's little recital that touched off things between her parents in earnest. For on the heels of the tussle over directions, we somehow found ourselves back on the Marx Brothers—bickering, to be precise, over their relative talents.

"It really disturbs me," I observed tartly, "that you don't think Harpo was the funniest."

"And it disturbs me," she retorted, "that you don't think Groucho was the funniest."

"Yeah, right. I don't even believe that you really believe Groucho *was* the funniest. That's just the obvious thing to say."

"The truth is, you can't even talk about any of them being funny as individuals. They're funny as an ensemble."

"Hah! That's the stupidest thing I ever heard. It's the statement of a person who doesn't appreciate the Marx Brothers at all!"

She stopped. "Harry, what are you so angry about?"

"I'm not angry. I'm merely investigating your alleged sense of humor."

At that, she just glared at me, her eyes reflecting less pain than white heat.

But then, we each have a pretty good idea, finally, how far the other can be pushed; and realize, too, that when it gets this bad, as it has only a few times in our years together, it's because the issues so assiduously being avoided are of such fundamental concern to both.

And so, in very short order, I was letting her know what it was that had been running through my head these past several days: that, dammit, things were a shambles. My career was a mess, and—it was time to stop kidding ourselves—if things didn't pick up soon, we were going to have to make some hard choices.

As I expected, this sobered her. Money talk, no matter how melodramatic, always does.

But then, out of nowhere: "Why don't you just admit it, you're ambivalent about my working?"

"I'm not ambivalent about your working. What I'm ambivalent about is your wasting everybody's time." I paused. "Also, by the way, you've been unbelievably distant lately. Do you know how it feels to be treated that way?"

"Harry, I've been *thinking* about this project. A lot. I know you don't think it's important, but it is to me." She stopped. *"Do I know how it feels?* Do you realize how preoccupied you get when you're working hard on something? I put up with it all the time."

"Yeah, but I didn't marry the writer, you did."

I hadn't intended to say quite so much, and we both smiled.

"And I'm sorry," I added, "but why won't you just admit this project is dead?"

"Because it isn't yet!"

"Look," I said heatedly, "they're taking advantage of you and you're just letting them! Believe me, I've seen it happen; they're just going to keep making you write proposals on spec, and when they drop you, they'll make like it's *your* fault. And you're going to be miserable and angry."

"So I'll be miserable and angry. What, you don't think I'll get over it?"

There was a long silence.

"Listen," she added softly, "I know you're probably right. But I've got no credits at all. None. They don't even have to give us this chance."

I was momentarily struck dumb. Never, in all our time together, had I ever heard such an admission, obvious as it might have seemed to an outsider, escape her lips. "I guess not. Maybe . . ."

"In case you don't know, this hasn't been an easy time for me either. I'm really not used to putting myself on the line."

"Listen, all right, it's fine for Thursday. If I can just have some work time this weekend."

"Good."

For ten minutes we drove on in silence.

"So what would you think," I heard myself wondering aloud, still looking for *my* due, "if I tried my hand at a new career? I was reading an article about Ralph Lauren the other day. Do you have any idea how much he makes with those horsey clothes of his?"

"Right." She was smirking. "Good thought. That's just where you belong—in women's fashion." A beat. "How did you come by this amazing capacity to lose perspective, anyway? God, you make things so much harder on yourself than they have to be!" She stopped again. "I'm going to tell you something, and I don't care if you believe me or not. Your work is richer than it's ever been—because you see so much more complexity now, you feel things so much more deeply."

I didn't know about the writing, and frankly, at that moment I didn't much care. But she was right about the rest.

As I stared out at the highway, the question presented itself with absolute clarity: How had it happened? How had I gotten so lucky? This person was not only a best friend, she was my auxiliary conscience; someone with whom to share the trek through this culture overloaded with options, trying to make the right choices for the right reasons.

As it happened, Priscilla's project would not pan out; they would be jerked around, seemingly to no end, for a full month more. But the following year, on the basis of that work and another exhaustive series of outlines and proposals, she would get a network assignment, a teleplay for a prime-time series.

She had also, by then, learned to drive.

By then, too, I was up to a good 40 percent of the child care—oddly enough, with only slight effect on my professional output; and was no longer surprised that even Charlie, for comfort, turned as readily to me as to his mother.

Not, evidently, that this is anything to gloat about. "That's about right," agreed Priscilla, hearing of my estimate. "Now, what about 40 percent of the housework?"

"I'm sorry for snapping at you before," she picked up finally, all those months ago on the road. "On top of everything else, I'm exhausted."

"I am too."

There was a long pause.

"I didn't tell you what happened with Charlie this morning," she said. "I came out of the shower and he looked at me in the most quizzical way, like he was seeing me for the first time. 'Mama,' he said, 'do you have a penis?' So I said, 'No, darling, I don't.' He wandered away, but five minutes later he was back, looking extremely worried. 'Mama, do you have toes?' "

I laughed. "What'd you tell him?"

"He made me show them to him. He was really frantic to know." A beat. "Harry, he's so adorable right now. He's so involved in making those sexual distinctions, trying to figure out who he is."

"I know. I only hope he does a better job with it than the rest of us."

We drove for a while in silence, the mind wandering. *"We are the world,"* I began singing softly, *"We are the children . . ."* A vagrant thought: "Remember that video? You think if John Lennon had been alive, he'd have been in it?"

"Probably." She paused. "And also Yoko. Who knows, a little screeching might have livened it up."

I laughed, my heart full to bursting. "I love you."

"I love you."

Keeping my eyes on the road, I reached back, and we clasped hands. Before me loomed the sign for the approaching exit.

"Now," I said, "is it Route 17 *East* we want or 17 *West?*"